Eloquent Gestures

**The Transformation of
Performance Style in the Griffith
Biograph Films**

Roberta E. Pearson

University of California Press
Berkeley / Los Angeles / Oxford

Photos on page 81 courtesy of the Museum of Modern Art Film Stills Archive, New York.

University of California Press
Berkeley and Los Angeles
University of California Press, Ltd.
Oxford, England

Library of Congress Cataloging-in-Publication Data

Pearson, Roberta E.
Eloquent gestures : the transformation of performance
style in the Griffith Biograph films / Roberta E. Pearson
p.   cm.
Includes bibliographical references and index.
ISBN 0-520-07365-7 (cloth).—ISBN 0-520-07366-5
(pbk.)
1. Silent films—United States—History.   2. Motion
picture acting.   3. Movement (Acting).   4. Griffith,
D. W. (David Wark), 1875–1948—Criticism and
interpretation.   5. Biograph Company.   I. Title.
PN1995.75.P43   1992
791.43′0973—dc20   91-30658
                                           CIP

Printed in the United States of America

9   8   7   6   5   4   3   2   1

The paper used in this publication meets the minimum
requirements of American National Standard for
Information Sciences—Permanence of Paper for
Printed Library Materials, ANSI Z39.48-1984. ∞

Kathy: Movies are entertaining enough for the masses, but the personalities on the screen just don't impress me. I mean, they don't talk—they . . . don't act—they just make a lot of dumb show.

Don: You mean I'm not an actor—pantomime on the screen isn't acting?

Kathy: Well, of course not. Acting means great parts, wonderful lines—speaking those glorious words. Oh, you can laugh if you want to, but at least the stage is a dignified profession.

Don: Dignified!

Kathy: And what have you got to be so conceited about? You're nothing but a shadow on film—a shadow— you're not flesh and blood.

Singin' in the Rain

Contents

Acknowledgments

Many people have offered various kinds of assistance in the process of a project that has gone from dissertation proposal to book. Perhaps pride of place should go to William Simon, who emerged from his office one day saying, "Why don't you write a dissertation on silent film acting?" Robert Sklar, my dissertation advisor, and Robert Stam, the other member of my core committee, helped bring the idea to fruition, contributing their own perspectives along the way. Jay Leyda and Brooks McNamara also served on the committee. Ann Harris and the rest of the staff of the Film Study Center at New York University's Department of Cinema Studies always had stacks of Biographs ready for viewing and kept the Steenbecks running. New York University's Graduate School of Arts and Sciences provided a Dean's Dissertation Fellowship that gave me nine months of writing time. Carol Zucker and Vivian Sobchack both published early versions of chapters: "The Modesty of Nature: A Semiotic Approach to Acting in the Griffith Biographs," in Carol Zucker, ed., *Making Visible the Invisible: An Anthology of Original Essays on Film Acting* (Metuchen, N.J.: Scarecrow Press, 1990), and "Cultivated Folks and the Better Classes: Class Conflict and Representation in Early American Film," *Journal of Popular Film and Television* 15:3 (Fall 1987): 120–28. David Paletz harassed me both about finishing the dissertation and revising the manuscript for publication, and, in retrospect, I thank him. Ernest Callenbach read the manuscript in dissertation form, told me how to turn it into a book, and has been a wonderfully encouraging editor. Pamela MacFarland Holway and Ellen Stein provided painstaking copyediting leavened with intelligence and humor.

During the revision process, Charles Musser shared many prepublication versions of his various books and articles with me, as well as some excellent advice. Richard deCordova kindly gave me a copy of his dissertation. Tom Gunning read the manuscript at two crucial stages, offering insightful criticisms and suggestions, many of which I have incorporated. James Naremore provided a very helpful reading of the first draft of the book. William Uricchio gave me moral support throughout the sometimes trying manuscript review process and made suggestions about the form of the conclusion when I was heartily tired of the whole project. Chapter 7 reflects our discussions about two forthcoming coauthored works, *Cultural Crisis, Cultural Cure? The Case of the Vitagraph "High-Art" Moving Pictures* (Princeton University Press) and *"The Nickel Madness": The Struggle Over New York City's Nickelodeons* (Smithsonian Institution Press). David Black saved countless hours of my time by marking films for frame enlargements, and Cathy Holter produced legible images from much-used 16mm prints. My cats, Henry and Keaton, together with the Duke University basketball team, provided much-needed distraction. And now for the usual disclaimers: I apologize to anyone I have omitted from the above list. And none of the above bears any responsibility for errors, incorrect interpretations, or anything else that reviewers may criticize.

1

Introduction

Amuse yourself with a little armchair time travel. Your companion is an imaginary New York City lawyer by the name of Josiah Evans, a man with a civic conscience who belongs to several progressive reform organizations. It's an unusually hot evening in the spring of 1909, Josiah's wife Lydia has taken the children to visit her parents in Connecticut, and he has taken to the Manhattan streets, seeking fresh air and distractions. Barely paying attention to his progress, he wanders down Broadway, past the expensive ladies' stores, and eventually finds himself on the Bowery in front of the Electric Theatre, a storefront picture show festooned with luridly colored posters.

Josiah has seen moving pictures, though not recently. A few years ago, before his marriage, he had occasionally visited Koster and Bial's Music Hall in search of light amusement. He was even there on that memorable night in April 1896, when Edison's marvelous Vitascope premiered. But in the last few years these new ''nickelodeons'' have been springing up like mushrooms on every street corner. Although Josiah has not paid a great deal of attention to the rapid growth of this new industry, he is aware that some of his friends, who belong to organizations such as the People's Institute and the Women's Municipal League, are quite concerned about the effect of moving pictures on the susceptible immigrants and workers. They argue constantly about whether this form of entertainment should be dismissed as a ''cheap amusement'' like the dance hall and the penny arcade or embraced as something with real potential for social or moral uplift. At the end of last year, Mayor George B. McClellan, Jr., persuaded of the deleterious nature of the moving pictures, caused considerable controversy by revoking the licenses of more than five hundred of these storefront theatres.

Well, why not see what all the fuss is about? Giving in to the impulse, Josiah hands his nickel to the woman in the box office and walks in. He pauses to permit his eyes to adjust to the dim lighting and immediately begins to understand why some of his stuffier acquaintances talk about the nickelodeon as a blight on the landscape. More than two hundred people, men, women, and children, Italians, Chinese, and Russian Jews, are crammed elbow to elbow in a small, badly ventilated, darkened room, illuminated only by the flickering pictures projected at the front. What a ripe breeding ground for physical and moral contagion!

The picture ends, the lights come up, and Josiah finds a seat in the back, as close as he can get to the exit. When he has settled himself as comfortably as possible on his hard wooden chair, a young woman steps in front of the screen and warbles a sentimental ballad accompanied by a series of crudely colored, vulgar, magic-lantern slides not at all like the exquisitely rendered fairy-tale slides that his children enjoy at home. A Western—taken, he warrants, just west of the Hudson—and a comic chase follow the song. All fail to impress him. The picture flickers, the actors move first like frenzied puppets and then like drugged, underwater swimmers, and a torrential downpour of scratches obscures every scene. The pianist thumps her badly tuned instrument with total disregard for the story, playing a lively rag for a tragic leave-taking and a funeral march during the chase.

After a pause, there appears on the screen an engraved image of an eagle perched over the words "American Mutual and Biograph Company." The audience is watching *A Drunkard's Reformation,* the tale of a young husband and father who has fallen prey to the evils of drink. Coming home intoxicated, he smashes crockery, yells at his innocent young daughter, and speaks harshly to his pretty wife until she persuades him to accompany the child to the theatre. There, the father sees a temperance melodrama and, ashamed, renounces his wicked ways. The film ends happily with the little family sitting serenely by the hearth in the glow of the fire.

Josiah enjoys the moving picture because the players remind him of the blood-and-thunder stage melodramas (some just like the play that the young father sees in the film) that he used to sneak in to see as a kid. The acting of the young wife as she depicts her misery and desperation particularly affects him. She collapses into her chair and rests her head on her arms, which are extended straight out in front of her on the table. Then, in an agony of despair, she sinks to her knees and prays, her arms fully extended upward at about a forty-five degree angle. In those cheap melodramas he had so enjoyed as a youth, he saw many an actress appeal to heaven in just such a manner. Emerging into the twilight, Josiah thought that, though he had benefited from his experience by gaining a fuller understanding of the problem of the nickelodeon, he was not likely to contract the "moving picture habit."

The years pass. One evening, shortly before the Christmas of 1912, Josiah

A Drunkard's Reformation: The despairing wife.

finishes work a little earlier than usual and decides to pay a visit to the nick-elodeon—it will be a welcome relief from the preholiday uproar at home. Since 1909, the moving pictures have become a familiar part of his life, though he still hasn't actually seen very many of them. Lydia has become involved in the activities of the National Board of Censorship, the group of private citizens sponsored by the People's Institute who pass on the suitability of new moving picture shows. She spends a couple of afternoons a month watching moving pictures with the review board and even subscribes to journals such as *The Moving Picture World, The New York Dramatic Mirror,* and the new *Motion Picture Story Magazine.* She says she needs to keep herself informed about the industry, but Josiah suspects she reads these magazines for pleasure as well. And he himself has stolen the occasional peek.

He goes to the Rialto Theatre on 14th Street, which just recently changed its programming from vaudeville to moving pictures and is conveniently near his Fifth Avenue office. The Rialto is certainly very different from the crowded, smelly, storefront theatre he went to a few years earlier. He buys his ticket, and a uniformed attendant ushers him to his plushly upholstered seat. Looking around, he sees that the clientele has also changed. Although there are still a number of patrons who seem to be recent immigrants and/or working people, women and children of his own class, who seem to be taking a break from their Christmas shopping, form a significant part of the audience.

The lights dim, though the room is not nearly as dark as the nickelodeon had been, and the program begins. To Josiah's delight, the Biograph Company's eagle again appears on the screen, heralding what will undoubtedly be an enjoyable picture, for Lydia and many of her friends believe that this company's films are among the finest made by the American manufacturers. As Josiah watches this Biograph, titled *Brutality,* he notices similarities between it and the moving picture he had seen on his memorable trip to the Bowery. This time, a decent young man takes to drink after marrying his sweetheart, and

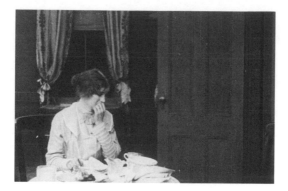

Brutality: The despairing wife.

their idyllic home life quickly deteriorates. Finally, in a reprise of *A Drunk-ard's Reformation,* the couple attends a vaudeville show that features a tem-perance melodrama, and the husband swears off liquor.

But this moving picture does not remind him of the blood-and-thunder melodramas of his youth. The acting is the equal of Mr. Gillette's in *Sherlock Holmes* or even of that in the Belasco play he and Lydia had attended last night. Particularly impressive is the young wife's despairing reaction to her husband's harsh treatment and abandonment. After he leaves for the saloon, the wife walks back to the dining-room table covered with the debris of their evening meal. She sits down, bows her head, and begins to collect the dishes. She looks up, compresses her lips, pauses, then begins to gather the dishes once again. Once more she pauses, raises her hand to her mouth, glances down to her side, and slumps a little in her chair. Slumping a little more, she begins to cry. How differently this actress portrays her grief from her counter-part in *A Drunkard's Reformation.* A lot has changed in those three-and-a-half years since his first visit to a nickelodeon.[1]

The Purpose of the Book

Our imaginary companion, though acquainted with the cinema primarily vicariously, nonetheless was astute enough to note the striking differences in the portrayals of despair by the wives in *A Drunkard's Reformation* (Biograph, 1909) and *Brutality* (Biograph, 1912). The years between the appearances of these two films saw a major transformation in cinematic acting. Not just at Biograph but at every American studio, actors moved from a performance style heavily influenced by theatrical melodrama to a style allied to "realist" movements in literature and the theatre.

To avoid confusion, I should at the outset indicate precisely how I shall use the term *performance*.[2] I wish to adopt the excellent definition offered by Richard Dyer:

Performance is what the performer does in addition to the actions/functions she or he performs in the plot and the lines she or he is given to say. Performance is how the action/function is done, how the lines are said.

The signs of performance are: facial expression; voice; gestures (principally of hands and arms, but also of any limb, e.g. neck, leg); body posture (how someone is standing or sitting); body movement (movement of the whole body, including how someone stands up or sits down, how they walk, run, etc.).[3]

Until recently, with a few exceptions to be mentioned below, film scholars have neglected the study of performance in this limited sense, concentrating instead on such other cinematic codes as narrative, mise-en-scène, and editing.[4] Neither classical or contemporary film theory nor historical inquiries into specific national cinemas have provided the means to assess the contribution that actors and their performances make to a film's overall meaning. A central component of cinema as text and cinema as institution has been widely ignored and, when not ignored, undertheorized.

This book examines acting styles in the American cinema between 1908 and 1913, years that film historians have come to designate as part of the transitional period, that is, the period between the "early" or "primitive" cinema (1894–1907) and the standardization of representational practices in 1917. Rather than attempting to account for the hundreds of films made during this period, I shall look instead, for reasons to be enumerated below, at the Biograph films made by D. W. Griffith. By focusing on Griffith's Biograph films made during the transitional years, I hope to trace the emergence of a performance style that came to dominate the classical Hollywood cinema and, by extension, world cinema.

Between the years 1905 and 1913, changes in film content, exhibition venues, and even the audiences pointed toward the increasing "respectability" of the cinema. Since the mid-1970s film historians have paid a great deal of attention to the pre-1917 or pre-classical Hollywood cinema, much of their work centering on the important modifications in both textual signifying practices and conditions of production and reception that led to film's changing social status.[5] Through focusing on one signifying practice, performance, this book may further our understanding of a crucial period in the history of the American cinema, during which film, once a cheap amusement patronized primarily by immigrant laborers in urban centers, changed into an acceptable mass entertainment patronized weekly by millions of Americans of all classes. This book is thus addressed to early cinema historians as well as all those interested in cinematic performance.

Related Works

Although film scholars have recently paid increasing attention to both acting/performance and stardom, only two books, Charles Affron's *Star Acting* and James Naremore's *Acting in the Cinema*, deal specifically with "what the performer does in addition to the actions/functions she or he performs in the plot and the lines she or he is given to say," though both, because they examine famous actors, also touch on issues of stardom.[6]

Affron's book examines three of Hollywood's most glittering stars—Lillian Gish, Greta Garbo, and Bette Davis. His analysis of their key films contains extensive and detailed descriptions, supplemented by numerous frame enlargements, of actors' gestures, movements, and facial expressions. Although Affron asserts that his purpose is "to illustrate certain techniques for the analysis of star acting, and how we perceive star acting in context," he explicitly disavows any attempt at general theorization: "It would be absurd to derive a stylistics of screen acting from three stars, or from any number of stars for that matter."[7] He predicates his method upon humanist faith in the unique individuality of both stars and scholars, hence overtly valorizing the "essential distinctness" of each of his stars and covertly valorizing his own judgments and appreciations, all of which leaves me wondering precisely how we might go about deriving a stylistics of screen acting that would enable us to transcend the unique individuality of stars and scholars.[8]

Naremore's *Acting in the Cinema* represents a major step beyond Affron's idiosyncratic musings. In the first section of his book, Naremore reflects on a host of complex issues with which any generally applicable theory of performance must come to terms, including such difficult problems as distinguishing performance from everyday life, defining performance space, and distinguishing between "actor" and "character." Although Naremore probably would not claim to have resolved these problems, he does give them more intelligent and sustained attention than any previous analyst, thereby producing the most theoretically insightful and sophisticated book yet on acting per se and laying a firm foundation for subsequent scholarship. The last two-thirds of Naremore's book may be seen, in part, as an attempt to derive a "stylistics of screen acting" from what Affron would term a "number of stars." Naremore discusses Gish in *True Heart Susie*, Chaplin in *The Gold Rush*, Dietrich in *Morocco*, Cagney in *Angels with Dirty Faces*, Hepburn in *Holiday*, Brando in *On the Waterfront*, and Grant in *North by Northwest*, as well as the ensemble acting in *Rear Window* and *The King of Comedy*. And here Naremore's book suffers from the same failing as Affron's: it presents assessments of individual performances predicated mostly on textual analysis and the judgments of the analyst and uninformed by the larger social, historical context.

Two other books, though not focused mainly on performance, present historical perspectives that make them directly relevant to this project. Richard Dyer's admirable *Stars*, mentioned above, presents the definition of performance that I have adopted here, which usefully restricts the area of investigation and encourages description rather than evaluation. Such description can, however, be judgmentally weighted. Moreover, simple description cannot tell us how the performance signs function within the overall meaning of the text, that is, how the actor conveys meaning. Assessment of the meaning of performance requires not only description but interpretation, as Dyer himself well knows.

Although Dyer addresses himself only briefly to film acting, as opposed to stardom, his insistence on the acknowledgement of culturally and historically specific codes provides a necessary first principle for further investigation. Dyer's performance signs (facial expression, voice, gestures, body posture, and body movement) are all extremely complex and ambiguous, potentially subject to multiple interpretations if inquiry is limited to the interaction between texts and analysts. Reducing this ambiguity requires applying extra- and intertextual knowledge, as well as some notion of reception, to contextualize textual analysis. As Dyer says, "The signification of a given performance sign is determined by its place within culturally and historically specific codes."[9]

Tom Gunning, a leading member of the new coterie of early film scholars that has emerged in the past fifteen years or so, has written an invaluable study of the first two years of D. W. Griffith's career at Biograph.[10] Gunning presents a thoroughgoing, detailed, and reliable textual analysis of the early Biographs, charting the many transformations in signifying practices that occurred in 1908 and 1909. He also attempts to correlate these textual transformations with simultaneous changes in film industry organization, constructing his argument with painstaking research and copious detail.

Gunning does, at several points in this massive work, discuss acting and the different kinds of performance styles used by actors in the Griffith Biographs. As we might hope to see in an early film scholar, he displays sensitivity to bygone cultural codes and begins his first sustained consideration of acting by immediately correcting a common misperception: "All too often modern critics dismiss melodramatic acting (and the acting in early films) as wild undisciplined overplaying. Rather it was a conscious system of conventional signs for portraying characters' emotions."[11] At a later point he briefly addresses the change from the "melodramatic" style, which he argues characterizes early Biograph performances, to the "more naturalistic performance style in the acting of the later films."[12]

In subsequent chapters I shall have frequent occasion to refer to Gunning's work, which forms such an important prelude to my own project, but, for the moment, I merely wish to question his terminology. Consider the two films seen by our imaginary New York City lawyer, *A Drunkard's Reformation,* released in April 1909 and starring Linda Arvidson as the wife and Arthur Johnson as the husband, and *Brutality,* released in December 1912, with Mae Marsh and Walter Miller playing the couple. Gunning, and many others, would probably characterize Arvidson's depiction of despair as melodramatic and Marsh's as naturalistic. Yet such characterizations cannot adequately either describe or account for the major transformation in cinematic acting represented by the contrast between these two performances.

Even by the nickelodeon period (1908–1913) the adjectives "melodramatic," "naturalistic," and "realistic" had been so indiscriminately applied to such greatly diverse theatrical styles and performers as to lose any precise meaning, and the intervening decades have added to their numerous connotations. After encountering these terms in their various guises, one begins to feel like Alice trying to converse with Humpty Dumpty, who tells her: "When I use a word it means just what I choose it to mean—neither more nor less."[13]

The concepts of realism and naturalism have had wide currency in dramatic criticism since Shakespeare's time at least. To quote Hamlet's advice to the players: "O'erstep not the modesty of nature; for anything so o'erdone is from the purpose of playing, whose end, both at the first and now, was to hold, as 'twere, the mirror up to nature." Phrases from this speech crop up again and again in nineteenth-century dramatic criticism to support myriad and often contradictory positions. In the next chapter, we will look at some of the various nineteenth-century meanings of realism and naturalism in both literary and dramatic contexts.

While the ideas of realism and naturalism are venerable, the word *melodrama* and its adjectival form *melodramatic* are of more recent vintage. Initially, *melodrama* and *melodramatic* referred to a theatrical form that originated in late-eighteenth-century France and became extremely popular throughout the nineteenth century in both Britain and the United States. Although various sub-genres, such as the gothic and the domestic, emerged and disappeared over the years, certain elements remained constant. Plots centered around imperiled virtue, black villainy, and fantastic coincidences that allowed the former to triumph over the latter. Heightened emotion and exciting situations mattered far more than coherent narrative progression. Stock figures of no psychological depth inhabited these improbable plots: most importantly, the pure heroine, the gallant hero, and the dastardly villain.

With the decline of melodrama's widespread appeal at the end of the century and its relegation to the inexpensive theatres frequented by the working classes, *melodramatic* became a term of opprobrium, with negative connotations that have persisted to this day. In film studies, however, the concept of melodrama has become increasingly fashionable, film scholars applying "melodramatic" to such diverse phenomena as *The Birth of a Nation*, the 1940s woman's film, Fassbinder's oeuvre, soap operas, and the latest network miniseries. Such widespread and indiscriminate usage has rendered the term all but meaningless.[14] In dealing with the transition in acting styles between 1908 and 1913, then, one must jettison the kind of imprecise terminology used by Gunning.

This discussion of the work of Affron, Naremore, Dyer, and Gunning points to two primary requisites in any study of performance. First, any such study should avoid devolving into idiosyncratic analyses of the scholar's favorite actors predicated on personal biases. In other words, a more broadly applicable analysis of performance necessitates augmenting textual analysis with other methodologies that, in a sense, correct for personal bias. Second, broadening the scope of inquiry beyond the text and thus contextualizing one's own preferences requires constant awareness of the cultural and historical specificity of performance codes and of the implicit judgments inherent in familiar descriptive terms such as melodramatic and naturalistic.

Affron and Naremore's tendency to fall back on their own unsubstantiated perceptions, a failing that characterizes most writing to date on cinematic acting, is not unexpected in light of John Thompson's observation that "normative considerations are absolutely basic to the cinema . . . as an institution." Yet "the dream of a non-normative, descriptive-analytic discourse on the cinema arises not only out of the desire for truth but from a wish to escape the tedium and frivolity of the judgmental."

Clearly, film scholars can never entirely escape the "frivolity of the judgmental." Nor should we profess that we have, for such a claim would reek of social scientific positivism. While we must realize that we remain creatures of our own historical moment, such a realization carries us a good distance along the road toward the development of historically sensitive approaches to the analysis of performance styles, which might approach a "non-normative, descriptive-analytic discourse."

As Thompson again points out:

> Performance norms present as clear a case of cultural relativity as could be asked for. Not only the experience of non-Western performance traditions, not only the accessibility of sufficiently detailed descriptions of acting in our own culture in previous centuries, but even the short history of the sound cinema illustrates how one framework's good is another's alien, stiff, laughable.[15]

The study of cinematic performance demands that we not depend upon our own aesthetic judgments, which we tacitly deem eternal and unchanging. Rather, we must acknowledge history by attempting to understand the aesthetic standards of another time and place, of a culture very different from our own. As I shall suggest below, the adducing of intertextual evidence provides one route of access to these forgotten aesthetic standards.

We cannot easily arrive at a method for analyzing performance that simultaneously transcends personal preferences and deals with a rich and complex historical context. Indeed, the difficulties inherent in such a task have dictated the narrow focus of this project on films made by one director at one studio during one five-year period. Yet I believe that the narrowness of the focus does not preclude the wider application of the pluralistic methodological approach suggested in this book.

Why Griffith?
Why the Transitional Period?

My membership in a generation of film scholars trained to debunk auteurism, as well as in a coterie of early film historians who have contested Griffith's position as the founder of modern "film language" may make my decision to rely here on Griffith and the Griffith Biographs seem strange and, perhaps, even wrongheaded. But while this book is ultimately more concerned with acting than with Griffith, there are compelling reasons, having to do both with Griffith/Biograph and the changes in the film industry circa 1908–1913, for choosing the Griffith films to exemplify the transition in acting style.

As early as 1910, Frank Woods, Spectator of *The New York Dramatic Mirror,* had written of the Biograph director's "striking aptitude for taking raw acting material and molding it into finished and polished form."[16] Woods could not mention Griffith by name, because Biograph continued to insist that its employees remain nameless long after other studios had begun publicizing both actors and production staff. Freed from this cloak of anonymity after his departure from the Biograph Company in 1913, D. W. Griffith took out a full page advertisement in *The New York Dramatic Mirror* touting himself as the "producer of all great Biograph successes," responsible for "revolutionizing Motion Picture drama and founding the modern technique of the art." The advertisement listed, as one of Griffith's major accomplishments, "restraint in expression, raising motion picture acting to the higher plane which has won for it recognition as a genuine art."[17] This advertisement heralded the start of an intensive campaign for personal recognition. The single-handed creation of a new and uniquely cinematic acting style figured largely in the myth of the great director that Griffith enthusiastically fostered. In interviews after the *Mirror* advertisement (published under such revealing titles as "The Man Who Made the Movies" and "The Genius of the Movies") writers eagerly collaborated in Griffith's self-promotion, crediting him with a profound impact on film acting. "It was Mr. Griffith who made moving pictures real, who insisted that actors act naturally."[18] Griffith was said to have invented the close-up, or at least to have brought the camera close enough to permit this "natural" acting:

> David W. Griffith was the first to bring the camera close enough to the face to catch the natural play of expression. Actors no longer rely on the waving of arms and legs for the interpretation of character and plot. So far reaching were the results of this innovation that it may be considered the most important single contribution ever made to pictures outside of mechanical invention.[19]

Griffith was also said to have taught a new generation of actors the "restraint in expression" necessary to a new style of film performance:

They [the actors] do not suggest the stage, and the result of their molding is a distinctive type of acting—as taught in the Griffith school, and for naturalness seldom approached elsewhere. Of course, it has conventions of its own, but they are not the conventions of screen emotions. Sweeping gestures, fainting on slight provocation, falling on arms of chairs to weep, and kindred actions that may be seen on the screen everyday, though seldom in life, give place to restraint. Grief, joy, love, jealousy . . . are registered by facial expressions, tentative movements and sometimes the immobility that follows emotions of stunning power.[20]

Among the press, both trade and popular, the consensus seems to have been that Griffith had greatly influenced film performance and all but single-handedly originated the new style. This perception certainly stemmed in part from Griffith's effective public relations, but many people, both within and outside the film industry, believed that Griffith and his actors had developed a performance style uniquely suited to the new medium of moving pictures. The unprecedented and unparalleled success of *The Birth of a Nation* probably ensured that the Griffith acting style became even more influential than during the Biograph years. Even today, when film scholars adamantly resist the great-man theory of film history, a prominent scholar still credits the Biograph director with "a true Griffith innovation, the new acting style."[21]

Further evidence for the impact of the Griffith Biograph's upon film acting comes from the trade press commentary on the films themselves. Griffith's first Biograph film, *The Adventures of Dollie,* was released in July 1908. By the next spring, the trade press had begun to agree that Biograph acting was some of the best, if not *the* best, to be found on the screen. Phrases such as "natural touches," "excellence," "splendid," and "superb" occur again and again with regard to Biograph acting. In a lengthy review of *Lady Helen's Escapade, The Moving Picture World* stated that "the Biograph Company . . . in the last few weeks, have by common consent placed themselves at the very head of American film manufacturers, alike for the technical and dramatic quality of their pictures."[22] Lest there be any doubt as to what was meant by *dramatic,* the *World* a month later asserted that any Biograph film "is one in which one is almost sure to see good acting."[23] Soon the *New York Dramatic Mirror* decided that Biograph acting was not only good but the best: "The Biograph Company at present is producing a better general average of dramatic pantomime than any other company in America."[24]

According to Lux Graphicus, a pseudonymous columnist for *The Moving Picture World*, the picture-going public as well as journalists recognized and responded to the excellence of Biograph performance. "They worship that silent Biograph heroine and know that the handsome leading man will always give good acting." The writer's account of his visit to the Bijou Dream to see *The Way of Man,* released in late June 1909, provides a rare glimpse at the reactions of a nickelodeon audience:

The title appeared and there was a sudden hush . . . and the people leaned forward expectantly . . . a man on my left who had been interjecting criticism, muttered to himself, "Now we shall see something good" . . . I saw interest and expectancy in every face. . . . "Why," said the man on my left, "you can see them thinking." This man unconsciously voiced the feeling of the entire house. We saw the three leading characters thinking. We were conscious of aught else. . . . Now this picture held the attention of the audience right up to the very last foot of film.[25]

Aside from Griffith's and the Biographs' leading role in the acting transition, compelling pragmatic reasons also dictate the choice of this particular studio's output. Our knowledge of the majority of films made between 1908 and 1913 derives from advertisements and reviews in the trade press, for a great many of the films themselves have been lost. The products of the Biograph studio are the major exception; virtually all the films made during Griffith's tenure survive, either in the paper prints deposited at the Library of Congress for copyright purposes or in some other form.[26] This almost-complete run of films provides a unique record of day-to-day and month-to-month changes in performance style. Although these films constitute an invaluable resource, the lack of a comparable record from another studio limits our ability to generalize: strictly speaking, all conclusions are drawn with regard to the Biographs only, though, as I have argued above, these films seem to have had a major impact on film acting at other studios.[27]

In addition to the films themselves, the amount of written material about Griffith and the Biographs, both primary and secondary, far surpasses that available for any other director or studio of the time.[28] Thirty-six reels of microfilm photographed from the Griffith Collection at the Museum of Modern Art contain many interviews with Biograph actors as well as an unedited version of the memoirs of Billy Bitzer, Griffith's longtime cameraman. All of the Biograph Bulletins (which advertised the company's product to film distributors and exhibitors) have been collected and published.[29] Several autobiographies supplement these primary sources.[30] Of the numerous secondary sources two stand out, the first Gunning's, and the second the production records and cast lists in *D. W. Griffith and the Biograph Company.*[31]

All the above does not, of course, justify the valorization of Griffith as the "Great Director" and the concomitant dismissal of early film as "pre-Griffith" cinema. One can defend the decision to study film performance between the years 1908 and 1913 on historical grounds completely unrelated to the presence of David Wark Griffith at 11 East 14th Street. The year 1908 saw the culmination of many significant changes in both film texts and film industry, which established the basic pattern for the nickelodeon era. By 1913, the year that Griffith left Biograph to strike out on his own, the nickelodeon era had virtually come to a close.

By 1908 the fictional narrative or story film was the major product of the

American film industry. Controversy typical of scholarship on the early cinema exists concerning the exact point at which the story film became dominant. Robert C. Allen locates the shift in the years 1907 and 1908: "A dramatic change occurred in American motion picture production: in one year narrative forms of cinema (comedy and dramatic) all but eclipsed documentary forms in volume of production." Allen notes that in 1908 story films constituted 96 percent of output.[32] More important, from my perspective, the percentage of dramatic films (as opposed to comedies and actualities) increased from 17 percent in 1907 to 66 percent in 1908.[33] Charles Musser argues that Allen's methodology is fundamentally flawed in its reliance on "quantification of subject by title."[34] Instead of counting titles, Musser presents data about the quantity of actual film footage, both negative feet and print feet, statistics that he claims much better reflect what people were really watching. Actuality titles outnumber fiction titles, but the latter seem to have been both longer and more popular. Musser concludes that "from the summer of 1904 onward, story films were made in substantial quantities and consistently outsold actualities that companies like Edison continued to produce, although with decreasing frequency."[35] Allen has acknowledged that Musser "corrects my use of incomplete data in computing the number of narrative films made during a given period."[36] But the implications of the statistics remain at issue. Did, as Musser asserts, the fiction film give rise to the nickelodeon, or did, as Allen asserts, the nickelodeon give rise to the fiction film? Fortunately, for my purposes, the advent of the fiction film, and its relation to the nickelodeon, does not matter as much as the narrative structure of the fiction film, which did indeed undergo a transformation circa 1907–1908. Gunning argues that in the early Biographs changes in editing, camerawork, composition, and other systems of meaning contributed to the formation of a "narrator system" that subordinates all these other elements to the need to tell a story. For example, Griffith incorporated into his early films some of the "special effects," such as stop motion, used in Biograph trick films, not as "the central attraction" to be "admired for its mechanical virtuosity and the wonder it creates," but as a way to develop narrative logic or characterization."[37]

The development of "narrative logic or characterization" through internal means was a relatively new strategy in 1908. As Musser has shown, prior to 1907, most film narratives were not self-sufficient, leading film manufacturers and exhibitors to employ a variety of devices to effect narrative coherence: intertextuality, redundancy (e.g., the chase), sound effects, and lectures.[38] But increasing demands for films from the rapidly proliferating nickelodeons created a desire among the manufacturers for "production efficiency and maximum profits."[39] The old system of representation was inadequate to these needs, and a new system arose based on strict linear temporality and the use of parallel editing and matching action.[40] Internally coherent narratives predicated on new modes of representation are linked, Gunning suggests, to an increasing psychologization and individuation of film characters: "The approach to characterization in the *narrator-system* asserts its hold on *story* through an expression of *psychology,* by which I mean the portrayal of interior states, such as memories or strong emotions, which are then seen as motivation for the action of characters."[41] I argue below, in Chapter 4, for a strong connection between the psychologized character and the transition in performance style.

The dominance of the fiction film, with emerging internally coherent narratives and rudimentary psychologization, coincides, as Richard deCordova has shown, with increasing journalistic attention to the actor and film performance: "Before 1907 there was no discourse on the film actor. Textual productivity was focused elsewhere, for the most part on the apparatus itself, on its magical abilities and its capacity to reproduce the real."[42] By 1907 journalists acknowledged the existence of film actors, but only insofar as their actions were important to the construction of a coherent narrative. Prior to 1908, deCordova observes, "acting was a profession associated with the legitimate stage, and the contention that people acted in films was neither immediately apparent nor altogether unproblematic."[43] Not until 1908 did the press begin to talk of film acting as an "art" worthy of comparison with the legitimate stage.[44]

Musser's work on the status of film actors complements deCordova's. Though he dates the fiction film from 1904, he says that a group of professional motion-picture actors did not become established until 1908. Prior to 1908, film studios had hired theatrical actors, who often kept their moving-picture work secret. Around 1907 the film manufacturers began to hire actors on a regular basis, developing the stock companies characteristic of the nickelodeon period.[45]

The emergence of internally coherent narratives centered on individuated characters combined with the development of resident stock companies makes 1908 an important year in the history of film performance. Instead of simply chasing their colleagues from shot to shot or reenacting topical incidents, actors must have begun to think about the characters they were portraying. Having a stable cast and the time to rehearse before the actual shooting, the director could help the actors in the construction of their characters. But 1908 is notable for changes not only in the films and the mode of production but also in the entire structure of the film industry.

By this year the film exchanges and the nickelodeons had wrested control of distribution and exhibition from the production companies and were consequently, from the producers' perspective, garnering too large a proportion of the profits. Led by the Edison and Biograph studios, the producers attempted to redress the balance, forming (along with six other companies) the Motion Picture Patents Company, or, as it was popularly known, the Trust.

The Trust derived its powers from pooling patents on film stock, cameras, and projectors. Film exchanges (the middlemen in the distribution chain), which were governed by the cartel's standards, now had to rent films rather than buy them outright, and only licensed exhibitors, who paid a weekly royalty on their patented projectors, could rent Trust films from the exchanges.

Aside from hoping to rationalize distribution and exhibition and improve their profit margin, the producers formed their cartel in response to increasing calls for censorship and regulation of exhibition sites. When films ceased to be a scientific and educational novelty and became primarily an amusement—and worse yet, in some eyes, an amusement for the "lower classes"—various sectors of the society predictably began to advocate government control of film content. The nickelodeons' reputation as dark, dirty, and immoral exacerbated the problem. When on Christmas Eve of 1908 New York City Mayor McClellan ordered all the nickelodeons closed, only a court injunction prevented him from keeping them closed. This near-crisis led the industry to help form the National Board of Censorship, an independent body that reviewed films before their release, recommending cuts and even suppressing some films entirely. The contemporary debate about the social function of entertainment, which partially accounts for the formation of both the Trust and the Board of Censorship, also relates to the shift in performance style, as will be discussed in Chapter 7.

By 1913 the nickelodeon era drew to a close, as several trends soon culminated in the film form and industry organization of the classical Hollywood cinema, different in many significant respects from the earlier period on which this book focuses. By this year, the Motion Picture Patents Company was in decline, as was the nickelodeon. More important, in terms of performance style, the short fifteen-minute films of the nickelodeon era had given way to the longer "feature film," and the star system came close to full flower.

Although the Motion Picture Patents Company was not declared illegal until 1915, by 1913 the rise of the "independents" had thoroughly undermined the Trust's power. Many of these independents, headed by such entrepreneurs as William Fox and Carl Laemmle, had already established organizations that would form the nucleus of the Hollywood industry. The year 1913 also saw the appearance of the picture palaces, a standard of lavishness that had been emerging for several years. Magnificent organs and even full orchestras replaced the badly tuned piano of the old nickelodeons, and elaborate stage shows replaced the amateur singers. Perhaps of more consequence for the industry, middle-class men, women, and children now frequented the picture shows they had once despised as unsuitable for decent society. Film was well on its way to becoming a mass medium.

Although American film manufacturers had, as early as 1909, experimented with longer films consisting of three to five fifteen-minute reels, the entire film lasting from thirty minutes to a little over an hour, the distribution system for the most part prevented screening the separate reels in one showing. In 1912 and 1913 many foreign multi-reelers, such as Sarah Bernhardt's *Queen Elizabeth* and the Italian *Quo Vadis,* were being shown as "feature" films, a development with which American producers felt forced to keep pace. The advent of the feature film had profound implications for both the rationalization of studio production practices and narrative structure, the latter, in turn, affecting performance style, since signifying practices are mutually interdependent.[46] As Kristin Thompson suggests, the feature film promoted the new acting style by "allowing, even encouraging, more time for character development."[47] I would add that the feature film, with its greater character development, modified, but did not fundamentally alter, the acting style of 1913.

From roughly 1909 to 1912, according to Richard deCordova, film actors were discussed in the press as "picture personalities." The actor's personality was seen as coinciding with that of her or his film characters: "The site of interest was the personality of the player *as presented on film.* There was thus a kind of restriction of knowledge about the players to the textuality of the films they were in."[48] By 1913, with the emergence of the star system, the press began to discuss actors' private lives, the people they "really were" off the silver screen. "In a very short period of time," deCordova notes, "the journalistic apparatus that supported the star system became geared toward producing an endless stream of information about the private lives of the stars."[49] The intertextual framework for the reception of actors and acting thus expanded considerably, seriously complicating any analysis of performance. Both the shift to the feature film, with its concomitant changes in narrative structure, and the advent of the star system, with the expansion of the intertextual framework, make 1913 an appropriate cutoff date for this investigation.

The Plan of the Book

As I said above, any study of performance that aspires to more than personal idiosyncrasy must correct for personal bias by augmenting textual analysis with other methodologies and must also remain constantly aware of the cultural and historical specificity of performance codes. This book, then, takes a pluralistic methodological approach, looking at the transformation of performance style in the Griffith Biographs as the result of a complexly overdetermined interaction among text, intertext, and context. Close textual analysis of both performance style and narrative structure is combined first with intertextual evidence concerning performance style in the nineteenth-century theatre and the reception of cinematic performance in the trade press and second with contextual evidence concerning the cultural position of the film medium during the period.

The next two chapters attempt to ground the discussion of Biograph performance style firmly in the late nineteenth and early twentieth centuries. Chapter 2 draws on intertextual evidence concerning the performance styles of the nineteenth-century stage to develop a terminology and a descriptive methodology that strive to escape both my own unsubstantiated perceptions and the aesthetic judgments of late-twentieth-century culture. Chapter 2 thus sets forth a diachronic, semiotic model of performance, predicated on historical intertextual evidence, that enables the close textual analysis of chapter 3 to trace the gradual changes in acting taking place over the five years Griffith spent at the Biograph Company.

The remainder of the book then attempts to account for this transformation. Chapter 4 contains a close analysis of some key films, exploring the interaction among performance, narrative, and other textual signifying practices. Chapters 5 and 6 look at Griffith and his actors, taking what might be called a modified auteurist perspective. Chapter 7 first examines trade press discourse, showing that the transformation in performance was industrywide and hence contextualizes the Griffith Biographs within the film industry as a whole. The chapter also connects the shift in performance style to the overall shift in film's cultural status. The performance style emerging in the Griffith Biographs, then, can be seen as an aspect of the film industry's very complicated response to a perception of imminent crisis.

2

The Theatrical Heritage

"Despite the stylized pantomimic gestures employed by Linda [Arvidson] and Arthur Johnson, . . . some small transcendence of types and situations was achieved."[1] Richard Schickel, the author of one of the more recent additions to the rapidly growing Griffith bibliography, thus assesses Griffith's first film, *The Adventures of Dollie*. Schickel might find *Dollie* laudable in all other respects, but to him the acting is on an equal—that is to say equally bad—footing with that of any other 1908 one-reeler. A few pages later, Shickel discusses the results of the Biograph Company's 1909–1910 sojourn in Los Angeles: "There was still, even in Griffith's films, plenty of posturing, exaggeration, excessive movement, . . . but in fact he was managing to tone this down and sometimes . . . to almost totally eliminate it."[2] Schickel seems to see the transformation in acting style as a simple, linear progression from the bad "posturing, exaggeration, excessive movement" to the good "deliberation and repose" that was being praised in the *New York Dramatic Mirror*.[3]

In the past, many writers on the early silent film committed similar errors of historical solipsism, devaluing not just the acting but also other signifying practices, such as editing. The films and signifying practices of the pre-Hollywood era were often depicted as necessary but faltering steps along the yellow brick road to the Emerald City of the classical Hollywood cinema. More recently, an intensive reevaluation of the pre-Hollywood period has done much to correct this teleological perspective.[4] Instead of dismissing the early silent films as primitive or preliminary, scholars now appreciate that their signifying practices constitute the road not taken and strive to understand the ideological determinants of their abandonment.

The Adventures of Dollie: "Stylized pantomimic gestures."

Yet surprisingly, even a scholar who has contributed a great deal to the reevaluation of the early silent cinema takes a somewhat teleological perspective on silent-film performance style. Janet Staiger, in "The Eyes are Really the Focus: Photoplay Acting and Film Form and Style," draws on evidence from the film-trade press and theatrical history to discuss performance style between 1908 and 1913, producing a creditable essay. In the first paragraph, however, Staiger contrasts the "graceful, intense, restrained and illusionistic" style of the "great actresses of the teens" with the "older film acting style of broad gestures, grotesque facial grimaces and contorted body movements."[5] Though Staiger never explicitly denounces the old style, the opposition between "graceful" and "intense," on the one hand, and "grotesque" and "contorted," on the other, unavoidably valorizes the new style. This valorization, inadvertent though it may be, blurs the possible ideological implications of shifts in performance style.

Recourse to intertextuality can help deal with the problem of a teleological perspective insensitive to the aesthetic standards of a bygone age. As the paradigms of auteurism and psychoanalysis, previously so influential in cinema studies, have given way during the past few years to new paradigms derived from British cultural studies and reader response/reception theory, the primacy of the text has simultaneously given way to a concern with intertextual and contextual matters. Film scholars increasingly supplement textual analysis with knowledge of how a particular text both relates to other texts and functions in the larger culture. Indeed, many theorists, including Tony Bennett and Janet Woollacott in *Bond and Beyond: The Political Career of a Popular Hero,* argue that the text by itself has no independent existence, is "an inconceivable object":

> The case of Bond throws into high relief the radical insufficiency of those forms of
> cultural analysis which, in purporting to study texts 'in themselves', do radical vi-

olence to the real nature of the social existence and functioning of texts in pretending that 'the text itself' can be granted an existence, as a hypostatised entity, separated out from the always variable systems of inter-textual relations which supply
the real conditions of its signifying functioning.[6]

A text, then, can only exist within and because of an intertextual framework. Intertextuality should not be conceived in the narrow art-historical sense
of direct influence. Rather, intertextuality refers to those texts, both "traditional" ones such as books, paintings, and plays, and less tangible ones such
as broadly diffused cultural conceptions, which form a framework for the reception of a particular text. As Jonathan Culler observes:

> Intertextuality thus becomes less a name for a work's relation to particular prior
> texts than a designation of its participation in the discursive space of a culture: the
> relationship between a text and the various languages or signifying practices of a
> culture and its relation to those texts which articulate for it the possibilities of that
> culture. The study of intertextuality is thus not the investigation of sources and
> influences as traditionally conceived.[7]

Because intertextuality conditions both production and reception, one cannot describe and account for the transformation of acting style in the Griffith
Biographs without reference to the intertextual frames within which these
films may have been produced and received. What was the shared frame of
reference between producers and audiences, derived from culturally prevalent
conceptions of "correct" performance style, that conditioned the production
and reception of acting in the Griffith Biographs?[8] I shall refer to this shared
intertextual framework as a code, by which, if you will, the producers encoded
their messages and the audience decoded them.[9]

Intertextuality, then, can help to temper a teleological perspective. But how
might we deal with the problem of value-laden terminology, which I raised in
the previous chapter, and avoid the use of such terms as "melodramatic,"
"realistic," and "naturalistic"? Rejecting these terms, and following
Humpty Dumpty's advice that Alice become the master of her words, I shall
invent my own terms for the old and new performance styles.

Between 1908 and 1913 the intertextual frame about performance style
shared by the Biograph producers and their audience gradually shifted. In
1908 the producers and audience derived the frame of reference primarily from
their knowledge of theatrical conventions, which were by that time associated
with the melodrama. Performance style was "histrionically" coded. By 1913
the shared intertextual frame derived primarily from knowledge of culturally
specific notions about the mimesis of everyday life. Performance was "verisimilarly" coded. I shall henceforth refer to the old style as the *histrionic code*
and the new style as the *verisimilar code*.

The Histrionic Code

The *Oxford English Dictionary* defines *histrionic* as "theatrical in character or style, stagey." The histrionic code is, in a sense, reflexive, referring always to the theatrical event rather than to the outside world. Until the second half of the nineteenth century, most English and American actors in most theatres performed in a self-consciously theatrical fashion, ostentatiously playing a role rather than pretending to be another person. Disdaining to mask technique in the modern fashion, actors proudly displayed their skills, always striving to create a particular effect. Performers, audiences, and critics all knew that a theatrical presentation was an artificial construct meant to bear little resemblance to any off-stage reality. Audiences and critics condemned as inadequate those who did not demonstrably act: the pleasure derived not from participating in an illusion but from witnessing a virtuoso performance.

The actors remained always aware of the spectators, "playing to the gallery." The stars stood at center stage, facing front, as close to the footlights as possible. At their climactic speeches, they would "make points," striding across the stage in deliberate fashion to call for applause. The audience entered into the spirit of the occasion, applauding more frequently than is the current custom, and even encoring favorite speeches. At times the audience would demand the reenactment of entire scenes, displaying a particular fondness for the repetition of heartrending, pitiful deaths.

The actors moved in stylized fashion, selecting their gestures from a conventional, standardized repertoire passed on not only through an "oral" tradition and stock-company training but through descriptions and illustrations in acting manuals and handbooks.[10] As early as the eighteenth century, "various attempts had been made to select and classify the gestures that were appropriate for use on the stage."[11] These manuals instructed actors on the facial expressions and arrangement of limbs and head necessary to portray a vast gamut of emotions. For example:

> Rage or Anger expresses itself with rapidity, interruption, rant, harshness and trepidation. The neck is stretched out, the head forward, often nodding and shaking in a menacing manner against the object of the passion . . . the feet often stamping; the right arm frequently thrown out menacingly, with the clenched fist shaken, and a general and violent agitation of the whole body.[12]

Just as many schools of acting flourished throughout the century, the instruction manuals proliferated. We may question how accurately the manuals reflect actual theatrical practice, because many of them were directed at either would-be thespians or amateurs. Nonetheless, the manuals provide the best available data about the histrionic code, recording gesture and movement in much more detail than do contemporary reviews or memoirs. My explication of the histrionic code depends mainly on instruction manuals and other books propounding the Delsarte system, one of the most popular and influential of the various schools of acting.

François Delsarte was a Frenchman who headed a theatrical academy in Paris and died shortly after the Franco-Prussian War. Founding his system upon the observation of human behavior, he assumed that posture mirrors emotions, a different posture corresponding to every shade of feeling. Delsarte devised exercises that taught his students to reproduce these postures, making a connection between "real life" and the stage, which the histrionic code denied. As one of his American disciples, Geneviève Stebbins, put it, "The actor's art is to express in well known symbols what an individual man may be supposed to feel. . . . But unless the actor follows nature sufficiently close to select symbols recognized as natural, he fails to touch us."[13] But Stebbins goes on to warn against a thoughtless and slavish reproduction of everyday behavior: "Strict fidelity to nature is nonsense. Art must always idealize nature, and when it fails to do this, it fails in its proper expression."[14]

Why equate Delsartism with the histrionic code? Delsartism thrived at the end of the nineteenth century, by which time histrionically coded performance had all but vanished from most stages. Moreover, Delsarte and some of his more faithful disciples professed to follow nature, a practice that was anathema to many of those championing histrionically coded performance. Delsarte, it would seem, desired to challenge the hegemony of the histrionic code, but the wholesale acceptance of Delsartism perverted its founder's intentions. His system, in its debased form, became emblematic of histrionically coded performances. His followers forgot about following "nature sufficiently close" in their enthusiastic determination to "idealize nature."

The Delsarte system enjoyed an American vogue, largely due to the proselytizing of Steele MacKaye, one of the important actor managers of the late nineteenth century, who also lectured widely and established the first dramatic school in New York City. Delsarte's enthusiastic American proponents applied the master's precepts to everything from dance to oratory, in the process rendering the system mechanical and artificial, a mere cookbook of theatrical emotion. They jettisoned theory, observation, and any notion of following nature, devising "correct" poses for each emotion and state of mind. Delsarte instruction books illustrating these poses resemble others of the period, and many of the pictures would today strike even the nonspecialist as immediately familiar. As any five-year-old child familiar with Saturday-morning cartoons could tell you, the right hand raised to the forehead, left arm extended backward, means "mine woes afflict this spirit sore."[15]

Delsartism's vast popularity and the great wealth of available information make it the obvious primary source for evidence about the histrionic code. One can also argue that the Delsarte postures reflect actual practice. After reading the manuals and examining the pictures, one discovers striking similarities among Delsarte postures, descriptions of melodramatic acting, and performances in the early Biographs. By the end of the nineteenth century, melodrama's appeal had waned and it was presented mainly at the cheaper or "popular"-priced theatres, such as those clustered along New York's Bowery. On these stages the histrionic code, banished from the boards of the higher-priced theatres, still flourished. And when the popular-priced theatres and the melodrama faltered circa 1907–1908, histrionically coded performances survived, though now in the nickelodeon rather than the cheap theatre.

If one were so inclined, it would be possible to present numerous instances, complete with frame enlargements and plate reproductions, of poses found in both Delsarte manuals and the early Biographs. Two factors invalidate this tactic. First, though strong similarities existed, one must not overstate the case: Biograph performance style, as will be seen, did not exactly duplicate either Delsartism or any other school. Second, the interesting parallels between Biograph and Delsarte style lie not in specific poses but in the overall principles of histrionically coded acting shared by the two.

Rather than present massive amounts of data sans interpretation, offering a fruitless plethora of examples, I shall instead seek to explicate these common underlying principles through reference to the semiotics of gesture and language. A linguistic model, while generally applicable to neither cinema nor gesture, does further our understanding of certain highly structured forms of gestural communication. The highly structured histrionic code shares several characteristics with natural language, a fact that greatly facilitates verbal description both of the workings of the code and of individual gestures.

Limited Lexicon

A gesture is not a word or a syllable but a whole phrase which cannot be further broken down. There seem to be no gestural equivalents to what linguists call phonemes and morphemes. Umberto Eco labels this phenomenon a "super sign," defining it as a sign "whose content is not a content-unit but an entire proposition; this phenomenon does not occur in verbal language but it does in many other semiotic systems."[16]

The resemblance of gestures to phrases or even whole sentences rather than words normally precludes a gestural dictionary, since there are an infinite number of possible gestures. This distinguishes both cinema and gesture from natural language systems. As Metz says of cinema, "One of the great differences between this language system [cinema] and natural language is due to the fact that, within the former, the diverse minimal signifying units . . . do not have a stable and universal signified. In a natural language each morpheme (moneme) has a fixed signified."[17]

Though the Delsarte system encompasses a multitude of possible postures/emotions, it does not encompass an infinity of possibilities and hence may be said to have a limited lexicon. Each emotion/state of mind must be represented by a particular, precise arrangement of the torso, limbs, and head. In actual practice, it is unlikely that any two actors could have faultlessly reproduced one another's exact poses, so that an infinity of possible poses did, in this sense, exist. But this is akin to individual pronunciation of a standard vocabulary, which some semioticians have referred to as an idiolect.[18] The Delsarte system did theoretically sanction a platonically ideal pose for each emotion. In a lecture delivered in the early 1870s Steele MacKaye stated, "The actor who is a follower of Delsarte is taught to express an emotion according to the laws of the emotion—the use of the appropriate and most powerful physical presentation of the impassioned thought."[19]

Though MacKaye's interpretation of Delsarte was more subtle and complex than that of the next generation of "Delsartians," this statement could be seen to countenance the publication of gestural lexicons giving students the "Delsarte" vocabulary.[20] The vocabulary, however, consisted not of words but of phrases. Eco's concept of the "super sign" corresponds to the way the "Delsartians" themselves thought of gesture: "But one gesture is needed for the expression of an entire thought, since it is not the word but the thought that the gesture must announce."[21]

Although it is not my intention to become the Dr. Johnson of the Biographs, a few entries from the Biograph gestural dictionary may help to illustrate the concept of the limited lexicon:

"resolution or conviction":   fist clenched in air, brought down sharply to side of body.

"despair, shame":   hands covering face or head buried in arms.

"fear":   arm extended, palm out toward fearful object, other hand perhaps clutching throat.

"Help me, Lord":   arms fully extended above head, sometimes hands clasped.

"feminine distress":   hand to cheek or hands on both sides of face.

"Honey, you and I are going to have a great future together":   gesture performed by a man, when he and his lady have finally transcended all obstacles to togetherness, in which one hand is raised as in the fascist salute, palm down and fingers spread, and waved slowly from side to side.

Analogical Versus Digital Communication

Digital communications, such as formal language systems, involve "discrete, discontinuous elements and gaps."[22] Barthes claims that this discontinuous character has in the past been considered necessary for signification to occur at all.[23] Gesture is, however, an analog communication, involving "continuous quantities with no significant gaps."[24] This continuous flow of signifiers, along with the lack of a minimal unit, makes it extremely difficult for the analyst to segment gestural signification. Indeed, Patrice Pavis asserts that the analyst should not even attempt segmentation: "We define gesture as that which cannot be limited or isolated, as that which cannot be isolated from the flow of communication without damage resulting."[25]

Because gesture cannot be segmented, the one-to-one correspondence between signifier and signified of verbal communication does not exist. A. J. Greimas states that the semiosis of the gesture will consist "in the relation between a sequence of gestural figures, taken as the signifier, and the gestural project, considered as the signified."[26] The recipient understands this gestural project only by translating it into another sign system, that of verbal language.[27] Barthes points out that this sort of translation is common in the case of analogical systems. "These systems are almost always duplicated by articulated speech . . . which endows them with the discontinuous aspect which they do not have."[28]

Though most gestural communication systems are unsegmented and analogic, the histrionic code, with its emphasis on the isolation of gesture, does resemble segmented, digital communications such as speech.[29] Actors deliberately struck attitudes, holding each gesture and abstracting it from the flow of motion until the audience had "read it." An author of one of the Delsarte instruction manuals advises: "But one gesture is needed to express an entire thought. Consequently, the gesture must be held until the impression which caused it melts away, and gives place to another impression."[30] One need only look at the early Biographs to observe the holding of gestures, but a 1907 *Atlantic Monthly* article confirms that this attitude-striking was also integral to melodramatic acting. The writer describes the heroine's gestures as she declares her innocence: "For gesture, one hand may be slightly extended and upraised, the other pressed timidly upon the breast; and at the close of the word [*innocent*] the eyes should fall, the head drop forward with sweet submission. This position may be maintained for several seconds. Then the gallery will clap."[31]

Not only were aspiring actors told to "rest long enough in a gesture,"[32] they were urged to avoid excessive movement, which might detract from attitude-striking. Dion Boucicault, one of the premiere names in theatrical melodrama, warned against superfluous gesture: "Let the gesture be exactly such as pertains to what you say . . . and no more. Do not use *gesticules*— little gestures—that is fidgety."[33] The elimination of the small gestures brings about the physical equivalent of silence between the grand, posed gestures, resulting in the "discrete, discontinuous elements and gaps" of digital communication.

Opposition

Another hallmark of natural language not shared by most gestural communication is opposition.[34] Indeed, Ferdinand de Saussure often insisted that language is nothing but a diacritical system of differences, that the meaning of a language system derives solely from paradigmatic oppositions. The presence or absence of phonemes in morphemes or of morphemes in sentences can entirely change the meaning of a word or sentence. Natural language exhibits a perfect binary opposition: the distinction between *cat* and *pat,* for example, stems solely from the opposition between *c* and *p.*

Opposition in histrionically coded acting is more a matter of degree. Actors had to decide: (1) the length of time of the gesture; (2) the stress and speed of the gesture; and (3) the direction of the gesture, each of which involves not two but a whole range of choices.

1. Length of time.   Though actors might be told to "rest upon a gesture," the histrionic code did not demand that each gesture be held for precisely the same number of seconds. Instead, actors varied the time of gestures for dramatic effect. Both the emotional intensity of a particular scene and the scene's place within the narrative determined the time that a particular pose might be held. At the climax of each act, always an emotional high point, melodramatic casts often froze in place, forming a motionless tableau that might last for several seconds before the curtain fell.

2. Stress and speed.   The weight and speed of gestures also constituted significant oppositions. Generally, slow, languid movements connoted resigned despair, pensiveness, calm content, quiet love, and similar states of mind. Fast, forceful movements connoted anger, fear, unbearable misery, grief, and other more active, and often negative, emotions. *The Actor's Art,* from 1882 (not a Delsarte book) tells us "a calm thought will prompt a quiet action. The arm will move slowly without abruptness." However, should "the sentiment be strong, the thought will prompt the arm to rise rapidly."[35] Once again, actors suited the stress and speed of the gesture to the progress of the narrative: early Biographs often begin with slow, languid gestures, climax with fast forceful gestures, and resolve with slow, languid gestures.

3. Movement.   The final significant opposition concerns the direction of movement with regard to the actors' bodies: toward the feet or the head, toward or away from the body, parallel or perpendicular to the body. Movements directed upward may indicate acceptance, pleading, or an appeal to heaven, while movements downward indicate conviction, resolution, or the act of rejection. Boucicault was quite insistent on these distinctions: "Why in the attitude of appeal do you put your hands up *so?* You cannot appeal *that* way [with the palms downward]. Why in depreciation do you put your hands downward? You cannot do it *that* way [the palms upward]."[36] Movements close to the body may indicate pleading, acceptance or shame, whereas movements away indicate rejection, fear, repulsion. Generally, the closer the movements to the center of the body, the calmer the emotion, while stronger emotions result in movements upward, downward, or outward. The greater the extension of the arm in these directions the more intense the emotion. The author of *The Actor's Art* states, "So long as in their movement the hands do not rise above the waist, they express sentiments of a quiet nature, . . . but so soon as the hands are raised above the waist, and therefore reach the chest . . . their expression assumes much greater force, more intensity."[37]

To summarize, the histrionic code is always marked by a resemblance to digital communication and a limited lexicon, but performers had to choose the time, stress and speed, and direction of their gestures. And since the performance of gesture could vary, an actor could use various combinations of oppositions to suit the movements to the nature and intensity of the character's state of mind. By looking at the quality of the gestures in the early Biographs we can conceive of a range of options between what I shall term the checked and unchecked histrionic codes, the latter more closely resembling conventional, stereotyped notions of melodramatic acting. In the unchecked histrionic code, gestures are quickly performed, heavily stressed, and fully extended, the arms being held upward, downward, or outward from the body. Often these gestures are repeated, either immediately or a little later in a series. Slower, less stressed, and less extended gestures, the arms remaining closer to the body, characterize the checked histrionic code.

The Verisimilar Code

By the penultimate decade of the last century, those connected with the theatre realized that the old style of histrionically coded performance had given way to a new style, to verisimilarly coded performance. "The stage may be said to have undergone . . . a revolution."[38] Or, as Gus the Theatre Cat put it more eloquently, "The theatre's certainly not what it was."[39]

The concept of mimesis goes back to Aristotle and *The Poetics,* while the terms "verisimilar" and "vraisemblance" appear frequently in structuralist literary theory. My use of *verisimilar* derives specifically from the work of Tzvetan Todorov. Todorov says that "we speak of the work's verisimilitude insofar as the work tries to convince us it conforms to reality and not its own laws. In other words, verisimilitude is the mask which is assumed by the laws of the text and which we are meant to take for a relation with reality.''[40] Verisimilitude should not be equated with reality; it refers, rather, to a particular culture's coded expectations about the artistic representation of reality. Reality in this sense is a cultural construct, a matter of commonly held opinion rather than that which is presumed to have some objective existence outside the text: "verisimilitude is never anything more than the result of opinion; it is entirely dependent on opinion, public opinion.''[41]

Verisimilitude, predicated as it is upon intertextuality rather than personal experience, frees the historian from having to make claims about some extra-textual historical "reality." As Fredric Jameson tells us, "history is *not* a text" but "is inaccessible to us except in textual form, or in other words, . . . it can be approached only by way of prior (re)textualization.''[42] There is no need to replicate Erving Goffman's work in a 1913 context in a futile attempt to determine how closely the Biograph actors' gestures approximated the gestures of their "real life" counterparts. Instead we can try to discover, through reference to other texts, the 1913 audience's coded expectations about the representation of everyday behavior. That the coded expectations may have had little relation to the way people actually behaved matters not at all: "For a particular society . . . the work that is realistic is that which repeats the received form of 'Reality.' It is a question of reiterating the society's system of intelligibility.''[43]

Let me illustrate the point anecdotally. During a film studies conference in New Orleans, a group of my colleagues and I took an after-dinner stroll along the banks of the Mississippi. Inspired by the setting, we began to storyboard a murder for the first scene of a projected film noir, *The Third Beignet*. We agreed that the principals would be followed to the riverbank in a long tracking shot. We agreed that the murder itself would be presented in quick-cut montage. But we disagreed over the background music. Two street musicians competed for our attention: a cornet player along the riverbank rendered a mournful version of "All of Me," and a bagpiper in Jackson Square played whatever bagpipers play. I argued that we should use the bagpipe for its sheer unconventionality. With the piping clearly audible to all, one of my colleagues countered, "There are no bagpipes in New Orleans." And he was right. As far as our hypothetical audience was concerned, there are indeed no bagpipes in "the city that care forgot." The "society's system of intelligibility" about a cinematic New Orleans includes cornets but not bagpipes.

An anecdote from the period in question may be more persuasive. In a 1912 article, "Stage Realism," the author questioned the theatre's obsession with the "approximation of life," making his point with a story about Sir Henry Irving, one of the leading actor-managers of the late-nineteenth-century British stage:

> There is a current anecdote . . . which relates how once Sir Henry Irving, at re-
> hearsal, upbraided a stagehand for the poor imitation of thunder the latter produced.
> "Please, sir," replied the man, "that wasn't me that made the noise. It's the real
> storm outdoors; it's ragin' so 'ard I couldn't 'ear you tell me when to begin."[44]

The extratextual storm violated Irving's expectations about the satisfactory
representation of thunder, which to convince him had to sound not like "real"
thunder but like "stage" thunder. But if we are tempted to mock our grand-
parents' naivete we need only recall the false, timid sound of the shots on the
evening news compared to the loud reports on our favorite action-adventure
shows.

As Henry James well knew, "the real thing" is not always the most convincing. In his short story of that title, he tells of a gentleman and his lady
who, having fallen on hard times, serve as artist's models. When the artist
begins to illustrate a book with an upper-class setting, the couple, possessing
the requisite breeding and bearing, expects a long engagement. The artist
finds, however, that his cockney char and Italian servant man make far more
suitable subjects: when he draws them they simply appear more aristocratic
than the "real thing."[45] James intended to show that there is no foolproof
recipe for verisimilitude.

> You will not write a good novel unless you possess the sense of reality; but it will
> be difficult to give you a recipe for calling that sense into being. Humanity is im-
> mense, and reality has a myriad forms; the most one can affirm is that some of the
> flowers of fiction have the odour of it, and others have not; as for telling you in
> advance how your nosegay should be composed, that is another affair.[46]

What was the late-nineteenth- and early-twentieth-century recipe for calling
a sense of reality into being? What were this particular culture's coded expectations about the artistic representation of reality? Ideally, one would answer
this question through immersion in the multitude of surviving texts: from the
dime Western to "great" literature such as the novels of Henry James. Following such an immersion, one might emerge with what Raymond Williams
would call "the structure of feeling" of the period:

> This structure of feeling is the culture of a period: it is the particular living result of
> all the elements in the general organization. And it is in this respect that the arts of
> the period, taking these to include characteristic approaches and tones in argument,
> are of major importance. For here, if anywhere, this characteristic is likely to be
> expressed; often not consciously, but by the fact that here, in the only examples we
> have of recorded communication that outlives its bearers, the actual living sense,
> the deep community that makes communication possible, is naturally drawn upon.[47]

Obviously, the recreating of the period's structure of feeling would in and
of itself constitute a book, if not a life's work, even if such a task were possible

or theoretically justifiable. Forced to be selective about the relevant intertexts for the structure of feeling or the intertextual framework, what texts do we select? Because we are concerned with the fictional representation of reality it behooves us to turn to a body of work that self-consciously addressed this issue. In the mid-nineteenth century a literary movement arose that scholars have dubbed nineteenth-century or modern realism. *Realism* is, as I have said, a term to be handled carefully, but it can be useful when properly defined. In this case, both the writers themselves and literary critics have rather precisely defined the characteristics of the nineteenth-century realist novel.

Verisimilitude has been debated since Plato and Aristotle, and, as Erich Auerbach has shown, the emergence of modern realism was a highly gradual process with numerous antecedents.[48] Through identifying and listing some of the primary ingredients, we can, despite James's demurral, reproduce at least to a degree the late-nineteenth-century recipe for literary verisimilitude. Having done so, we can seek points of contact between this construction of reality and the verisimilar code in performance. In what follows I have to some extent relied on secondary critics but where possible have used period writers, assuming that the latter were perforce more strongly imbued with their era's structure of feeling and of "the received form of Reality."[49]

Most realist writers adopted as their first premise the notion that literature should indeed have some connection to the actual experience of day-to-day life. W. D. Howells, the foremost champion of the realist movement among literary critics, asserted that "we must ask ourselves before we ask anything else, Is it true?—true to the motives, the impulses, the principles that shape the life of actual men and women."[50] These writers deliberately opposed themselves to a fiction that they perceived as mannered, stylized, and artificial. To turn once again to the doyen of literary realists, listen to Henry James's Mark Ambient, "The Author of Beltraffio," telling his young admirer about his wife's conception of the novel: "[It] is a thing so false that it makes me blush. It's a thing so hollow, so dishonest, so lying, in which life is so blinkered and blinded, so dodged and disfigured, that it makes my ears burn."[51] Ambient desired to be "truer than I've ever been. . . . I want to give the impression of life itself."[52] Or, as James said elsewhere, "the only reason for the existence of a novel is that it does attempt to represent life."[53] Clearly, this was a hallmark of the new verisimilar performance style—the assertion rather than the denial of a connection between the stage and everyday life.

Two techniques that the realists used to achieve "truth" and the "impression of life" relate directly to the emergence of the verisimilar code. According to A. C. Benson, writing in 1912, the "old inclination . . . was to brush aside all the vulgar, obvious and commonplace elements of life."[54] Scientific observation and recording of these commonplace elements would lead to the inclusion of facts, of little details. The aspiring realist would go about the world with a notebook, mental or actual, noting down the peculiarities and particularities of his fellow beings, then transcribe these minutiae onto the written page. A realist should literally draw from life: "realism in fiction consists in copying actual facts. . . . The realist is a photographer. His grocer has a peculiar way of tying up a package, his mother-in-law a trick of lifting her left eyebrow; the indefatigable realist secures a negative of each."[55]

Barthes argues that details, those "minute gestures, transitory attitudes, insignificant objects, redundant speech"[56] serve no narrative function but naturalize the text by contributing to an effect of the real. The details become "the very signifiers of realism. A *realistic effect* is produced, which is the foundation of the unacknowledged verisimilitude that makes up the aesthetic of all the common writing of the present."[57] As we shall see, the observation and inclusion of "realist" details figured largely in Griffith's instructions to his actors.

The realists also struggled to dispense with artificialities of plot and character, to give their fictional creations a psychological depth and plausible motivation. In their work they sought to capture the "God-given complexity of motive which we find in all the human beings we know."[58] The exploration of psyche became of paramount importance, and character the dominant element of the novel. In the realists' plots, characters precipitated events rather than simply reacting to them. Henry James summed up this doctrine in his famous questions about narrative construction:

> What is character but the determination of incident? What is incident but the illustration of character? What is either a picture or a novel that is *not* of character? . . . It is an incident for a woman to stand up with her hand resting on a table and look out at you in a certain way. . . . At the same time it is an expression of character.[59]

The rise of dramatic realism paralleled that of literary realism, both movements originating in the mid-nineteenth century.[60] Theatre historians generally point to the English playwright T. W. Robertson's 1865 *Caste* as the origin of a rudimentary dramatic realism, often dubbed "teacup" realism for the drawing-room society that it portrayed: "A plausible representation of actual life and manners and speech, with all the rhetoric and rhetorical conventions abolished, with no aim but the aim of illusion, was for the first time presented to an English playhouse audience."[61]

The dramatic realists shared with the literary realists the desire to represent real life in their work: "The realistic drama is not a poetical fancy of the inner vision, but a photograph of actual life."[62] Like the novelists, the realist dramatists emphasized the ordinary rather than the extraordinary. "Drama of the intimate type . . . aims to the reflection of actual life upon the stage, life stripped of the large meaning, but with as many of the commonplaces retained as possible."[63] The dramatic realists also rejected unbelievable plots and implausible characters. They wished to substitute for one-dimensional stock figures, whose personalities were often signified by their physical attributes, the more complex, multi-dimensional, and psychologized characters being created by the literary realists:

> A character came to signify a man fixed and finished: one who invariably appeared either drunk or jocular or melancholy, and characterization required nothing more than a physical defect such as a club-foot. . . . Because they are modern characters . . . I have drawn my figures vacillatory, disintegrated, a blend of old and new.[64]

The dramatic realists also paid attention to the insignificant, trying to get the little things right. Or as one hostile critic put it, "Petty details are to be substituted for largeness of conception and execution."[65] In the plays themselves, realist detail often meant dialogue that accurately reflected a character's social station or nationality, instead of the standard clichés of the melodrama.

Realist details became especially important not primarily in the texts but in their production. Throughout the second half of the nineteenth century, British and American theatrical producers increasingly sought the "realist effect" through sets, props, and costumes that reproduced in great detail their "real-life" models. The trend began with the productions of Robertson's plays at the Prince of Wales Theatre, which introduced the first fully developed box set to the English theatre. With its three walls, and implied fourth, all set within the picture frame of the proscenium arch, the box set at the Prince of Wales transferred the society drawing room, complete with furniture, sculpture, draperies, and fireplaces, to the stage.[66]

In the United States at the end of the century the famous producer David Belasco had become the prime exemplar of this sort of theatrical realism, which he carried to fantastic and, said some, unnecessary extremes. Theatre critic Sheldon Chaney accused Belasco of devotion to an "unimaginative realism" predicated on "photographic accuracy and naturalistic detail" that obscured a play's deeper meaning: "Belasco, in a recent magazine essay, epitomized his creed in one sentence: 'I believe in the little things.' . . . He believes that if he puts together enough little details that are 'real' or 'natural'—that is, true to the outer, material aspects of life—he can build a whole that will be artistically or spiritually true to life."[67] In his passion for accuracy Belasco put on stage wet rainstorms, working telephone switchboards, and once a Child's Restaurant set complete down to the food.[68]

Once Belasco set the standard, others followed his lead, and theatrical realism became synonymous with a mania for accurate and "lifelike" detail:

> Infinite pains are now lavished upon settings and costumes and properties, to make them accurate and complete and real. The stage is boxed in with sidewalks and ceilings. . . . Real meals are served to players who actually eat and drink. Real water trickles over realistic stones. Real horses and automobiles are pressed into

service. And the actor himself makes an earnest endeavor to say and do things on the stage as they are said and done in real life.[69]

The movement toward theatrical realism coincided with a new acting style, the verisimilar code. Crediting Robertson with the introduction both of rudimentary dramatic realism and realistic settings, theatre historians also trace the new acting style to the first productions of his plays.[70] Because both text and stage sought to evoke "real life," verisimilarly coded performance achieved a unity of effect that the self-conscious theatricality of the histrionic code could not. But the ephemeral nature of the acting makes it much easier to discuss Robertson's society dramas and box sets than the performances that took place in those painstakingly reproduced drawing rooms.

The writings of critics and of the actors themselves help us to visualize the new code. Given the fallibility of human memory, how reliable is this evidence? As any film scholar knows, ask any two people to tell you about a film, and you will get three completely different descriptions. We have no reason to assume that critics accurately recorded nor actors accurately reported what happened on stage. But by looking at nineteenth-century literary, dramatic, and theatrical realism we have attained a sense of that society's code of verisimilitude. This enables us to describe the verisimilar code by seeking homologies in the written evidence between the new acting style and literary, dramatic, and theatrical realism. In this way we have an intertextual control, if you will, on human fallibility.

As we have seen, the realists (literary, dramatic, and theatrical) all used details to create a "realistic effect." The passion for detailed accuracy which animated the set designers carried over to the actors. Verisimilarly coded performances included the little details, the realistic touches that actors referred to as "byplay." A critic defined subtle acting, by which he meant the new style, as "a temperamental ability to suggest the stage portrait by delicate hints and nuances rather than by obvious methods."[71] In 1867 one of the actors in a production of *Caste* at the Prince of Wales was said to establish his entire character by the way in which he filled his pipe.[72]

For the great English actor-manager Henry Irving, byplay was "the very essence of the true art." Believing "trifles make perfection,"[73] Irving built his characterizations on physical mannerisms, portraying Tennyson's Becket, for example, with a "piercing side-long glance and peculiar motion of the head."[74] Whereas actors employing the histrionic code behaved all the time as if they were on stage, and center stage at that, Irving added credible touches that suited his characters to their situations in life. In a lecture on acting, Irving revealed how he had learned to do this. During a production of *Guy Mannering,* Irving was cast opposite Charlotte Cushman to whom, at one point, he was to hand a purse of money. He handed her a "large purse full of coin of the realm, in the shape of broken crockery." This prop was traditionally used because, when hurled to the ground in righteous indignation by the virtuous young maiden whom it was supposed to persuade, "the clatter of the broken crockery suggested fabulous wealth."

> But after the play Miss Cushman . . . said to me, "Instead of giving me that purse don't you think it would have been much more natural if you had taken a number of coins from your pocket, and given me the smallest? That is the way one gives alms to a beggar, and it would have added realism to the scene."[75]

Irving learned his lesson well, as we can see from a description of his first entrance in one of his most famous roles, as Mathias in *The Bells*. Entering a house from a raging storm, he sat and listened to a conversation between two men:

> The process of getting rid of his coat, and brushing off the snow as he stands on the mat by the door being over, he works his way down to a chair . . . and there, taking off his boots, he begins to put on and buckle his shoes. . . . Irving . . . [buckles his first and then] his second shoe, seated and leaning over it with his two long hands stretched down over the buckles. We suddenly saw these fingers stop their work; the crown of the head suddenly seemed to glitter and become frozen—and then, at the pace of the slowest and most terrified snail, the two hands, still motionless and dead, were seen to be coming up the side of the leg.[76]

In this scene Irving had nothing to do but enter, sit, and listen, yet he used his costume (coat, boots, shoes) as props, simultaneously confirming the realism of the setting, keeping his audience's interest, and revealing his character. Irving was not the only actor to realize the importance of props, which became an important part of the new acting style. As André Antoine, founder of the Théâtre Libre, said, "Expression will be based on familiar and real props: a returned pencil or an overturned cup will be as significant and will have as profound an effect . . . as the grandiloquent exaggerations of the romantic theatre."[77]

The use of props, personal mannerisms, and "realistic" touches all contributed to distinctly individual characters. The standardization of the histrionic code had imposed a certain uniformity on dramatic characters: with each emotion and state of mind represented by a certain prescribed pose or gesture, characters expressed themselves in precisely the same fashion. A young woman and an old man both portrayed grief by raising the back of the hand to the forehead. As Antoine complained, "All the characters of the present day theatre have the same gestures and express themselves technically in the same manner, whether they be old or young, ill or in good health." Antoine wanted his actors to "include those thousands of nuances and details which have become indispensable in capturing the spirit of a character and building it logically."[78] The construction of character through detail and nuance is obviously related to the literary realists' giving their characters psychological depth. Remember what James said of the connection between character and incident: "for a woman to stand with her hand resting on a table and look out at you in a certain way . . . is an expression of character." James might almost have been giving stage directions for a verisimilarly coded performance.

Just as writers were urged to go about the world taking notes, actors were told to accumulate nuances and details by the scientific observation of real human beings. Tommaso Salvini, the leading Italian exponent of the new style, told of his training:

> I felt the need of studying, not books alone, but men and things and all the passions for good and evil. . . . I needed to study out the manner of rendering these passions in accordance with the race of men in whom they were exhibited, in accordance with their special customs. . . . I needed to form a conception of the movement, the manner, the expressions of face and voice characteristic in all these cases. I must learn by intuition to grasp the characters of fiction . . . seeking to give every one a personality distinct from every other. . . . I must become capable of identifying myself with one or another personage to such an extent as to lead the audience into the illusion that the real personage and not the copy, is before them.[79]

As is apparent from the above, the advocates of the verisimilar code held to the realist tenet that there should be some connection between artistic representation and the actual experience of day-to-day life. Byplay and observation could establish this connection, but for the most part both actors and critics had difficulty in characterizing the verisimilar code, in reducing it to a formula to be followed by neophytes. The writings about the verisimilar code consist largely of negative injunctions: "It is much easier to ascertain what good acting is not. To begin with, it is evidently not staginess—conventional gestures and conventional attitudes and conventional sonority of language."[80] Tyro actors were not told what to do, they were told what *not* to do: "the exaggerated and grotesque use of gesture and facial expression, the stilted and unnatural stride and strut . . . these, with many other inherited blessings from the Palmy Days where there was acting that really amounted to something, may easily be recognized and thrown out."[81] We can sum up most of the negative advice in one sentence: "Do not use the histrionic code!"

At the inception of a new artistic style, this definition by opposition is common practice. According to Mukarovsky, artistic tradition establishes the intertextual frames by which people judge and evaluate new art works. Mukarovsky calls these frames aesthetic norms, "a point of orientation serving to make felt the degree of deformation of the artistic tradition by new tendencies." Unlike legal norms which must always be followed, aesthetic norms exist to be "violated rather than observed."[82] This is particularly the case when the new styles make realist claims, the realism consisting to some extent in not following established practice. As Jakobson points out, practitioners of a new "realist" style often conceive of "the tendency to deform given artistic norms" as an "approximation of reality."[83] Thus, the literary and dramatic realists rejected one-dimensional characters, improbable coincidences, and high-flown rhetoric.

What did the adherents of the verisimilar code reject? Most fundamentally, they wished to substitute an easy "naturalness," a lack of self-consciousness, for the deliberate theatricality of the histrionic code. Proponents of the histrionic code criticized actors for not acting, while those of the verisimilar criticized actors for acting:

> The difference between the subtle and the blatant actor may be read in his demeanor. The latter betrays self-consciousness from the moment of his entrance. He has one corner of his eye for the audience, and he gives the impression that he is not altogether unconcerned regarding the effect that he is creating. When he has a good line, he recites it with an emphasis that will ensure that it will not be lost upon the house. When he gets a chance at an emotion, he takes hold of it and wrings the life out of it. He takes the stage with a "now watch me" air, and lets it be felt that he considers himself the center of gravitation. However forcible or stirring he may be, however good a reading of the part he may be giving . . . he is palpably acting.[84]

Instead of "palpably acting," actors were to "acquire the art of standing at ease upon the stage," shedding that "fatal self-consciousness which is the main cause of the artificial and redundant gesture."[85] William Gillette, a leading actor-manager and matinée idol, did much to propagate the doctrine of not acting, which he called the "illusion of the first time":

> Now it is a very difficult thing . . . for an actor who knows exactly what he is going to say to behave exactly as though he didn't; to let his thoughts (apparently) occur to him as he goes along, even though they are in his mind already; and (apparently) to search for and find the words by which to express these thoughts, even though these words are at his tongue's very end. . . . The Illusion of the First Time . . . extends to every part of the presentation . . . to the most insignificant item of behavior—a glance of the eye at some unexpected occurrence, the careless picking up of some small object which (supposedly) has not been seen or handled before.[86]

The "illusion of the first time" would, of course, be enhanced if actors ignored the audience, pretending that the hypothetical fourth wall truly existed. August Strindberg, in his Preface to *Miss Julie,* which Raymond Williams dubs his "manifesto of Naturalism," stated that he would like to be able to get "the actor to play for the audience and not with it"; although he did not dream "of seeing the full back of any actor through the whole of an important scene," he did "wish very, very much that decisive scenes would not be played as duets (next to the prompter's box) designed to be applauded, but at the place the situation dictates."[87] Belasco, as producer and moneyman, had more power over actors than a mere writer. When he told his players to ignore the audience, they did:

> I eliminated every movement . . . that did not seem natural. When two men sat down to talk things over, I had them sit there as they would if another wall had cut the stage off from the audience and they didn't move until they would naturally have moved. There was no striving for "keeping up the action."[88]

Just as contemporary practitioners and critics defined the verisimilar code in opposition to the histrionic, let me explain the opposition in the semiotic terms that I introduced earlier. The histrionic code is characterized by its limited lexicon and digital nature, while the verisimilar code has no lexicon and is analogic.

1. Verisimilarly coded acting had no standard repertoire of gestures, no limited lexicon. The style defined itself by the very abandonment of the conventional gestures of the histrionic code. Actors no longer portrayed emotions and states of mind by selecting from a pre-established repertoire but by deciding what was appropriate for a particular character in particular circumstances.

2. Whereas the histrionic code tended to resemble digital communication, the verisimilar tended to resemble analogical communication. The histrionic code depended upon gestural isolation, each gesture sufficiently distinct to be read by the audience. Actors struck attitudes and took poses, with intervening gestures omitted. When the new-style actors used gesture (and they were counseled to use it sparingly), they employed a continuous flow of movement composed of little details rather than broad sweeping motions.

3. Though opposition still operated in the verisimilar code, the oppositions were not as extreme as in the histrionic code. The verisimilar style no longer held gestures for dramatic effect and the fully extended, upward, outward, or downward movements of heightened emotion were dropped.

3

The Histrionic and Verisimilar Codes in the Biograph Films

The Histrionic Code

Film scholars may increasingly supplement textual analysis with knowledge of how a particular text both relates to other texts and functions in the larger culture, but close formalist analysis still remains an important methodology in cinema studies and other disciplines. Even Tony Bennett and Janet Woollacott, who believe that the text is "an inconceivable object," nonetheless do not suggest that "texts have no determinate properties—such as a definite order of narrative progression—which may be analyzed objectively."[1] In this chapter and the next, I shall focus on these "determinate properties"; in chapter 3, looking at the ways the Biograph actors employed the histrionic and verisimilar codes in the construction of their characters, and in chapter 4, theorizing a model of the interaction among the signifying practice of performance and other textual signifying practices and showing the workings of this interaction in the films themselves.

It may help to begin by formulating some general principles about the actors' use of the histrionic code at various points in the early Biographs. Most shots in these films fall into one of five categories: (1) the tableau; (2) everyday activity; (3) conversations; (4) heightened emotions and action scenes with more than one performer; and (5) gestural soliloquies in which an actor emotes while alone in the frame.[2] As a rule, the performances in these categories tend to range from the checked to the unchecked histrionic code.

1. Modified tableau. Although the Biographs borrowed the tableau from the stage melodrama, they somewhat modified its usage. In the theatre, performers used the tableau to convey intense emotions in nonverbal form, freezing in place with arms fully extended outward, downward, or upward at an act's climax. A contemporary print depicting the second act of *East Lynne* shows the actors in the act-ending tableau: In the center a man sits in a chair, hands clasping head in an agony of despair. A young girl kneels at his feet, her right hand reaching up in supplication. To the left, an elderly gentleman has both hands raised high above his head in an appeal-to-heaven posture. To the right, a stern woman points at the girl with her left hand, while her right hand is held perpendicular to her body, the finger pointing to the door in one of the most parodied of all histrionic gestures.[3]

Obviously, the Biographs retained the goal of expressing strong emotion in nonverbal fashion but somewhat modified the technique. The actors eschewed fully extended gestures and kept their arms close to their bodies, expressing emotional intensity through a comparative lack of movement rather than absolute stillness. The only motionless tableau in the Biographs occurs in *A Corner in Wheat* (1909) at the moment when the poor line up to buy the overpriced bread and become perfectly motionless, contrasting with the frenzied activity of the Wheat King's party.

Usually, the actors make small gestures that contrast markedly with the more common broad gestures of the histrionic code and thus convey the impression of relative motionlessness. In the last shot of *A Drunkard's Reformation*, Arthur Johnson and Linda Arvidson sit in front of the fire with their little girl. The child sits on the floor before her father's chair, the mother sits on the arm of the chair. Arvidson has her arm around Johnson, and they hold hands. With his free hand, Johnson gestures to the girl, as if to credit her with his reformation.

2. Everyday activity.   In scenes of everyday activity characters are shown going about their normal routine prior to the introduction of narrative disequilibrium. They might be shown at work, like the farmers plowing their fields in the opening shot of *A Corner in Wheat,* or at home, like the happy family at the beginning of *The Lonely Villa* (1909). In these shots, gesture helps to establish a character and that character's relation to other characters. The characters often handle props, such as books, or the tools of their trade, that prevent fully extended outward movements.[4] Gestures tend to be close to the body, fairly slow, unstressed, and not held for any significant time.

In the first shot of *Lady Helen's Escapade* (1909), Florence Lawrence portrays a bored, wealthy woman. She sits in a chair beside a table on which her arm rests, her hand dangling loosely over the front. When a maid offers food, she rejects it with a languid wave of the hand. Then she heaves a sigh, shoulders visibly moving, and yawns. All her gestures are slow, and with the exception of the wave, her arms and hands stay close to her body.

Above left: *Lady Helen's Escapade:* A languid
wave of the hand. Above: *The Voice of the Violin:*
The conversational gesture. Left: *A Summer Idyl:*
The conversational gesture.

   3. Conversation.   In the Biographs, conversations among characters involve a great many gestures of a type we might call, to use a semantic term,
"diectic" or "anaphoric"—the gestural equivalent of verbal "shifters," personal pronouns and words indicating place, such as *here* and *there*.[5] In the
films, these meanings are expressed by inward movements, indicating *I* or
here, and outward movements, indicating *you, there,* or similar ideas. In *A
Convict's Sacrifice* (1909), the released convict, James Kirkwood, talks to a
laborer, Henry Walthall, who is eating his lunch. Kirkwood points to the food
and to himself and Walthall hands him the dinner pail. Then Walthall asks his
boss to hire Kirkwood, pointing at himself and then the convict, as if to vouch
for his behavior.
   Conversational gestures usually fall somewhere between the contained
stillness of the tableau and the frantic extended movement of the gestural soliloquy. In *The Voice of the Violin* (1909), Arthur Johnson proposes to Marion
Leonard. He declares himself with both hands on his chest, then extends his
arms one on either side of the woman. No, she says, with her hand on her
chest, then points to him, then puts her hand back on her chest. We can see
the gradual modifications in the histrionic code by looking at another marriage
proposal, from a film released the following year: In *A Summer Idyl* (1910),
Walthall proposes to a society woman (Stephanie Longfellow), who rejects

him. He leans closer to her, his hand on his chest, then extends his other hand to her palm up. Then he takes her hand in both of his. She says no, and he pleads with right hand extended to her, left hand on his chest, the fingers relaxed. All his motions are slow and graceful, and his arms are never fully extended outward like Johnson's.

Because Walthall stresses his gestures less than Johnson, the performance does not connote the same degree of theatricality. This becomes clear in comparing the way each actor places his hands on his chest. Johnson uses both hands with the palms flattened, to modern eyes parodying a lover declaring himself, as the pose absolutely reeks of theatricality. Walthall places one hand lightly on his chest, the palm slightly raised and fingers slightly cupped. Though Walthall employs a conventional gesture, the lack of emphasis reduces the deliberate self-consciousness of the histrionic code.

4. Heightened emotions and action scenes.   Categories 4 and 5 most closely resemble the stereotyped ideas of ''melodramatic'' acting, as performers tend to resort more to the unchecked histrionic code. The arms are fully extended upward, outward, or downward, the gestures are often more heavily stressed and quickly performed than in everyday activities or conversation, and poses are held longer. In *A Test of Friendship* (1909), Arthur Johnson receives the news that he has been ruined (financially, not morally, this latter being a woman's prerogative). His hands clutch his head and then come down, fingers spread, as his arms are held straight out to his sides. He bows his head, and his hands drop to his sides. He then looks up and clenches his fists.

In *The Call of the Wild* (1908), we see two performers enacting heightened emotions. A woman (Florence Lawrence) rejects the proposal of a ''civilized Indian'' (he wears a suit and attends parties). The veneer of civilization immediately vanishing, the rejected suitor (Charles Inslee) leads an Indian band on the warpath, captures his beloved, and proceeds to work his will upon her. He kisses her, and she falls to her knees, arms outstretched. Her left hand points to her chest and then to heaven, while her right hand points to him. He points to his Indian followers, as if to say, ''I am one of them.'' She points to heaven again, her arm straight up and fully extended. Finally seeing the light, he raises both arms, sinks to his knees, lowers his head on his arms. She then points off screen right, as if to say, ''Come back with me.'' Here we see a mixture of the diectic gesture and the unchecked histrionic code.

5. Gestural soliloquies.   In the gestural soliloquy, the quality of the gesture remains the same as with heightened emotions, but the quantity increases. In the previous category, no single performer enacts an elaborate series of gestures because the other actors collaborate in creating an emotional effect or in telling the story. Gestural soliloquies often occur at emotional high points

The Hindoo Dagger: The gestural soliloquy.

in which the characters undergo emotional catharsis. The characters in this situation often have only one point to make: "I am angry," "I am grief-stricken," or "I am desperate," and employ a series of gestures (sometimes repeating the same gesture), all of which express the same state of mind. While narratively redundant, the cumulative effect of the gestures is to increase the emotional impact, in keeping with the heightened emotional states characteristic of the melodramatic form. Though this repetition runs counter to injunctions against "the useless multiplication of gesture," each gesture remains distinctly separate, preserving the digital nature of the histrionic code.

In *The Hindoo Dagger* (1909), a woman's lover (Harry Solter) discovers her body and, thinking he will be accused of murder, enacts his distress. Kneeling at her side, he puts both hands on top of his head, then holds the backs of his clenched fists to his forehead, then puts his hands to his throat. He raises his arms in appeal to heaven, then waves clenched fists in the air, and finishes by crossing his arms over his chest. *The Tavern Keeper's Daughter* (1908), like *The Call of the Wild,* relates a tale of lust, villainy, and redemption. This time the pursued virgin takes refuge in a cabin occupied only by a crib and a baby. The villain (George Gebhardt) charges in, overlooks the woman, but spies the baby. In best melodramatic tradition, the child precipitates a reformation, and the villain enacts a gestural soliloquy. He sinks to his knees by the crib, beats his breast, raises clenched fists in the air, puts bowed head in hands, spreads arms wide, looks up to heaven, crosses himself, and slumps forward, head in hands. Then he rises, puts one forearm to his eyes and his other hand to his chest. All these gestures could be translated into one or two verbal phrases: "I am sorry," or "Forgive me."

The gestural soliloquy was also used to trace a character's thought processes, though the verisimilar code would better suit this function. In this case, rather than simply heightening emotional effect, the soliloquies serve to advance the narrative. In *A Burglar's Mistake* (1909), a husband (Harry Solter) contemplates suicide. As he holds the gun, he sees a toy that his young child has left in his office. He gestures to the door with his free hand, his arm extended behind him. Then he makes a fist in the air and brings his arm sharply down and up in a semi-circle as he decides on a course of action. Note, however, that the performer's gestures might be incomprehensible without the presence of the toy, showing precisely how difficult it is to discuss performance in isolation from other signifying practices.

The Verisimilar Code

Describing the operation of the verisimilar code in the Biographs presents a more daunting task than describing the histrionic. Because the verisimilar code was intended to mimic reality and create individual characterizations, one cannot turn to mechanical formulations and prescriptions such as are found in the histrionic-code instruction manuals. Nor can one evolve general categories, illustrating each with examples, as with the histrionic code. But the discussion of the theatrical verisimilar code in the previous chapter, in conjunction with the recent work of film scholars, can point to the key characteristics of the verisimilar code in the Biograph films. As we have seen from looking at the verisimilar code in the theatre, byplay and props formed an important part of this performance style. In addition, as Gunning, Thompson, and Staiger have all asserted, use of the face and eyes constituted an extremely important component of the new style of acting in the cinema, which makes sense given the differences between the two media.[6]

The New York Hat (1912) seems a particularly appropriate starting point for the discussion of the verisimilar code, because its inclusion in the Museum of Modern Art's circulating Griffith collection made it quite well known. As one of the few Biographs in common circulation, *The New York Hat* contributed to Griffith's reputation among film scholars as the originator of ''subtle, restrained'' acting. It also features Mary Pickford, one of the ''Griffith actresses'' whom posterity has judged to excel at the new style, and Lionel Barrymore, a Broadway-trained actor in one of his first film roles. Both Barrymore and Pickford have scenes in which the characters' thoughts are revealed through a combination of gesture, expressions, glances, and props, so that we can begin our discussion with a look at two sequences that combine all the key components of the verisimilar code.[7]

Just before her death, Pickford's mother writes a letter requesting that her minister, Barrymore, buy her daughter an occasional gift. Barrymore buys Pickford the fancy New York hat of the title. The town gossips immediately begin to circulate slanderous rumors, and Pickford's harsh father tears up the hat. All ends happily as the misunderstanding is cleared up, and Barrymore and Pickford seem destined for a rosy future.

The New York Hat: The verisimilar code.

In the second shot of the film, Barrymore opens the mother's letter and the packet of money that accompanies it. As he reads the letter, his mouth opens in surprise. He picks up the money with a thoughtful expression and looks straight out, almost at the camera, while holding the money. He looks at the letter again and laughs. Placing his hand flat on the desk, he mouths "I'll do it." He nods his head "yes" and looks at the letter again while smiling.

In a four-shot scene, Pickford examines her old hat, decides it won't do, and asks her father for a new one. In the first shot, the standard three-quarter shot of 1912, the father sits at his desk on the left and Pickford stands on the right side of the frame, her right hand at her side and her head slightly tilted as she looks up at a mirror on the wall next to her and straightens her jacket. In a cut to a medium shot, Pickford takes a hat off the wall and brushes off the top with a sad expression. She puts the hat on, examines her reflection, and glances in the direction of her father. An intertitle states, "Daddy, can I have a new hat?" In three-quarter shot again, Pickford stands with one hand out to her father and the other touching her hat, but he gestures her away. In another cut to medium shot, Pickford takes a pair of gloves from a hook near a mirror, and straightens the mirror. She arranges the gloves in her left hand, smiles, and looks in the mirror. Looking doubtful, she takes the hat off, hangs it up, and shakes her head. Again she looks in the mirror, looks at the gloves, smiles and smooths her hair with her hand. Even without the intertitle, Pickford's performance clearly establishes her character's decision to ask for the hat and her shifting emotions, as she first tries to make do with the old hat and then decides to do the best she can without it.

Although the various elements of the code all work together to externalize mental processes, as in the above example, one can better understand the actual operation of the verisimilar code by isolating, insofar as possible, each component. We start by examining several examples of byplay, the small, realistic touches the actors called "bits of business," which are the performance equivalents of Barthes's realistic effect.[8]

The God Within (1912) with Henry Walthall, Lionel Barrymore, Blanche Sweet, and Claire McDowell, recounts the intertwined fates of two couples. Barrymore seduces Sweet and leaves her pregnant, while Walthall's wife, McDowell, announces to her husband that she too is expecting a child. McDowell dies in childbirth, Sweet's baby is born dead, Sweet acts as a wet nurse to the motherless child, and all turns out well as Walthall and Sweet form a family at the end. The acting of the principals is verisimilarly coded, and all four employ bits of business in their interchanges with other characters.

Near the start of the film, Barrymore comes to tell Sweet that he is leaving town. She sits alone, waiting for him, and when she hears his knock, wipes away her tears, clasps her hands in her lap, and smiles. As they talk, she stands close to him, her hand stroking his lapel, and then leans closer to whisper that she is pregnant. Barrymore rubs the back of his neck in perplexity and then gestures to the door with his thumb. As McDowell tells Walthall that she is pregnant her actions are similar to Sweet's. She takes his sleeve, fingers his collar, puts a hand on his shoulder, and whispers in his ear. When the doctor proposes to Walthall that he take Sweet into his home, Walthall scratches the back of his neck as he thinks. At the film's end, Barrymore comes to Walthall's cabin and proposes to Sweet. Walthall returns home and also proposes to her. Sweet picks Walthall, signaling her decision by taking his hand. The two men converse over the seated woman, and, as they talk, Sweet tilts her head so that her cheek touches her and Walthall's linked hands, the small gesture registering her character's fulfillment and happiness.

These kinds of small gestures can be combined to create the verisimilar equivalent of the gestural soliloquy, in which characters express intense emotions. But while the intent is the same, the nature of the gestures is vastly different. In *The Lesser Evil* (1911), Blanche Sweet is trapped in a boat's cabin, with only the captain standing between her and a crew of would-be rapists. She stands at the cabin door, hands around the bolt, looking upward and perfectly still except for the slight movement of her hands on the bolt. She

The Lesser Evil: Blanche Sweet fears a fate worse than death.

then reloads the captain's gun, opens the door to hand him the weapon, then rebolts the door. She leans against the door, her right hand on the bolt and left hand to her face.

The impact of this scene admittedly depends on her expression as well as her gestures, but Biograph actors were fully capable of fulfilling Strindberg's wish that important scenes be acted with the back to the audience. To return to *The God Within,* Walthall has a gestural soliloquy at his wife's deathbed. His hat in his hand, he looks down at his wife and baby while he raises his hat to his mouth as if to stifle a sob. He turns his back to the camera, showing only about one-quarter of his face in profile, bows his head, and raises his hand to his eyes. After a moment, he turns slightly back, wipes his eyes, looks down again, and kneels at the bedside. He rests his head on his upraised hand while his fingers pull at his hair. Until he kneels, we do not get a good view of his face, and his grief is indicated by posture and hand movements alone.

The byplay in *The God Within* externalizes thoughts and emotions and delineates character. But "bits of business" could also directly establish character type or create psychological complexity. In *The Broken Cross* (1911), the residents of a boarding house include a gum-chewing, slovenly servant girl and a hip-swinging, eye-batting manicurist. In *The God Within,* Barrymore reveals his character's bravado and untrustworthiness by hooking his thumbs in his waistcoat pockets. In *A Child's Remorse* (1912), Claire McDowell plays a mother described by the *Biograph Bulletin* as having a "pettish nature."[9] She makes her entrance pushing back her sleeves and smoothing down her dress and then places her hands on her hips, posing for her husband's admiration. When he ignores her, she clenches her fists and gestures to herself as if to say "Look at me!" She then makes a sweeping downward gesture of both hands down the front of her skirt. In *Friends* (1912), Mary Pickford plays the darling of the mining town whom all the men admire. While awaiting her

The Way of Man: The use of a prop.

beau, she smooths her curls; when he fails to arrive, she stamps her foot impatiently. In the same film, Walthall plays a fastidious prospector-dandy, who returns from the gold fields to see Pickford. Standing at the bar before going up to her, he flicks dust off his sleeves and straightens his cuffs. Earlier, upon unexpectedly encountering an old friend, he had surreptitiously brushed away a tear, an action perhaps not consonant with the dandy image but which adds depth to his character and prepares for his later good-natured renunciation of Pickford.

Byplay also entailed the use of props. In an early example from *The Way of Man* (1909), Florence Lawrence portrays a woman scarred by an accident who sees her fiancé with another woman. Retreating to the next room, she leans over the back of a chair for a few seconds, her arms straight down the chair back. Then she walks slowly to front center, hands at sides, staring dully ahead. She picks up a hand mirror, looks at her reflection, puts a hand over the mirror, and shakes her head. She then puts a forearm to her forehead. With the exception of the last gesture, Lawrence does not use her customary histrionic gestures but embodies her character's thoughts through body posture, a slight movement of the head, and the look in the mirror. In a scene from *The Inner Circle* (1912) the use of props augments the fully developed gestural byplay of the verisimilar code. An intertitle, ''The Lonely Widower and his child,'' precedes the film's first shot. A little girl sits in a chair in a tenement room, and her father (Adolphe Lestina) enters. He walks slowly, head bowed, and carries a flower. He looks at the child, smiles slightly, sniffs the flower and turns to look at a picture on a table behind him. His hand barely raised from the table, he extends his bent index finger toward the picture, then rests his hand on the table. The father turns to his child and offers her the flower, but she is sleeping. He straightens, looks at the picture, places the flower in front of it, rests his hands on the table, and looks up, before waking and hugging the child.

The Lesser Evil: Blanche Sweet thinks of her beau.

In this shot the gestures and props develop the portrait of the Lonely Widower announced by the intertitle, but Lestina communicates his sorrow for his dead wife with an upward glance, and his pity for his orphaned child by looking from the picture to her. This brings us to the second important element of the verisimilar code, the use of the eyes and the face. As in Lestina's case, the direction of the look often suffices to convey a character's thoughts (given the narrative context, that is). In another example from *Friends,* Walthall returns from the gold fields unaware that Barrymore has preempted his place in Pickford's affections. As he and Pickford embrace, he looks over her shoulder to see the picture of Barrymore she has left out. A dawning realization crosses his face, but the mere fact of his seeing the photo indicates that the character's suspicions have been aroused. In *Her Father's Pride* (1910), Stephanie Longfellow and Charles West declare their love by look alone. After an intertitle, "The Inevitable," the two look at each other until she bows her head and walks away. His eyes follow her as he smiles. In another sexual interchange based on glances, this time in *One Is Business, The Other Crime* (1912), we see an early instance of the controlling male gaze that figures so largely in feminist film theory. Edwin August stands at a doorway admiring his wife, Blanche Sweet, who has completed dressing for dinner. His eyes sweep up and down her body as he looks her over, then smiles, and shakes his head as if to say, "You're really something!" She looks shyly away, averting her gaze.

As the trade press would have said, "You can really see the actors think!" Occasionally, the later Biographs devote entire shots to a character's thoughts, with the actors reflecting on the previous action and moving very little if at all. In *Friends,* after Pickford receives a visit from Barrymore she lets him out and remains motionless, her hand on the doorknob and her eyes moving from side to side. In a similar scene in *The Lesser Evil,* Blanche Sweet has just gotten a proposal from her longtime beau. She pauses at the front door of her house, with her hands at her sides and her head down. She looks up slightly, smiles, then goes into the house. Nor is it only women mooning over their sweethearts who pause in reflection. In *Friends,* the doctor tells Walthall to wait outside while he goes inside to deliver the baby. Walthall stands for a moment with his hand on the doorknob, motionless except for his eyes moving from side to side as he contemplates his wife's fate.

One Is Business, The Other Crime contains an extended instance of the "reflection shot," as the four main characters, a rich couple (Edwin August and Blanche Sweet) and a poor couple (Charles West and Dorothy Bernard) all consider their futures. August has been bribed with a thousand dollars which West, unable to find employment, tries to steal, but Sweet apprehends him, in the process discovering the note offering her husband a bribe. West returns to his wife, and the poor couple thinks about their hopeless lot, while August, in his study, considers Sweet's demand that he return the money, and Sweet, in her bedroom, awaits his decision. In a sequence of eleven shots, the film cuts between Sweet, August, and the poor couple.

1. Sweet walks toward a chair in her bedroom.
2. August fingers the money, starts to put it down on the desk, but instead thrusts it into his pocket.
3. Sweet sits in a chair. She stares ahead, closes her eyes, slumps her head, and rests her arm on a table.
4. West arrives home, sits in a chair by the window, and makes a gesture rejecting something.
5. August takes the money out of his pocket, shakes his head and puts it back, then paces to the rear of the frame.
6. Sweet stands at the back of the frame, arms folded. She drops her hands to her sides, walks forward, yawns, shakes her head, and turns her back, brushing the back of the chair with her hand as she turns.
7. Bernard comes over to sit and talk with West.
8. August turns off the light and sits in a chair by the window, smoking a cigar.
9. West and Bernard sit at the window almost perfectly still.
10. As August sits quietly, "sunrise" illuminates the room. He gets up, takes the money out of his pocket, walks to the desk, and writes a note.
11. Sweet stands, hands on the back of the chair. She looks at the door angrily and exits.

As with the above sequence, many of the "thinking" and "reflection" shots cannot and should not be separated from the editing patterns of which they are a part, nor, for that matter, from the entire narrative context. This is particularly the case with the reaction shot that reveals mental processes precisely through the accumulation of shots. With the 1911 films, the three-shot–point-of-view pattern began to be standardized, as several films feature sequences in which characters look through windows and then react to what they see, the reaction shot sometimes in closer scale than the rest of the film (*The Chief's Daughter, Enoch Arden, His Mother's Scarf, The Two Sides*).

The Code Shift

By 1912 most performers, under most circumstances, in most Biographs employed the verisimilar code, some being more adept at it than others. Using the word *adept* comes perilously close to making a value judgment about good and bad acting. What does *adept* mean in this context? Those performers skilled in the new style used smaller gestures, gave them less emphasis, and melded them into a continuous flow. The less skilled retained elements of the histrionic code: while they might not use conventional gestures, their movements tended to be larger, more emphasized, and more discrete. Skilled performers also used more byplay and bits of business to construct their characters. Those performers whom subsequent generations have valorized as good (i.e., Blanche Sweet, Bobby Harron, Henry Walthall, Lillian Gish, Mary Pickford, Mae Marsh) are the ones who mastered the verisimilar code, so that it is possible in this instance to identify the components of "good acting" or at least specify what most people probably mean by "good acting" in the Biographs.

By 1912, however, the histrionic code had not entirely vanished. Actors still represented conversation with diectic gestures and the occasional conventional gesture.[10] In *The Black Sheep* (1912) a father warns off his daughter's suitor (Charles West). The father gestures with his thumb over his shoulder in his daughter's direction, raises his hand like a police officer halting traffic, and shakes his head. In *The New York Hat,* the village gossips tell Pickford's father (Charles Mailes) about the minister's purchase of the hat. Their leader (Claire McDowell) takes his arm, points offscreen, and touches her hat. The father points to his chest, then his head, looks severe, clenches his fists, nods, and says thank you.

The histrionic code persisted not only in conversations but also during emotional high points. In *The New York Hat,* the father comes upon his daughter wearing the new hat. He spreads his arms wide with fists clenched, as he asks where she got it. When she answers, he runs his hands across the top of his head and yells at her, raising his clenched fists in the air. In *The Lesser Evil,* Sweet's fiancé (Edwin August) sees Sweet being kidnapped. He raises his hands high above his head, staggers back, and waves his arms.

Perhaps it was only actors less skilled at the verisimilar code who resorted to the histrionic at times of great emotion? This does not seem to be the case. Even such a master of the verisimilar code as Henry Walthall, capable, as we have seen, of portraying intense grief with his back to the camera, uses histrionic gestures. In *The God Within,* when the doctor wishes him to take his baby to Sweet, Walthall makes the standard gesture of rejection, his hand near his head, arm bent at the elbow and then brought downward and out in a thrusting-away movement. Is editing perhaps the explanatory factor? To some extent, certainly, but the histrionic code can appear in a reaction shot. In *The Inner Circle,* Lestina looks through a window, seeing his daughter in the house under which he has just planted a bomb. He staggers back, arms wide, clenching his fists.

Just as the histrionic code lasts into 1912, we can find traces of the verisimilar as early as 1908. In *One Touch of Nature* Florence Lawrence's child has died. She sits quietly staring ahead until she picks up the child's doll and gently strokes its head, the use of the prop seeming to inhibit histrionic gestures.

The presence of the two codes in films made during the same year, and, sometimes even in the same film, prevents simply declaring that the verisimilar code replaced the histrionic on a precise date in a certain film. While one can identify 1910 and 1911 as the crucial transitional years, during which the codes mingle more frequently than previously or subsequently, we cannot reduce the matter to a question of chronology, providing lengthy and tedious year-by-year descriptions of acting. Nor can we hope to identify the simple linear causality of such factors as editing patterns or a closer camera.[11] Rather than considering performance in isolation or in relation to one other signifying practice, we must take into account the complex interaction of performance with the entire textual system. As Metz says, "The intrinsic consideration of a code does not tell us how it may be articulated with other codes (or with which ones), and at what level it may play a part in the general economy of a long and complex text."[12]

4

Performance Style and the Interaction of Signifying Practices

Theoretical Approach to the Interaction of Signifying Practices

Though a simple model of linear causality cannot adequately explain the transformation in cinematic performance style, a transformation in one signifying practice, narrative, crucially inflects performance in the Biographs. To elucidate this connection, I shall in this section present a model that theorizes the interaction among performance, narrative structure, and character-centered signifiers. *Signifying practices* refers to overall systems of meaning, such as editing, lighting, and camera work. *Signifier* refers to a particular element of a signifying practice, such as a jump cut, low-key lighting, or a tracking shot. While *narrative* is a signifying practice, it is clearly of a different order and may to some extent be considered a result of the cumulative effect of the other signifying practices or, in other words, a result of the interaction of signifying processes including performance.

During the years in which performance style changed from histrionically to verisimilarly coded, a concomitant change occurred in narrative structure, from ''pure melodrama'' to a degree of psychological realism resembling that of nineteenth-century literary and dramatic realism.[1] The ''pure melodrama'' relied on non-psychological causality as the mainspring of the narrative, while the ''realist'' narrative depended on character psychology. I quote David Bordwell about the role of character psychology in the classical Hollywood cinema; the ''premise of Hollywood story construction,'' Bordwell says, is causality, consequence, psychological motivations, the drive toward overcoming obstacles and achieving goals. Character centered—i.e., personal or psychological—causality is the armature of the classical story.

This sounds so obvious that we need to remember that narrative causality could be impersonal as well. Natural causes (floods, genetic inheritance) could form the basis for story action.[2]

Floods and other natural causes—Acts of God—did indeed provide the narrative causality for many a melodrama. In the "realist" narrative, however, psychological causality structures the narrative and, hence, the deployment of signifying practices: "Psychological causality, presented through defined characters acting to achieve announced goals, gives the classical film its characteristic progression."[3]

Clearly, the distinction between nonpsychological and psychological causality is relative rather than absolute: no film will conform entirely to either category. But the distinction remains useful for heuristic purposes, particularly given that we have already established the strong connection between the emergence of the verisimilar code in the theatre and the emphasis on the construction of individualized rather than stock characters.

What was the relationship between character and narrative in the melodrama, and how does it differ from that in the classical Hollywood style? What might the implications of these different relationships be for the deployment of other signifying practices? The Russian formalist Sergei Balukhatyi looked at the nineteenth-century French melodrama from a structuralist perspective, in the process furnishing an analysis of melodramatic character, as suggested in this excerpt from Daniel Gerould's paraphrased translation:

Characters in melodrama do not carry the full weight of real life; they are rather only outlined distinctly, being effective not in themselves, but as . . . points of attachment for the springs of the plot. Above all, characters in melodrama are devoid of individuality, either personal or everyday realistic; they are interesting to the spectator not . . . because of their . . . psychic substance, as are the characters in realistic, psychological drama, but only because of their role in interweaving plotline, their creation of dramatic situations.[4]

Can structuralist literary theory furnish any help in evaluating the validity of Balukhatyi's distinction between melodrama and the "realistic, psychological drama"?[5] Unfortunately for this purpose, structuralists such as A. J. Greimas and Vladimir Propp have tended to reduce character to a function of narrative, while ignoring the psychological characters of nineteenth-century realism. As Jonathan Culler says, "Character is the major aspect of the novel to which structuralism has paid the least attention and been the least successful in treating."[6] Most structuralists would reject Henry James's conflation of character and incident. Tzvetan Todorov, however, seriously, albeit briefly, reflects upon James's queries, contrasting narratives in which "everything is subservient to the psychology of the characters" to those in which "the characters are subservient to the action."[7] Todorov makes the distinction not through character analysis but by looking at the causal structure of the narrative:

> We might speak of an *immediate* causality as opposed to a *mediated causality*. The first would be of the type "X is brave—X challenges the monster." In the second, the appearance of the first proposition would have no immediate consequence, but in the course of the narrative X would appear as someone who acted bravely. This is a diffused, discontinuous causality, which is expressed not by a single action but by secondary aspects of a series of actions, often remote from one another.

Todorov chooses an example from *The Arabian Nights* to illustrate immediate causality: "Sinbad likes to travel (character trait)—Sinbad takes a trip (action)."[8] A narrative of "diffused, discontinuous causality" would motivate Sinbad through prior establishment of his love of travel, perhaps attributing his wanderlust to a stultifying youth spent on a Kansas farm during which he never ventured further than the general store in the nearest small town. A narrative of immediate causality dispenses with such niceties. Sinbad likes to travel because he likes to travel—because, that is, the narrative requires that he likes to travel. In the nonpsychological narrative of immediate causality, characters do not motivate the narrative; the narrative motivates the characters. As Seymour Chatman summarizes Todorov's argument: "the characters are deprived of choice and become . . . mere automatic functions of the plot."[9]

As Chatman suggests, to further differentiate the nonpsychological from the psychological narrative we must ask whether and to what degree the characters seem to control their own destinies. In the former, characters respond willy-nilly to external forces: fate, fortune, natural disasters, and so on. In the latter, they respond to their own (often contradictory) desires and emotions: love, hate, greed, etc. Self-doubt never disturbs the blackly evil or shiningly virtuous stock figures of the melodrama. To adopt Robert Heilman's terminology, they are whole rather than divided characters.[10] With no internal conflict and thus no internal motivation, external forces must create the necessary narrative disequilibrium. This is why, in the "pure melodrama," the characters often find themselves at the mercy of fate, which batters them for four acts and miraculously saves them in the fifth. As James L. Smith maintains, "It is this total dependence upon external adversaries which finally separates melodrama from all other serious dramatic forms."[11]

As we have seen, then, the relationship between character and narrative in the "pure melodrama" involves immediate causality and external motivation, while nineteenth-century realist literature and the Hollywood style derived from it involve mediated causality and internal motivation. Psychological filmic narratives driven by mediated causality and internal motivation, in which performance is generally verisimilarly coded, deploy signifying practices differently from nonpsychological narratives driven by immediate causality and external motivation, in which performance is generally histrionically coded. In the classical Hollywood style filmmakers reveal thoughts and emotions by selecting and combining signifiers from paradigms of equivalent signifiers. The actor's performance is only one among several signifiers revealing a character's mental processes. In the Biographs (and other films of this period) that resembled the "pure melodrama," performance alone often had to convey all the information about a character's thoughts and emotions necessary for audience comprehension of the narrative.

Because the histrionic code more nearly resembles spoken language than does the verisimilar code, an unaided histrionically coded performance can convey a great deal of narrative information. Barthes asserts that nonverbal sign systems are almost always translated into articulated speech: "Is not speech the inevitable relay of any signifying order. . . . Man is doomed to articulated language."[12] The histrionic code's resemblance to articulated speech facilitates this translation. But with the move to psychological causality the histrionic code became increasingly inadequate, its reliance upon standardized gestures making it unsuitable for the portrayal of individualized, psychologized characters.

The verisimilar code abandoned the conventional gestures, replacing them with gestures coded by cultural expectations about how particular characters in particular situations might behave in real life. Tailoring gestures and expressions to an individual character, the verisimilar code contributed to the creation of credibly psychologized individuals, in the process helping to forge the inextricable link between character and narrative of the classical style. To quote Bordwell again: "If characters are to become agents of causality, their traits must be affirmed in speech and physical behavior, the observable projections of personality."[13]

Nonetheless, admirably suited as it was to psychological causality, the verisimilar code's lack of resemblance to natural language hampers its translation to articulated speech and hence its ability to convey sufficient information in the absence of other signifiers. As Barthes tells us:

> an image inevitably involves several levels of perception, and the reader of the image has at his disposal a certain freedom . . . every glance at an image inevitably implies a decision; i.e., the meaning of an image is never certain. . . . The image freezes an endless number of possibilities; words determine a single certainty.[14]

The possibility of multiple interpretations of an actor's expressions and gestures gave rise to an unwelcome polysemy, posing problems of narrative clarity. In 1911, a writer in *The Moving Picture World* complained about the failure of the verisimilar code to pin down an unambiguous meaning.

Nothing that is not clear and plain as daylight will be wholly effective as drama. . . . The pantomime actor can picture the emotion perfectly; the audience will see it and sympathize, but like one who sees another man in grief and doesn't know why he looks so sad; it can guess the reason but guessing isn't knowing.[15]

Though an avid partisan of the new style, even Frank Woods of *The New York Dramatic Mirror* realized that performance might "improve" at the expense of narrative clarity. In 1909 he said, "The whole problem . . . is one of approximating reality and at the same time making the story clear."[16]

As does the caption of a photograph, the addition of other signifiers closes off the "endless number of possibilities," giving the acting the precise meaning necessary to the flow of a coherent narrative. Consider the Kuleshov experiment, in which the actor's expression by itself meant nothing and yet, in concert with other signifiers, was thought to externalize immediately identifiable emotions.[17] Verisimilarly coded performance imparts information about a character's thoughts and emotions in conjunction with other signifiers. Those signifiers that work in conjunction with performance, aiding in the revelation of a character's thoughts and emotions, I shall refer to as *character-centered*.

A brief discussion of filmic narrators may help to clarify the concept of character-centered signifiers. In "Genette and Film: Narrative Level in the Fiction Cinema," David Black addresses the question of narrative level in films with voice-over narration, using Genette to elucidate the problems of authorial agency that such films pose. Referring to the character Walter Neff, in *Double Indemnity* (Billy Wilder, 1944), Black says; "Diegetically, he is posited as the narrating agent responsible for the story; in fact his claim to that position is challenged by no less a pretender than the narrative agency of the film itself (to which he as a character owes his existence), with all its recourse to extra- and non-verbal devices."[18] Black refuses to ascribe this agency to characters, directors, writers, or the camera, but rather labels it the "intrinsic narrator . . . whose narrative agency is congruent with the discursive activity of the medium itself."[19] Thus, while characters may occasionally seem to authorize the diegesis, they are always subordinate to the intrinsic narrator, which at times only seems to relinquish its authorial authority to varying degrees.

In general then, those signifiers over which the intrinsic narrator seems to grant the character some control are the most character-centered. In other words, character-centered signifiers seem to be authorized by the characters rather than by the intrinsic narrator, with the degree of seeming authorization varying from signifier to signifier. For example, a tracking shot that follows character movement seems, to some degree, to be character-authorized while a point-of-view shot has a higher degree of character-authorization. This determination of character authorization admittedly involves close calls at the plate, but unlike the umpire, we are aided by numerous replays of the players' actions.[20]

The Interaction of Signifying Practices in the Biographs

As suggested above, the transformation of performance style is inextricably linked with the shift from the pure melodrama to the realist psychological narrative. Though the Biographs can more readily be assigned to the melodrama than to any other genre, not all Biographs, and perhaps no single Biograph, would meet all the criteria of "pure melodrama," for melodrama is not a static genre but, like all genres, is subject to change over time. By 1913 most Biographs differed from the "pure melodrama" by substituting psychological causality for coincidence and psychologized individuals for stock figures, yet they still resembled the melodrama more closely in many respects than the classic nineteenth-century realist novel and drama from which the psychological causality of the classical Hollywood style derived. Two Biographs from 1909 located along the range from pure melodrama to psychological realism illustrate the workings of the interaction of performance, narrative, and character-centered signifiers.

The Rocky Road, released January 3, 1910, closely resembles the pure melodrama and indeed descends from the popular temperance melodrama. The *Biograph Bulletin* publicity even references the film's antecedents by foregrounding its nonpsychological narrative causality. The promotional copy is subheaded "A Story of Fate's Capriciousness," and the blurb elaborates on this theme, almost apologizing for the film's melodramatic reliance upon fate and coincidence: "Coincident as the episodes may appear they are evolved with a convincing consistency rarely found in dramatic stories of this type."[21]

The film, like *A Drunkard's Reformation* and *Brutality,* shows the miseries that a husband's drunkenness brings on his family. As the film begins, the husband (Frank Powell) carouses in a saloon with his companions, then returns home to abuse his wife (Stephanie Longfellow), who is caring for their sick daughter (Edith Haldeman). The man deserts his wife, who goes mad and roams the streets carrying the child and looking for her husband. She encounters a peddler who gives her a cloak for the daughter and, after further wandering, collapses in a haystack. Thinking she hears her husband, she abandons the child, who is found and adopted by a kindly farm family. The wife, suffering from amnesia, becomes a maid to another kindly family in the same neighborhood. Meanwhile, the husband, as an intertitle puts it, "gets work in a distant village and resolves to brace up." Another intertitle announces "Later. The Husband Favored by Fortune," and we see the husband quitting his job as a laborer and driving off in a chauffeured limousine that breaks down outside the house where his daughter (by now, Blanche Sweet) is celebrating her eighteenth birthday. After a couple of meetings the father proposes to his daughter, but before the wedding day a chance encounter with her husband causes the wife's memory to return. On the wedding day itself, the wife passes her daughter's home, sees her husband drive off to his wedding, and staggers to the door, where a friendly maid (Kate Bruce) lets her in. Sitting at the table she sees a picture of her husband and learns he is about to be married. The maid tells the story of the bride's adoption, producing the cloak the peddler had given the mother years before. The horrible enormity of her knowledge full upon her, the mother rushes to the church just in time to prevent the ceremony. After "The Terrible Revelation" (as an intertitle puts it), she collapses into her husband's arms while the wedding guests look away and the minister raises an arm to heaven, the company forming a tableau.

The narrative of *The Rocky Road* endows the main characters, the husband and wife, with single character traits that lead to immediate action. The husband drinks. He abuses and deserts his wife. The wife goes mad. She abandons her child. The husband resolves to brace up. He gets a job. The factors that might have contributed to the husband's drunkenness and subsequent reformation or the wife's madness and sudden cure are simply irrelevant. The film does not tell us about the husband's miserable childhood or the wife's previous history of mental instability. Instead, fate and implausible coincidence motivate the characters. Two kind-hearted families in the same neighborhood fortuitously shelter both mother and child. The husband, having been favored by fortune, is fortuitously stranded on his daughter's doorstep. The wife fortuitously sees her husband before the wedding day and passes her daughter's house on the day itself. In the nick of time, the old cloak leads the mother to her appalling realization—articles of clothing, along with birthmarks and lockets, being the staple melodramatic devices for identifying long-lost children.

His Lost Love was released on October 16, 1909, a few months earlier than *The Rocky Road,* but despite its earlier date this film much more closely resembles the realist, psychological narrative, indicating that there was certainly no inevitable progression toward the classical Hollywood style. In the *Biograph Bulletin* publicity for *His Lost Love* a subheading beneath the film title focuses on human causality: "A Brother's Sacrifice and Its Outcome." The copy refers to the film's reliance on internal motivation, speaking of the "struggle against self" of two of the characters.[22]

The film involves the romantic attachments and misalliances of two brothers (James Kirkwood and Owen Moore) who are both attracted to Mary Pickford. Although Kirkwood loves Pickford he selflessly renounces her after she and Moore fall in love. They are married, Pickford's sister (Marion Leonard) comes to visit, and a mutual attraction grows between Leonard and Moore. An intertitle, "The Old Struggle Against Self," precedes a scene in which Moore struggles to remain faithful to his wife but gives way to temptation.

After Pickford has a baby, the sister attempts to leave, but her farewell to Moore is observed by Pickford. Moore and Leonard go off together, leaving Pickford collapsed in Kirkwood's arms. After her inevitable death, Kirkwood vows to raise the child.

Contrast the intertitle "The Old Struggle Against Self" with "Later. The Husband Favored by Fortune" of *The Rocky Road*. In *His Lost Love* all four characters to some extent control the course of their futures. Pickford rejects Kirkwood for Moore. Kirkwood renounces Pickford and later adopts her baby. Moore wavers between honor and dishonor. Leonard flirts with the husband but then decides on the honorable course. At this point, fate intervenes with Pickford's accidental witnessing of her sister's departure precipitating her death. Just as the motivation is largely internal, causality is mediated. Kirkwood adopts the child at the end of the film because he loved the mother at the beginning.

These two films allow us to explore the correlation among performance, psychological causality, and character-centered signifiers while holding relatively constant the factor of chronology. If the hypotheses about the interaction of signifying practices are correct, there should be noticeable differences in performance style and the deployment of signifiers even though the films were made only a few months apart. The differences are indeed striking. The unchecked histrionic code is employed throughout most of *The Rocky Road*, while the performers in *His Lost Love* employ a mixture of the verisimilar and checked histrionic codes, resorting to the unchecked histrionic code only in one climactic shot. *The Rocky Road* contains gestural soliloquies in which performers externalize the same intense emotion through the repeated gestures of the unchecked histrionic code, unaided by character-centered signifiers, but in *His Lost Love*, decision-making and thought processes are externalized through performance, props, and editing.

Close analysis of a few shots from each film, starting with the gestural soliloquies of *The Rocky Road*, makes clear the contrast. In shot 4, the husband stands outside his house, making his decision to abandon his family. He smiles, raises his fingers in the air in an "I have an idea!" gesture, indicates the house, with thumb over shoulder, moves his hand as if pushing the house away, raises his hand to his ear, and brings it down to his side in resolution, then clenches his fists in the air. After a cut to the interior, shot 6 shows the mother outside the house. She enters the shot holding both arms raised level with her head, points left (in the direction the husband exited), clenches her fist, and reenters the house. Here both characters have reached decisions, but only the conventional gestures indicate this, for we are in no way privy to the thought processes leading up to the decision.

In shots 12, 13, and 22 we again see conventional gestures performed in unchecked fashion. In shot 12 the mother returns home from the saloon after looking for her husband. She enters the house, raises the back of her hand to

Left: *The Rocky Road:* "I have an idea!" Right: *The Rocky Road:* "I am distressed!"

her forehead, while her other hand is raised at her side. Taking the child with her, she exits into shot 13, the house's exterior, where she raises her hand to heaven, then points off left again. In shot 22 the conventional gestures are used in repeated series to portray the mother's anguish at the loss of her child. She returns to the haystack where she had left her child and, not finding her there, raises her left hand to her breast while her right hand is clenched at her side. She points with her left hand, moving her right hand to her breast, and then puts both hands on her breast. She reaches down to where the child was, puts her hands back on her breast, reaches down again, puts both hands back on her breast, and walks off. Throughout the shot, the actor has told us only one thing: "I am distressed."

In *His Lost Love* much of the information is conveyed by conversational gestures, glances, and byplay that are entirely absent from *The Rocky Road*. In the film's first shot, Kirkwood proposes to Pickford. Frank Powell, the father, sits rear left, and Pickford sits left of the central table. Kirkwood enters right and leans on the table near Pickford, while the father rises to stand behind them. Kirkwood gestures to himself, then to Pickford. She touches her chest tentatively as if to say "Me?" Kirkwood and Powell both hold their hands out to her in confirmation, then Pickford sits next to Kirkwood on the table. He holds her hand, kisses it, and looks up at her. She looks down bashfully, and they hug. In the third shot, Moore talks to Pickford, sitting next to her on the table and putting his hand over hers. Kirkwood reenters, places a hand on Moore's shoulder, and gestures offscreen, as if telling him he is wanted. Moore walks to the door and watches while Kirkwood takes Pickford's hand and then kisses her. Moore sneers, clenches his fist, and makes a small downward movement, giving a checked version of the conventional gesture of resolution. The glances and byplay combine with the conversational gestures to set up the triangle.

The title "The Old Struggle Against Self" precedes a five-shot sequence

His Lost Love: Conversational gestures.

in which Moore is torn between fidelity and desire, the verisimilar code working in concert with props and editing (and the occasional conventional gesture)
to illuminate his thought processes. In shot 7, set in Moore and Pickford's
living room, Leonard stands at a table looking at a book (an important prop).
Standing behind her, Moore raises his hands as if to embrace her, but Pickford
enters with a nurse, looking weak. She sits, puts her hand on her stomach, and
Moore crosses to her, pats her head, and holds her hand. Leonard gestures
offscreen and walks to the door. Moore walks over to her and she asks a question. He looks to Pickford, then back to Leonard, and shakes his head. She
leaves, and he remains in the doorway, looks at Pickford, shakes his head
again, and clenches his fist and hits his thigh in a gesture of frustration. Then
he walks to Pickford and picks up her knitting (another important prop). The
ninth shot shows Pickford's sister in church, handing a note to an old man and
sending him to fetch the music book she forgot. In shot 10 Pickford knits and
Moore reads. The old man delivers the note, and Moore exits, about to take
the book to his sister-in-law. Pickford stops him. Moore puts the book on the
table and walks over to Pickford, who shows him the little garment she is
knitting, lowering her head in embarrassment. Moore takes it from her, fingers
it, and then sinks to one knee and rests his head on his forearm in a conventional remorseful pose. Pickford puts a hand on his shoulder, and Moore rises
and kisses her. Standing with his hand on her shoulder, he makes a pushing-
away gesture, a sort of negative wave, toward the door, which is associated
with the sister. He then walks over to the table and leans on it, looking down
at the book, which he finally picks up. After another cut to the sister in church,
Moore reaches his decision. Still standing at the table holding the book, he
looks up and right, away from Pickford, who is looking at him. Through conversational gestures he tells her he will deliver the book. At the door, he hes-

His Lost Love: Knitting as a prop.

itates, looks at Pickford and then at the book, and this time makes a negative wave at Pickford.

The conventional gestures of *The Rocky Road* indicate the characters' decisions, but the mixture of conventional gestures, glances, and byplay in *His Lost Love* makes the audience privy to the decision-making process: Moore changes his mind several times as he waffles between wife and sister-in-law. Yet without the props (book and knitting) and the editing (cutting to the sister in church), Moore could not so clearly reveal his character's mental processes.

In the climactic scene of *His Lost Love* we see the use of the histrionic code in the absence of other character-centered signifiers. In this shot, in which Pickford learns of her husband's betrayal and husband and sister-in-law leave together, all four performers use the unchecked histrionic code. Leonard and Moore stand in the entrance hall as she tells him she is leaving. With one hand on her breast, she uses her other hand to push against Moore's chest, points offscreen (indicating Pickford), then points to the door. Moore grabs her hands and kisses them, but she shakes her head. Pickford enters, clenches her hands on either side of her face, extends her arms, and sinks to the floor. Kirkwood enters, pushes Moore and Leonard apart, points at Pickford, and spreads his arms wide as if to ask, "What are you doing?" Leonard raises her hands in a "stop" gesture, puts her hands on her chest ("It's my fault"), extends her left hand backward ("I shall leave"). Moore takes her hand and points to his chest ("I'm going, too"). Kirkwood raises his hands in fury as Pickford, still on the floor, clutches at his jacket and pleads, until he lowers his hands to her shoulders. Moore and Leonard leave, Pickford reaches out in their direction, then collapses into Kirkwood's arms.

In looking at *The Rocky Road* and *His Lost Love,* we have controlled for chronology while investigating the relationship among performance, psychological causality, and character-centered signifiers. But chronology must also be accounted for. Hence we shall look at two Biographs, *After Many Years,* released in November 1908, and a June 1911 remake of the same subject, *Enoch Arden,* both based on Tennyson's narrative poem, "Enoch Arden."[23] Biograph did not use Tennyson's names for the characters in *After Many Years,* which the *Bulletin* described as "a subject on the lines of Enoch Arden, although more intensely heart stirring than the original story,"[24] but for clarity's sake I shall use Tennyson's names for the characters in both films.

In the films, Enoch Arden, a fisherman (Charles Inslee [1908], Wilfred Lucas [1911]), marries Annie Lee, his childhood sweetheart (Florence Lawrence [1908], Linda Arvidson (1911)), who chooses him over Philip Ray, another childhood friend (Harry Solter [1908], Frank Grandon [1911]). The couple have children, Enoch goes to sea, and he is shipwrecked on a desert island for ten years. Philip repeatedly proposes to Annie, who strives to remain true to Enoch. In *After Many Years,* she rejects Philip, while in *Enoch Arden* she accepts him for her children's sake. Finally, Enoch is rescued, in *After Many Years* returning to find that Annie has been faithful and in *Enoch Arden* to find that she has married Philip Lee and borne his child. In the earlier film, Enoch is joyously reunited with his family, while in the later film Enoch looks at Annie, Philip, and the children, vows Annie shall never know of his return, and conveniently dies.

The films were chosen because, of all the Biographs, they are the only pair of original and remake. Although Griffith often recycled themes, situations, and entire plots, *Enoch Arden* comes closest to the modern concept of the remake, in which the same characters enact a narrative similar to that of the original. Both films tell the same story, *Enoch Arden* restaging many scenes from *After Many Years* but using different signifiers to impart the same narrative information. Comparison of these scenes tests the hypothesis that the transition from the histrionic to the verisimilar codes entailed the increasing use of character-centered signifiers. While the plots are similar, differences in causality and motivation place *After Many Years* closer to the pure melodrama than *Enoch Arden,* allowing a test of the hypothesis that the verisimilar code is associated both with psychological narratives and character-centered signifiers. The later film, a two-reeler rather than the standard (for Biograph) one-reeler of the period, devotes the extra time to a prologue establishing the love triangle and to several scenes around Enoch's departure. *Enoch Arden* actually shows Annie rejecting Philip in favor of Enoch, a rejection reenacted each time that Philip proposes after Enoch's shipwreck. The prologue, by creating a "diffuse, discontinuous causality," strengthens the understanding of Annie's internal conflict and more strongly motivates her steadfastness than in *After Many Years.* Awareness of the love triangle also provides stronger motivation for Enoch's despair and Philip's persistence.

As "diffuse, discontinuous causality" strengthens internal motivation in *Enoch Arden,* immediate causality weakens internal motivation in *After Many Years.* In this film, Enoch leaves his wife with great reluctance, but seems to

After Many Years: Enoch and Annie.

have no choice in the matter. Two sailors arrive, presumably to tell him that his ship is sailing. Enoch is a sailor—he must sail. In *Enoch Arden* the title character signs on for a voyage only after an agonized decision. Although both characters are shipwrecked by fate, the later Enoch at least has chosen to make the voyage. This choice invests his leave-taking scenes with far more poignancy, for there is always the possibility that he might change his mind.

The close analysis focuses upon seven scenes included in both films that employ different signifiers and in which the performers use different degrees of the histrionic and verisimilar codes. As a general rule, the fewer the character-centered signifiers, the more active the performance. We need to look at whether the text simply presents an actor's performance, thus requiring the actor to convey all the relevant information, or attempts to close off the meaning of the performance through character-centered signifiers.

1. Introduction of the characters.   In *Enoch Arden* the verisimilar code and character-centered signifiers together give us far more specific information about Annie, Enoch, and Philip than we receive in *After Many Years.* In the first shot of the earlier film, Enoch and Annie walk together in a garden beside a large bush that runs the diagonal length of the frame. They have their arms spread wide as if to embrace the scenery, to which they gesture. Annie runs a little ahead, making the quick movements typical of youthful Griffith heroines. Enoch catches up with her, she points to the bush, picks a rose, puts it in Enoch's lapel, and the couple kisses twice. So far we know only that the couple is in love and, given intertextual knowledge of other Griffith films, that they are probably married since the heroine permitted two kisses. With the exception of the rose, the histrionically coded acting alone indicates the couple's love. Not until the next shot does the appearance of their baby confirm the couple's married status.

In *Enoch Arden* the first three shots introduce the three main characters and

Above left: *Enoch Arden:* Annie. Above: *Enoch Arden:* Philip. Left: *Enoch Arden:* Enoch.

instantly establish the love triangle. The first shot shows a rocky beach where much of the subsequent action takes place. Annie enters slowly, pensively tapping a stick against her hand, looks to the right, then sits on a rock, tracing patterns in the sand with the stick. In the second shot Philip stands at a window looking screen left. He has his right hand raised as if reaching out to somebody, presumably Annie, whom he sees through the window. He lowers his hand, puts on his hat, and exits. In the third shot Enoch stands in front of his house toying with a vine and looking left. With the exception of Philip's raised hand, the minimal gestures in these shots express the characters' general affect, but the props, editing, and direction of gazes tell the story. The slow, distracted fashion in which Annie and Enoch handle their props tell us they are thinking, but the intercutting and matching looks between Annie and Enoch tell us what they are thinking about.

The fourth shot unites the points of the triangle established by the first three shots. Enoch stands in the background, watching Annie and Philip talk. It is interesting to compare Enoch's reactions in this and the next shot. Standing in the back of the frame, Enoch does nothing but look at Annie and Philip. The

Enoch Arden: Annie gives Enoch the locket.

next shot shows waves crashing against rocks, setting the tone for the performance. Enoch enters, looks back left to establish that he has just exited the previous shot, clenches his fists, makes a downward movement, points to himself, and exits, having decided to confront Philip. This shot illustrates how much more an actor alone in the frame must do to externalize thoughts and emotions, even though the editing pattern and his glance establish his connection with the other characters, making an unchecked histrionic gestural soliloquy unnecessary.

  2. Enoch's departure.   *After Many Years* shows the couple's misery at parting only through histrionically coded performances featuring extended and redundant gestures. Saying goodbye in long shot on the front porch of their house, the couple embraces, Annie holding the baby. Enoch points to his chest and then upward to the heavens, and raises his hand to his forehead in the classic gesture of despair as he tears himself away from Annie's arms. Turning to leave, he clenches his fists in the air before pausing to lean over the porch railing and kiss Annie once more.

  Enoch Arden stages the departure in several shots, with editing, props, and a closer camera reinforcing the couple's emotions. In the first shot (shot 13), Annie, screen left, kneels at a cradle, while her two older children play screen right. Enoch enters the space in the middle of the frame which the composition has left for him, looks at the baby, touches the children, then stands, back to camera, facing the window in the center background. Reaching a decision to leave, he raises his clenched fists to his head and lowers them, engaging in the most histrionically coded gestures of the departure sequence. Enoch signs on, then we see the family in the same composition as before, only this time in close to a medium shot, Enoch and Annie kneeling by the cradle. The next

After Many Years: Annie talks to Enoch's portrait.

shot, the closest in the entire film, is a medium close-up of the couple. Annie cuts a curl from the baby's head, puts it in a locket, and hangs it round Enoch's neck, toying with it while speaking to him. As the couple talks, the close camera clearly shows the exchange of sad glances, which the stage business with the locket reinforces. There is no need for histrionically coded gestures here, nor in the shot in which Annie reacts to Enoch's departure.

When Enoch's ship sails away, Annie and the two children stand on the beach, their backs to the camera. Shots of them are intercut with shots of Enoch arriving on board and the ship sailing out of the frame. In the last shot of this beach sequence, Annie and the children stand in three-quarter shot, their backs to the camera, Annie watching the boat through a telescope. She lowers the telescope, takes the children's hands, and shakes her head, all slowly and without great emphasis. The emotional impact of this depends not on the performance alone but on the emotional resonance established by the earlier leave-taking as well as the intercut shots of the departing Enoch.

3. Annie's reaction to Enoch's shipwreck. Both films feature cross-cutting to establish a psychic connection between Annie and her shipwrecked husband, though in the 1908 version Annie already knows of Enoch's misfortune. In the third shot of *After Many Years*, Annie leans over a crib and Philip enters holding a newspaper that he shows her, shaking his head. Annie conventionally displays feminine distress, placing her hand to her face and backing away from him. Phillip leaves Annie alone to externalize her misery with the aid of two props. Standing in the right background, she holds the newspaper in her fully outstretched arms and talks to a picture, which only repeated viewings have revealed as a portrait of Enoch. Because neither newspaper nor portrait is clearly shown, the histrionically coded performance serves as the

Left: *After Many Years:* Annie grieves for Enoch. Right: *Enoch Arden:* Annie grieves for Enoch.

dominant signifier in the shot, at least for a present-day viewer accustomed to the conjunction of narrative significance and compositional centrality.

Later in the film, Griffith for the first time experimented with cross-cutting between characters in different locations to create an emotional link between them.[25] In the eighth shot, Enoch on his island performs a gestural soliloquy of frustration and despair, ending by kissing a locket around his neck. The ninth shot shows Annie in medium close-up, the closest shot of this film, standing on the front porch where she had bid Enoch goodbye. She reaches out her left arm until it is fully extended perpendicular to her body, then her right hand in the same gesture, clasps a handkerchief between both hands and collapses crying. Aside from a rather general indication of loss and despair, the unchecked histrionic gestures here have no intrinsic meaning, gaining their intelligibility only from the conjunction with the previous shot. A more checked degree of the histrionic code might have worked here, but given the relative novelty of the closer camera and the experimental nature of the cross-cutting, it is not strange that the performance is constructed as if it alone revealed Annie's emotions.

In *Enoch Arden,* Annie reacts in much the same manner. In shot 33 Enoch is washed up on the island. In shot 34 Annie stands on shore facing the camera, then sits down, her back to the camera. Shot 35 returns to Enoch, and in shot 36 Annie realizes Enoch's peril. In medium long shot (the camera now having crossed the line to show her front), she shouts her husband's name, both arms extended outward like the 1908 Annie. Her eyes widen, she shouts again, her body bends forward, she gathers her children to her and looks heavenward. Since this shot constitutes Annie's emotional high point, it follows that the histrionic code, associated in the melodrama with extreme and exces-

Above left: *Enoch Arden:* Enoch looks at the locket. Above: *Enoch Arden:* Annie thinks of Enoch. Left: *Enoch Arden:* Enoch "looks" at Annie.

sive emotion, should be used, even though the repeated intercutting with Enoch closes off the meaning of the performance more than the editing in the 1908 version.[26]

4. Philip's proposals.   Later in the 1911 film the connection between Annie and Enoch is established through more than performance. After the children have grown up, Philip, whom Annie has already rejected, proposes twice more, to be accepted the second time. The editing in these sequences, coupled with the direction of the characters' glances, fully explains Annie's reluctance, leaving little for the performance to signify. The first proposal is preceded by a shot of a now-bearded Enoch looking at the locket Annie gave him. In the next shot, Annie, the children, and Philip are in Annie's house. After Annie says no to Philip simply by turning her head away, Philip goes to sit with the children, and Annie gazes slightly to the left of the camera. In the next shot, Enoch lies on the beach, looking off right, his gaze almost meeting

Annie's. The use of the prop reinforces the meaning of the interlocking gazes, as Enoch looks at the locket, fingers it, then rests his head on his folded arms. The composition of the shot of Annie, Philip, and the children further works with the editing and the props. Annie, the children, and Philip are arranged precisely as were Annie, the children, and Enoch during Enoch's departure scenes, with Philip now in Enoch's position. The immediate cut to Enoch shows the rightful holder of this place in the frame. A shot of Enoch also precedes the second proposal, as Enoch pauses at the edge of the frame, looks up as if at something offscreen, and then lowers his head in despair. In the following shot Annie accepts Philip.

In *After Many Years,* Philip proposes twice, with histrionically coded performance and props imparting the necessary information. The first proposal takes place in the garden where Annie and Enoch first appeared, the setting invoking Enoch's absence as do the composition and the editing in the remake. Philip and Annie walk toward the camera, he talking while she shakes her head. They pause, Philip picks a rose, places the hand with the rose on his breast, makes a declaration, and presents the rose to Annie. She shakes her head and pushes the rose away. Her left hand then gestures in the direction of the offscreen house, as if to indicate her continued loyalty to Enoch. Then, with arms fully extended on each side of her body, she shakes her head and walks slowly away, hands at her sides. The rose and Annie's gestures to the house evoke Enoch, but not as directly as the matching glances and intercutting in the later film. Annie's histrionically coded gestures of refusal in *After Many Years* are necessary because the audience, while reminded of Enoch, never sees him. In the second refusal of the proposal, Annie once more stands before Enoch's portrait, another invocation of his absence. After Philip asks his question, Annie walks to the picture, holds her arms fully extended toward it (in the same gesture she will later use standing on the front porch and reacting to the shipwreck), clasps her hands to her bosom, then once more extends her hands to the picture. Just as in Annie's reaction to the news that Enoch is lost, the prop works with the actor so little that Annie's performance borders on a gestural soliloquy.

5. Enoch's locket.   In *After Many Years,* the narrative neither singles out Enoch's portrait nor gives it emotional resonance, hence preventing it from augmenting the actor's performance to any degree. The same holds true of Enoch's locket. In the 1908 film we see the prop for the first time when Enoch, at the end of his gestural soliloquy of frustration and despair, looks at it, then kisses it. Because this is the locket's first appearance, it can serve only as a general symbol: people use lockets to remind them of loved ones from whom they are separated. The 1908 Enoch cannot illustrate his despair simply by looking at the locket. He must raise his hands over his head, clasp them behind

Top left: *After Many Years:* Enoch looks at the locket. Top right: *After Many Years:* Enoch in despair. Middle left: *After Many Years:* Enoch appeals to heaven for rescue. Middle right: *Enoch Arden:* Enoch grieves for his dead companion. Left: *After Many Years:* Enoch's homecoming.

his neck, then clench his fists at his sides. The later film shows the locket being given to Enoch, making it a signifier of a particular home and a particular family. The 1911 Enoch can lie quietly on the beach fingering the locket and tell us as much about his emotions as his 1908 counterpart does through gestural soliloquy.

6. The histrionically coded Enoch.   Despite the three years that separate the films, when Enoch is placed in circumstances similar to those of the 1908 version, he still, in 1911, uses the histrionic code. In both films, Enoch, awaiting rescue, sees a boat, which the film doesn't show. He must gesticulate wildly, both to attract the imaginary sailors and to convince the audience that the boat is indeed there. In *After Many Years,* Enoch jumps up and down on the beach waving a blanket, falls to one knee, hands clasped above his head in prayer and pleading, rises, puts hands to his head, staggers back, covers his face in despair, sinks to his knees, hands above head, then collapses full length on the beach.

The 1911 Enoch also uses histrionic gestures, though not in a fully elaborated gestural soliloquy. When this Enoch "sees" the ship, he is lying on the beach looking at the locket. He suddenly rises to his feet, his arms over his head. In the next shot he stands on the beach waving his arms over his head. The 1911 Enoch does perform a gestural soliloquy after the death of his companion, as it is his gestures alone which must externalize his great grief and distress. The man dies cradled in Enoch's arms. Enoch raises the man's head and lets it drop. His hands hover over the body, and his eyes widen. Then he starts back, crawling backwards on his knees. He stands, hands raised as if in surrender, turns, runs, turns again, hands raised. After a cut to Annie, the next shot shows the dead man. Enoch rushes into the shot, makes flailing movements at the body, then rests his head on the man's chest.

7. Enoch's return home.   Although *After Many Years* ends happily, both the 1908 and the 1911 Enochs have scenes in which they enact their dismay and desperation at seeing Philip with their families and assuming the worst. The denouement of *After Many Years* takes place in the film's last three shots, in all of which Enoch performs at the back or side of the frame unnoticed by the other characters (a theatrical convention of the time). In shot 13 Enoch enters the garden where he had walked with his wife in the film's beginning. He puts down his bundle, extends his left hand to the rose bush, and then kisses a branch, his right hand placed on his chest, his gestures reinforcing the emotional resonance of the setting. Then he looks left, starts back, and staggers back against the bush. Because we do not see what has so affected him, the sudden change in his emotions is momentarily puzzling. The puzzle is resolved when Annie and Philip enter, walk across the frame, and exit. Enoch holds his arms out toward them, sinks to one knee, head lowered, then raises his fists in the air in resolution. In shot 14, Enoch follows Annie and Philip as they walk along the path, clenching his fist in the air and bringing it down forcefully before exiting after them. Shot 15 shows Philip and Annie and the child standing in front of the house, while Enoch stands by a bush in front of the porch. He raises his hands above his head, puts them on his chest, takes

Enoch Arden: Enoch's homecoming.

out a dagger, and pauses as he is about to strike Philip. Annie and Philip go into the house, and Enoch sinks to his knees. Now he begins to interact with the little girl, and then with Annie, who reemerges, but from the time he sees Annie, Philip, and the girl until this point, Enoch's gestures have served as the sole signifiers of his thoughts and emotions and have had to indicate the swift changes in his feelings and intentions.

Compare this with *Enoch Arden,* in which Enoch's reactions are intercut with the happy family he sees through a window. The film's earlier use of this window has strengthened the poignancy of Enoch's exclusion from home and hearth. Immediately after Enoch's rescue, Annie and Philip are seen outside Philip's house, standing by the window. The next shot shows Enoch homeward bound. In the next shot, Annie, sleeping by the open window, starts awake and, as if in a trance, extends both arms toward the window, then shakes her head and puts her hand to her temple as if coming out of a daze. The reaching gesture, in conjunction with the editing, once again links Annie and Enoch, and in so doing links Enoch and the window. Immediately before

Enoch's appearance outside their house, Annie and Philip stand by the window, and they are shown framed by the window in the next shot, from the exterior. The next shot cuts to the interior, Philip closes the window, shutting out the world, and the family assembles. The very window toward which Annie had reached yearning for her returning husband now serves to separate him from his family, yet gives him an excellent view of all he has lost. The next twelve shots alternate between Enoch outside the house and the family inside.

Let's concentrate on Enoch's reaction shots. The series begins with Enoch in three-quarter shot looking in the window. Shot 78 is a medium shot of Enoch, his eyes widened in reaction, as is shot 80. Not until shot 82 does Enoch say "Annie," cover his mouth, and shrink back. In shot 84 he looks upward, presumably to heaven, and clenches his hand. Shot 85 cuts back to a three-quarter shot in which Enoch staggers back against the shrubbery, his hand on his chest. An intertitle states that Enoch has vowed that Annie will never know of his return, and shot 86 repeats shot 85. Compared to the 1908 Enoch, this Enoch has done very little: the performance is verisimilarly coded, and the editing closes off the meaning.

5

D. W. Griffith and the
Biograph Company

The historical record indicates that many people perceived Griffith as the prime mover behind verisimilarly coded acting, while the film record indicates that the Biograph actors gradually adopted a new acting style. But what evidence helps us to assess Griffith's involvement and influence in the transition to the verisimilar code? One might be inclined to treat Griffith's claims in *The New York Dramatic Mirror* and subsequent interviews with some skepticism, for to do otherwise risks succumbing to the ''great man, great artist'' theory of film history. But unilaterally discounting the historical personage ''David Wark Griffith'' when investigating Biograph performance style would be just as simpleminded.

This is not the place to rehearse yet again the weary debate on auteurism, auteur-structuralism, or whatever term now disguises an approach to film studies designed to let people watch their favorite movies without guilt. Having raised the specter of the author, however, perhaps I should specify what this chapter will *not* do. In ''Authorship and Hollywood,'' Stephen Crofts lists the four major conceptions of authorship current in film studies:

1. Author as expressive individual
2. Author as constructed from the film or films

    2.1 as thematic and stylistic properties impressionistically and unproblematically read off from the film or films

    2.2 as a set of structures identifiable within a body of films by the same author.

    2.3 as a subject position within the film.

3. Author as social and sexual subject.

4. Author as author-name, as function of the circulation of the film or films.[1]

We can immediately dismiss categories 2 and 4, which deal only with the film texts, since the previous chapter has already offered a structural analysis of the Biographs. Category 1 looks promising, including as it does "the real, live, tangible person who is conventionally identifiable as someone on set near the camera with a loud voice,"[2] but who in practice has been conflated with category 2.1. Most scholars have reduced the "author as expressive individual" to a bundle of "thematic and stylistic properties," constructed solely from the film texts, ignoring both the conditions of production and the historical context. Very few have interpreted the "expressive individual" as "someone on the set" making decisions that may partially determine textual signifiers. Hence, category 1 tends to be as textually oriented as category 2. Category 3 seems to consider the "real, live, tangible person." In fact, however, an admirable focus on intertextual, social, and historical determinants has thrown out of focus the director as a specific individual with specific ideas working in specific circumstances.

As presented by Crofts, auteurism either deals only with the texts or leaps directly to the historical and cultural context, skipping in the process an important intermediary step. This chapter attempts to take that step by looking at the historical David W. Griffith, considering his background and experiences, his ideas about film acting, and the institutional framework within which he worked. The relevant questions are: (1) What were Griffith's theatrical experiences? What acting style(s) might he have been exposed to? (2) What acting style(s) did Griffith himself employ both on stage and in film? (3) What do we know about Griffith's involvement in the preparation for and actual shooting of the Biographs? Who else at Biograph might have been involved in decisions affecting acting style? (4) What were Griffith's ideas about an appropriate film acting style and about the relationship of film to stage acting?

Griffith's Theatrical Experiences

The ephemeral nature of theatrical acting largely precludes precise knowledge of the acting styles of all but the most prominent actors, and even then the scanty evidence necessitates informed speculation. In the case of a relatively minor actor such as Griffith, evidence is elusive and, for the most part, nonexistent. Griffith, speaking of his touring days, admitted that "we acted in true 'high-falutin style.' "[3] Marshall Neilan, who in 1905 appeared with Griffith in *The Financier,* said that Griffith "played the villain and he was lousy."[4]

By "high falutin," Griffith presumably referred to the unchecked histrionic code, but what did Neilan mean by "lousy"? That Griffith employed the histrionic code which was by then passé, or that he employed the histrionic code inadequately even by the standards of those accustomed to the old performance style? Beyond these two comments and a few brief reviews, very little evidence about Griffith's theatrical acting survives.

George Pratt and Russell Merritt have, however, managed to piece together a fairly detailed record of Griffith's professional activities from the summer of 1895 through the winter of 1907.[5] Griffith spent most of this period touring with a variety of small, undistinguished companies that presented everything from Shakespeare to such popular standards as *East Lynne* and *Camille*. He usually had supporting roles and is only occasionally mentioned in reviews, none of which says much about his acting. The zenith of Griffith's stage career occurred in 1906 when he joined the company of Nance O'Neil, a well-known leading lady. Griffith stayed with O'Neil from February through May of 1906.

Merritt uses these data about Griffith's theatrical career to make a psychoanalytically inflected argument concerning Griffith's expression of biographical impulses in his Biograph films: "I will be arguing that by the time Griffith made his first film, he had gone through an adolescence marked by feelings of unexpressed anger, acute humiliation, and fear of women. His early experience in the theatre . . . generally intensified these emotions. Not until he discovered film did he find a way effectively to channel and redirect them."[6] Merritt, then, is not concerned with attempting to reconstruct Griffith's own acting style, a task I seek to accomplish by adducing information about the performers with whom Griffith worked as well as about the staging of his play *A Fool and a Girl*.

As he migrated from company to company, what kind of acting might Griffith have seen? Because many of the companies and actors with whom he was associated were fairly obscure, this is a difficult question, though one can assume that most actors in most second-rate touring companies at the turn of the century probably employed the histrionic code. Judging by his frequent mentions of O'Neil's name, Griffith seems to have considered the time spent with the O'Neil company as his most prestigious theatrical accomplishment. Luckily for us, her productions received extensive publicity, as she played major roles in major cities, and reviews and other sources provide a fairly clear picture of O'Neil's performance style. Both favorable and unfavorable critics often compared her with actors of the histrionically coded school. Reviewing her production of Ibsen's *Rosmersholm,* in which Griffith played Brendel, *The Boston Transcript* said: "She really is a survival from a past generation of acting. . . . She illustrates emotions as the players of an elder day used to picture them."[7] The same paper had earlier directly linked her with Delsarte:

From her beautiful arms and hands and the most exquisite use of the wrist and the open fingers in gesture . . . one could construct all the figures of the traditional poses, as given in Delsarte and the old French works for the expression and heightening of all the various passions and emotions. As with the arms and hands, so with the whole superb figure, all of its movements were "express and admirable."[8]

The Evening Sun, unimpressed by this throwback to an earlier style, accused O'Neil of "ranting, shouting, tearing and strutting about in awkward poses and impossible attitudes, with all of the airs and very few of the graces of the tragedy queens of fifty years ago."[9]

O'Neil herself summed up the critics' assessment when she said that they thought that "I am inclined to rant, to assume the ultra melodramatic which has gone out and was never artistic."[10] Her interpretation of Lady Macbeth would certainly seem to have verged on the "ultra melodramatic." Recalling seeing her in this role, Henry Goddard reported that "in the scene where she welcomes Duncan to the castle, she seized his hand and bent over it effusively." At the close of the banquet scene she "drops at her husband's feet as he sits, burying her face in his lap and sobbing convulsively as the curtain falls." In the ultimate test of any Lady Macbeth, the sleepwalking scene, she "starts backward so swiftly as to strike against the pillar at the corner of the stage . . . so violently that it awakens her. Glaring at the two attendants she utters a shrill scream."[11] Here we see the self-consciousness, the deliberate theatricality, and the attitude-striking of the histrionic code.

O'Neil was a theatrical atavism who nonetheless tackled the dramatic realists for whose work she seems to have been singularly unsuited. In a daring move, she played Ibsen's Hedda Gabler in New York at the same time that Mrs. Fiske, the female exemplar of the new style, appeared in the role in a nearby theatre. Mrs. Fiske garnered rave reviews, while O'Neil's interpretation was uniformly judged inferior. But though the critics may have objected, there were still audiences who appreciated the old style. Reviewing *Rosmersholm, The Boston Transcript* noted that "the subtleties and suggestions of modern psychological acting would probably baffle and weary them [the audience] as much as Miss O'Neil's forthright playing of the obvious gives them pleasure."[12]

In later life, Griffith would mention O'Neil but express profound admiration for Mrs. Fiske. Yet when he wrote his first play, *A Fool and a Girl,* his sympathies seem to have lain more with the O'Neil school, as suggested by a few of the stage directions:

Effie throws herself across chair, clutching wildly at his coat.

Effie catches hold of his hands as he takes her and throws her off.

Crouching on floor by door moaning.

Wearily picks up receiver [of telephone] then sinks to a heap on floor.[13]

Publicity stills from the play's only production (one week in Washington, one week in Baltimore) indicate that the actors used the conventional gestures and attitude-striking of the histrionic code, though whether at the playwright's behest or that of James K. Hackett, the producer and director, is unknown. In what appears to be a climactic confrontation, five men and two women stand on stage, the women in the center. The leading lady, Fannie Ward, later to star in deMille's *The Cheat* (1915), stands facing Allison Skipworth. Ward holds her right arm extended backward at a forty-five degree angle as she points at Skipworth with her left arm fully extended. Skipworth holds out her right hand, arm fully extended to Ward, while her left hand is placed on her hip. The gentlemen stand stiffly, hands at sides or on hips, or in one case leaning on knuckles on a table. In another photo of Ward, Skipworth, and a male actor, Ward sits on a fallen tree, one hand in her lap and the other hand pointing at a gentleman who sits at her feet.[14] The first photograph, especially, could well be a frame enlargement from a 1908 Biograph.

Griffith's Film Acting

The little evidence available leads to the conclusion that most of the performers with whom Griffith worked used the histrionic code, as did Griffith himself, though Griffith, as an aspiring man of the theatre, must at least have attended verisimilarly coded performances. Eyewitness accounts and films provide evidence of Griffith's notions of appropriate cinematic acting in 1907 and 1908.[15]

After the failure of *A Fool and a Girl*, a financially desperate Griffith became involved for the first time with the film industry, selling story ideas, appearing as an extra, and even playing a few leads. Between December 1907 and July 1908, Griffith appeared in twenty-three films that we know of, twenty-one at Biograph and two, *Rescued from an Eagle's Nest* and *Cupid's Pranks*, for Edison.[16] Wallace McCutcheon, who directed Griffith in his Biograph films, summed up his actor's talents in two words: "He stinks!" McCutcheon continued to employ Griffith not for his thespian abilities, but because he had story ideas and suggested "bits of business for other performers."[17] Henry Marvin, Biograph's vice-president and general manager, also worried about the skills of Biograph's new acquisition. In his unpublished memoirs, Billy Bitzer discusses Griffith's first film appearances:

> In the spring of 1908 when Mr. Griffith first got before the camera as an extra when my boss . . . Mr. H. N. Marvin . . . saw the picture . . . he could not help but notice that the character Mr. Griffith was playing, an innkeeper or bartender, in a picture with a ''What Ho, what'll it be me Hearties'' attitude accompanied with a swinging gesture of his arms . . . that the arms were a blur, looked more like fans than arms, for which I was blamed. . . . It would take a shutter of a hundredth of a second to stop the waving arms and some of the other quick movements of . . .

Rescued from an Eagle's Nest: Griffith's superfluous gesture.

Griffith. I figured the only thing to do would be to place this Griffith to the side of scenes and then if his gestures were wild, I could move the camera ever so slightly and he could do his waving out of the scene. [Griffith said later], ''Why didn't you tell me to slow down. I thought action had to be exaggerated the way I had seen them do it in Vitagraph pictures.''[18]

From this comment we can infer that in his initial appearances Griffith thought it necessary to adapt his stage acting style to the new medium, which he did by speeding up the fully extended, heavily stressed movements of the unchecked histrionic code.

Close analysis of *Rescued from an Eagle's Nest* (J. Searle Dawley, director, Edison Studios, 1908) and *At the Crossroads of Life* (Wallace McCutcheon, Jr., director, Biograph, 1908) reveals that it was not blurred arms that set Griffith apart from his fellow film performers but rather an intensely self-conscious theatricality combined with the making of narratively superfluous movements. In *Rescued,* Griffith plays a woodsman whose child is stolen by an eagle and carried to its nest. In the film's second shot, Griffith and two others cut down a tree. The situation makes histrionically coded gestures unnecessary: all the actors have to do is saw. But Griffith nonetheless pauses to gesture to his fellow workmen and then point at the tree, as if exhorting them to greater effort, though they seem to be working hard enough. In the sixth shot, Griffith and friends cut down another tree. After it falls, Griffith extends his left arm and swings it back and forth while smiling in what seems an entirely meaningless gesture contributing neither to story nor characterization. At this point, his wife rushes in and tells him about the kidnapping. She gestures upward, and he points upward three times in succession before leading the group offscreen with much arm-waving. Griffith and company chase the eagle until they reach the top of a cliff on the side of which the eagle resides. The men tie a rope around Griffith and lower him over the side. As he begins

Left: *At the Crossroads of Life:* Griffith pleads with his beloved (Museum of Modern Art Film Stills Archive). Right: *At the Crossroads of Life:* Griffith as rejected suitor (Museum of Modern Art Film Stills Archive).

his descent, and then again as he disappears, he raises his right hand in a wave, the gestures all but meaningless. After landing on the cliff ledge, Griffith kneels screen right over his stolen child and then, seeing the eagle, assumes an extremely theatrical posture. He looks around and extends his right arm fully before rising with both arms extended outward, right leg bearing his weight, knee slightly bent, and his left leg back, knee bent as if to kneel, then puts both hands to his head and holds the pose. Having killed the eagle, he kicks it over the cliff edge, accompanying the kick with a sweeping outward gesture of the right arm. As the eagle falls, he leans over and shakes his fist at it.

Griffith's excessive theatricality is even more apparent in *At the Crossroads of Life,* where at times he seems to be almost intentionally parodying the histrionic code. In his first scene in this film, he comes to visit his lover. As he enters through a curtained doorway, he looks right, then left toward the woman. He pauses to assume an ''I love you'' pose, both hands reaching out toward her. He advances toward her with hands still extended, takes her hands and kisses one, then holds her hand with his right hand while pointing toward the door with his left in a ''come away with me'' pose. He then takes both her hands in his again and leans in so that his face is next to hers. When a servant enters, they separate, Griffith holding his right hand extended sideways, the arm slightly bent, and the other hand near his chest, again striking an attitude. After the servant leaves, he kisses the woman again. She breaks away, but he keeps both arms extended toward her then drops his hands to his sides as he walks out. At the door he pauses again, points at her, talks, turns to leave, and clenches the hand that had been pointing, so that he exits with one arm extended backward and fist clenched. Later, at the denouement, the woman rejects him. He shakes hands with her, turning his head momentarily, then turns back thrusting his chin forward in a ''noble'' pose. He kisses her hand, steps back, still holding her hand and looking at her, and, turning away from her, he brings his hand up to his chest and then down again in a conventional gesture of rejection.

These two films illuminate Marshall Neilan's comment about Griffith's acting. It was not simply that Griffith used the histrionic code, it was that he used it inadequately. Judging both by his fellow performers in these films and by other films featuring histrionically coded performances, Griffith was a bad actor by the standards of the histrionic code. He took the self-consciousness and theatricality inherent in histrionically coded acting and exaggerated it, giving each gesture and pose a great and unnecessary emphasis.

Director Griffith

During the spring of 1908, the Biograph front office, facing a shortage of directors, offered Griffith the chance to make a film. Though Griffith had by this time been writing scenarios and acting in films for six months, he still felt less than sure of his directorial abilities and agreed only with the assurance that he be retained as an actor should his directorial debut fail. Originally hired as director simply to rehearse the actors, Griffith soon found himself, as Bitzer tells us, involved in all aspects of the films' production:

> Before his [Griffith's] arrival, I, as cameraman, was responsible for everything except the immediate hiring and handling of the actor. Soon it was his say whether the lights were bright enough or if the make-up was right. . . . . A cameraman had enough to do watching the rapidity of the action and keeping the hand-cranked camera going at a steady pace to prevent the film from buckling.[19]

The evolution of studio organization remains a disputed point among film historians. Bitzer's comment may be taken to lend support to Staiger's chronology, set forth in *The Classical Hollywood Cinema*. Prior to 1907, according to Staiger, one person, the cameraman, had control of all aspects of film production, from the selection of the subject to the final editing. As distributors and exhibitors clamored for more film, the studios instituted division of labor, switching from a "cameraman" system of production to a "director" system. Under this system, the cameraman retained control over technical matters such as lighting, but a variety of workers such as outside scriptwriters, stage managers, property men, and wardrobe mistresses took over his former jobs. The director, at this time often called the producer, oversaw the whole production and became recognized as the chief authority. By 1909 the film studios began to institute the "director-unit" system to meet the exhibitors' need for twenty to thirty new reels a week. Under this system the studios employed several directors, giving each his own cast and crew and requiring him to turn out one reel a week.[20]

According to Tom Gunning, "It is not certain how relations between cameraman and director had evolved at Biograph prior to Griffith's first films," though "it seems that Biograph had employed a director-cameraman team for dramatic films . . . for several years before Griffith appeared."[21] At any rate, Griffith was the sole director from June 1908 through December 1909, when the first non-Griffith unit began operation. By the time Griffith left in the fall of 1913, six directors were shooting Biograph films under Griffith's supervision.[22]

Charles Musser, who proposes a modification of Staiger's chronology, believes that Griffith may have had more authority at Biograph than did most directors at the time. Musser asserts that a collaborative system, in which films were codirected by cameramen and/or producers, and/or directors, "dominated American cinema until 1907 or 1908."[23] Around these years, a shift occurred to a hierarchically organized central-producer system, which Musser dates several years earlier than does Staiger.[24] Staiger's intermediary "director-unit" system, according to Musser, "simply never existed."[25] Musser argues that Griffith at Biograph is a unique case from which historians have drawn inaccurate generalizations.

> Griffith's role at Biograph represented a somewhat unusual variation of the central producer system, not some distinct interim category. This was a conjunction of at least two factors. First the subordination of Bitzer or Marvin to Griffith conformed more readily to preexisting practices at Biograph than at some studios. Secondly . . . his ability to work efficiently . . . meant that he could produce and direct two reels of film per week. . . . Soon he produced and directed some Biograph films while supervising the direction of others. Biograph thus allowed for a concentration of titles and responsibilities in one person.[26]

What precise responsibilities did Griffith have with regard to "the hiring and handling of actors" and other matters impinging on performance? What restrictions did the front office impose, and what input might other Biograph employees have had? Let us examine these issues by proceeding step by step through the production process, beginning with the matter of personnel. The front office seems to have granted carte blanche with respect to hiring, and Griffith established his own personal stock company, which remained remarkably stable over the years, given the mobile nature of the acting profession. The stock company began to be developed almost as soon as Griffith began directing. When Florence Lawrence started at Biograph in July 1908 there were only "three or four regularly employed actors and actresses who were paid on a weekly guarantee." But four or five months later Griffith had established a company[27] and continued to seek new talent throughout his Biograph years. One of his first acquisitions was a leading man for *The Adventures of Dollie*. Making the rounds of the theatrical agencies (with which he must have been all too familiar), Griffith encountered Arthur Johnson and entered into a two-year working relationship over a couple of drinks.[28] After this successful experience, Griffith made a habit of looking for new (to film) talent. He found Frank Powell at a theatrical agency. Meeting James Kirkwood at the Lamb's Club, he persuaded him to visit the studio and then persuaded him to accept employment.[29] Shortly after this, Kirkwood's fellow Lamb, Henry Walthall, came visiting and found himself acting in his first film. When the Gishes came to visit Mary Pickford they also made their cinematic debut at Griffith's behest, appearing in *An Unseen Enemy* (1912).[30] During the Biograph years, Griffith had an unerring instinct for acting talent and the requisite charm to convince the actors to enter the new medium. After a few years at the Fourteenth Street studio, many of Griffith's discoveries went on to great success in the film industry, and the Biograph Company boasted an impressive array of talent amongst its alumni.

Griffith had less freedom with respect to stories than he did with personnel. When Griffith arrived at Biograph, the studio already had a story department, in the person of Lee Dougherty and an inhouse writer, Stanner E. V. Taylor, Griffith's immediate predecessor as director. Even though the director was authorized to purchase story ideas, Griffith never had sole control over the subject matter of Biograph films but always consulted one or both of these men. Linda Arvidson recalled that Dougherty would read story submissions first, then go over them with Griffith to make the final selections.[31] According to Taylor, he, Dougherty, and Griffith would go to a rathskeller (probably Luchow's near the studio on 14th Street) every Sunday afternoon and "go over possible stories . . . scene by scene and what actors. Dougherty always sat in on story conferences for selection of stories."[32]

Whether or not these story ideas were turned into formal scripts that guided Griffith during the filming remains subject to debate. It was, during the nickelodeon era, standard industry practice for staff writers to prepare the script, often without consulting the director. Lawrence McCloskey, writer for the Lubin studios, said in 1913, "Now the director does not see the scenario until it is handed to him for production, complete in every detail. Should he disagree with the idea or about anything in the script, the point is agreed and settled before the play is begun."[33] But Griffith's associates have always adamantly denied that Griffith ever used a written script, or even notes, asserting that he kept complicated shot structures entirely in his head. "David never used a script," his wife flatly stated.[34] Even Mary Pickford, not the most enthusiastic of Griffith boosters, said, "D. W. Griffith never adhered to a script. In most cases, at least in the old Biograph days, I don't think such a luxury had even made its appearance in the studios."[35]

But scripts seem to have appeared at the Biograph studios before Griffith did. Taylor said, "Scripts at Biograph we always had. . . . There was always a script, 12, 15, 18 scenes."[36] Patrick Loughney has substantiated Taylor's claim by discovering five pre-1908 Biograph scripts in the Library of Congress archives. The scripts were deposited for copyright protection, but Loughney believes that they predated the films rather than being written after production. With a film such as *Tom, Tom, the Piper's Son,* logistics alone would have necessitated a script, given the involvement of twenty-two actors, rapid shifts between interiors and exteriors, and a shooting time of just one day. Moreover, the script contains material that is missing from the released film, the differences resulting not from someone writing a script based on the completed film but from someone encountering difficulties in filming the script. As further evidence, after the time of the earliest script discovered (*Personal,* 1904), the *Biograph Bulletins* get longer, perhaps as a result of the preexisting scenarios making the promotional writers' task easier.[37] Loughney has concluded that "the Edison and Biograph companies may have been using rudimentary screenplays as early as 1902."[38] Gunning believes that the logistical complexities of discontinuous shooting would have required Griffith to use "some form of shooting script."[39] On the evidence, it seems that scripts existed at Biograph both before and after Griffith's arrival and that Griffith deliberately kept the actors from seeing the scripts, suggesting to them that no scripts existed. That Griffith would deny he ever used a script is consistent with his penchant for self-promotion, lack of a prewritten script emphasizing his artistic autonomy and contributing to his construction of the myth of the great director.[40]

But why does it matter whether or not scripts existed and whether or not Griffith used them? First, the early Biograph scripts contain stage directions, including specific movements. In *The Nihilists* (1905), a man is "flung half dead upon a table, from which he falls, writhing in his agony to the floor." Later in the film, actors "stagger and stumble in their weakness," and at the denouement, the heroine, "with arms raised to heaven . . . gives thanks for the success of her efforts."[41] These directions clearly call for histrionically coded performances, but might not writers who submitted narratives of psychological causality have included suggestions for verisimilarly coded acting in their scripts? Frank Woods, who wrote as "The Spectator" of *The New York Dramatic Mirror* and was a vocal advocate of the verisimilar code, authored several scenarios for Biograph, beginning with *After Many Years.* If Woods had been involved in the development of scripts, one would expect that his firm convictions about appropriate cinematic acting would have found their way into the stage directions. Were this the case, Woods and many other writers may have significantly contributed to the transition to the verisimilar code. However, resolution of all this speculation must await further archival discoveries.

Second, it was customary at most studios to provide at least the principal players with scripts in advance of rehearsal and shooting. "The principals have probably read the play, and have done some rehearsing before a mirror but minor people depend upon instruction and rehearsal to learn their movements and expressions and to interpret a story they may never know."[42] Making the minor players totally dependent upon the director was standard operating procedure. "Only the leading members of a company prepare for their roles in advance. . . . The minor members . . . know nothing of the story until called for rehearsal. . . . The director explains the story, and tells the players how he wants to proceed."[43] But without scripts, Griffith's leading players would have been as ignorant of the story as the merest spear carrier. Griffith's withholding of scripts from his actors may be interpreted as a desire for absolute control over their performances. Because only Griffith knew the entire story, which he would disclose slowly during rehearsals, his actors would have been entirely dependent on him, even the leads lacking sufficient information to mount a convincing argument for their own interpretations.

While all directors rehearsed their actors, the time allocated to rehearsal seems to have depended upon the studio. In 1909 a studio visitor noted that the players sometimes received only one or two hours of rehearsal.[44] In 1911 *Moving Picture World* columnist E. W. Sergent commented that "the number of times that a scene is rehearsed varies with the director and with the intricacy of the action, five to ten times being an average."[45] At the time Griffith acted at Biograph one gets the impression that the studio did not encourage lengthy preparations. Arvidson describes the rehearsal that preceded Griffith's first Biograph screen appearance as a rather perfunctory matter, unduly hasty even for readying a very minor extra such as Griffith: "After a short rehearsal, an explanation of 'foreground' and instructions about keeping 'inside the lines' and 'outside the lines,' the camera opened up."[46]

By mid-1909, Griffith was already willing to devote half a day or more to rehearsal,[47] a good idea since the cost of film prohibited more than one take.[48] By 1911, "Griffith would rehearse six or even seven stories months ahead with various people doing the same parts."[49] He took up to a week to rehearse a one-reeler before production and rehearsed *Musketeers of Pig Alley* (1912) for ten days.[50] Bitzer spoke of Griffith "repeatedly rehearsing, sticking to it for hours, until he had the effect or some semblance of what he desired."[51]

Griffith became increasingly concerned with rehearsals during his Biograph years, and Biograph actors' reminiscences of the actual production process tend to center on rehearsals. We have more information about the company's preparation for shooting than we do about any other aspect of the production process. This is fortunate, for the rehearsals were a crucial factor in the transition from the histrionic to the verisimilar codes, giving Griffith a place to try out his ideas, to learn from his more experienced actors, and to train his neophytes. In 1911, when the verisimilar code became dominant, Griffith and his actors were using rehearsals to work out bits of business, to experiment with props, and to develop the psychologized, individuated characters associated with the new acting style.[52]

But when Griffith first began directing, rehearsals did not concentrate on the development of characterization, for the Biograph front office demanded quickly paced performances using the unchecked histrionic code. "Deliberation and repose would have been out . . . in the early days of the Biograph pictures as the films were sold for fourteen cents a foot and Mr. Griffith was told that the buyers would positively not pay for a foot of film that did not have action in it."[53] The actors objected in vain to this economic exigency, and Florence Lawrence devoted a section of her *Photoplay* memoirs to this issue, worth quoting at length for their valuable insight—running counter to Griffith's carefully constructed image—into Griffith's early career.

> What seemed to annoy us . . . and to hold us back from achieving greater artistic success was the speed and rapidity with which we had to work before the camera. Mr. Griffith always answered our complaint by stating that the exchanges and exhibitors who bought our pictures wanted action, and insisted that they get plenty for their money. . . . There was no chance for slow or "stage" acting. The moment we started to do a bit of acting in the proper tempo we would be startled by the cry of the director. "Faster! Faster! For God's sake hurry up! We must do the scene in forty feet. . . ." In real life it would have taken four minutes to enact the same scene. . . . The buyers of the films saw their money being wasted if there was a quiet bit of business being portrayed. They didn't want, as Mr. Griffith had said, "illustrated song slides. . . ." Following the appearance of the Film d'Art pictures, nearly all of the Biograph players asked Mr. Griffith to be allowed to do slow acting, only to be refused. He told us it was impossible since the buyers would not pay for a foot of film that did not have action in it.[54]

Mary Pickford's report of arguing with Griffith over performance style corroborates Lawrence's. Pickford states, with an annoying self-satisfaction, that she had sworn never to overact, a "revolutionary" concept at this time. Her declaration that she would not "exaggerate" precipitated, she says, one of many squabbles between actor and director, presumably because Griffith insisted on a rapid tempo.[55]

Both Lawrence's and Pickford's memoirs indicate that Griffith by no means began directing fully committed to the holy cause of bringing a new performance style to the screen. Indeed, at the start, Griffith seems to have been pro-histrionic and anti-verisimilar, a position in accord with his theatrical training, his own film acting, and his economic situation. As we have seen, Griffith's stage career had exposed him mainly to actors of the old school. As for his own film acting, despite Bitzer's remonstrations the front office kept him on, giving him no reason to think they found his style unacceptable. One imagines that the front office's opinions played a large part in Griffith's calculations at this time. So uncertain of himself that he agreed to direct only after being assured of job security, he was unlikely to confront the money men on issues of artistry at such a tenuous point in his career. Not until later did Griffith feel confident enough to risk challenging not only the front office, but the exchanges, exhibitors and, possibly, the audience:

> The Biograph's first experiments along this line [deliberation and repose] were undertaken with no little hesitation and fearsome doubt. Those having the responsibility for the change felt that they were treading on thin ice. So deeply rooted was the opinion that speed was the thing, that the experimenters were fearful that their attempts to introduce real acting into the films would be met with derisive laughter.[56]

When rehearsals became an integral part of Biograph productions, they were a multistep process, which a variety of sources enables us to reconstruct. At the "first reading," Griffith would assemble his troupe and outline the story to them. Mary Pickford reported that "we were taken aside and intelligently explained the theme of the story and the dramatic possibilities of it." This would be followed by tentative role assignments and preliminary rehearsals, during which players "walked through the scenes to get our positions." Not until after the first "few rough rehearsals" did Griffith make final decisions about casting.[57]

At most times during the Biograph years, Griffith had available several actors capable of playing the leads, and "no one had a cinch on a line of good parts."[58] An actor might play the lead in one film and appear as an extra at a garden party in the next. Preventing any one or two actors from becoming the "stars" of the company may have been part of the front office's economically motivated resistance to the impending star system, but such a strategy also fit well with Griffith's methods. Griffith constantly created jealousy and competition among his employees and somewhat capriciously handed out the plum assignments as a technique for controlling his actors, for punishing and rewarding them: "In their eagerness to get a good part in a movie, the actors behaved like hungry chickens being fed nice, yellow corn, knocking and trampling each other in their mad scramble for the best bits."[59] When making *Man's Genesis* in 1912, Griffith went to each of his ingenues and asked her to play the part of the young cave girl. Because the girl was to wear a grass skirt, showing her bare legs and feet, Mary Pickford, Blanche Sweet, Dorothy Bernard, and Mable Normand all refused. Griffith assigned the role to Mae Marsh, announcing at the same time that she would play the lead in *The Sands of Dee,* a part that all the other young women coveted.[60] For the same film, Griffith chose Joe Greybill over Edwin August for the male lead, having had a disagreement with the latter. The front office intervened, demanding that August be cast, and saying that he was to be in every romantic and society drama.[61] This is the only recorded instance of front office interference in Griffith's casting decisions.

After the final casting, rehearsals began in earnest. At first, the actors walked through their parts on a bare stage with nothing but wooden kitchen chairs, going through the action again and again while Griffith decided about lighting, editing, camera positions, and the placement of props.[62] By the time Griffith had satisfied himself with respect to these technical matters the actors' blocking would be automatic, and both they and the director would be ready to concentrate on characterization and emotions.[63]

This was the stage of the rehearsals in which players and director constructed the characters we see in the Biographs. What did Griffith actually do during these rehearsals? The answer depends to some extent on the source, but the general impression is that Griffith possessed the ability to obtain the best performances from his people, varying his tactics to suit the actor. Mary Pickford said, "Griffith knew the strengths and weaknesses of all his players and devised ways and means of bringing the actors out of themselves by his clever psychological handling. He could make an actor express himself in dramatic performances."[64]

Having explained the story and described the characters' actions and emotions, Griffith started rehearsals by trusting his performers' instincts. "You understand the situation. Now let us see what you would do with it. After giving the matter careful consideration, she [the actor] plays the scene after her own ideas. Mr. Griffith gives the actress a chance."[65] Allowing the actor some latitude of interpretation, Griffith at first offered only praise or gentle corrections: "He was your audience . . . he'd cry, laugh—he'd simply draw it out of you—his enthusiasm was infectious: 'That's fine, that's dandy—do it some more. . . .' He had the faculty of getting it out of you—He was magnetic."[66] Sometimes he would offer more specific suggestions in an attempt to make the performer feel her character's emotions. Gish tells of rehearsing for *The Mothering Heart:*

> As I rehearsed the scene, Mr. Griffith fed me the reactions of the injured wife: "You feel that you've been humiliated by your husband in public. You think that he doesn't love you any longer because you're carrying his child. You're afraid that he wants to get rid of you."
> With his intense voice coaching me, I felt the heroine's agony.[67]

Griffith would more actively intervene if the performers failed to meet his expectations: "if you weren't getting the scene as he felt you should, he would show you how it should be done."[68] Again and again, actors speak of Griffith acting out the parts, regardless of age and sex, showing his players the specific gestures and facial expressions with which to externalize thoughts and emotions. Given Griffith's limitations as a thespian, one may wonder at the efficacy of these performances, but his actors apparently found them inspiring. Blanche Sweet said that, "He'd show you so beautifully that you felt, 'Oh, I'd never be able to do it that way.'"[69] Others offer a more realistic assessment: "He was not very good, I am afraid what we call 'hammy.' "[70] Though Griffith had apparently not rid himself of his excessive theatricality, he did have an excuse for his performance style. "Griffith was hammy in showing what to do. . . . He said he exaggerated to show what he meant."[71] Having shown the players what he wanted, he then worked with them until he reached the desired effect: "he would act out the scene himself with exaggerated gestures that he would later modify in us."[72]

When praise, gentle criticism, and example all failed to elicit an acceptable performance, Griffith resorted to rougher tactics, willing to use any means to produce the necessary emotion. Thinking that Mary Pickford was giving a less than spirited performance, he began to badmouth her lover, Owen Moore. "As her eyes filled with angry tears, Griffith looked away, grimly satisfied. This was the look he wanted in the scene we were going to film. 'Camera,' he called."[73] Griffith even resorted to physical intimidation of a sort. When he tried out the Gish sisters for *An Unseen Enemy* (1912) he "pulled a real gun from his pocket and began chasing us around the room, shooting it off."[74] Desiring a frightened reaction from Mae Marsh, he would have a shotgun fired off a few feet away.[75]

As most of the above suggests, it would seem that Griffith paid most of his attention to his female actors, the "child-women" to whose thespian training he devoted himself. Claire McDowell, an older member of the troupe, contrasted Griffith's direction of her with his handling of the "girls": "I was a good dependable actress. He used to say I was a rest for him as he did not have to work so hard directing me. All the other girls were younger and without stage experience and he had to teach them every mood and move."[76] Anita Loos suggests that Griffith deliberately sought inexperienced youngsters to whom he could teach the "Griffith style": "Blanche Sweet seemed rather unsure of herself, as did all Griffith's young actresses; he wanted no positive traits to prevent them from being passive instruments on whom he could improvise."[77] Christy Cabanne, a Biograph actor/director, asserted that Griffith "showed Mary [Pickford] every move she made, same as with the others."[78] Pickford herself worried that Griffith was totally dominating her: "I was getting to be a machine under Mr. Griffith. I got to be an automatic doll. If he told me to move my left foot, I moved it. When he said, 'Look up' I did that just as unquestioningly."[79] According to Mae Marsh's description of Griffith's direction of her in *Man's Genesis* (1912), he did indeed treat her like an automatic doll, telling her exactly what to do and when to do it. On the first day's shooting he told her to go sit next to Bobby Harron and look at him as if she were very much in love. "He said, 'Just think that you're terribly in love and look up at him shy-like.' So I did, and he said, 'Look up at him again and then put your head down,' which I did. Then he said, 'Now get up and run away.' So I got up and ran away."[80]

Anyone wishing to mount an argument for Griffith as the "auteur" of the

Biograph verisimilar code would do well to concentrate upon the "Griffith actresses," but even here one must exercise caution. Remember that Mary Pickford in her autobiography claims to have argued with Griffith over performance style. It would be a mistake to paint Griffith as a directorial Svengali with a cast full of compliant Trilbys. On this point, let Griffith speak for himself: "I did not 'teach' the players with whom my name has been linked. We developed together, we found ourselves in a new art and as we discovered the possibilities of that art we learned together."[81] There is evidence that Griffith actually encouraged his casts' participation in the construction of their performances. Many of the actors recalling their Biograph years mentioned that Griffith willingly accepted suggestions and actively solicited their advice, sometimes calling the company from the dressing room and asking for their input.[82] Often, when a scene was not jelling properly, he left the studio, instructing the actors to solve the problem. On one occasion he told them that if they succeeded, he would ask the front office for a five-dollar pay raise. In the scene, the actors played guests at a bachelor party who were to toast the prospective bridegroom, Owen Moore. When Griffith returned, they lifted Moore up, set him on a table, raised their glasses, turned to Griffith and shouted, "Biograph! Hah! Hah! Hah! Ten Dollars, Ten Dollars, Rah! Rah! Rah!" They got the raise.[83]

The rehearsal process permitted the actors to devise bits of business that would flesh out their characters: "He couldn't bother with asking why you did this or that, or telling you about your character—what kind of walk you should use, what kind of clothes. It was up to you. You had to be creative. . . . We tried things out in rehearsal. If it was good, Griffith said 'Keep it in.' "[84] One of the most famous shots in a Griffith film originated in this fashion. During the rehearsal of the courtroom scene in *Intolerance,* Mae Marsh unconsciously twisted her handkerchief, and Griffith said "Keep it in"[85] The next chapter more fully investigates the contribution of the actor to Biograph performance style.

By the time of the actual shooting, little remained to be done. The cameraman's assistant put down the "lines," using nails and cord to surround the area that would be in the frame, and there would be a quick, final rehearsal for positioning.[86] When the camera began to crank, the actors were expected to do exactly what had been agreed upon in rehearsals. Improvisations were forbidden.[87] Griffith himself watched quietly, occasionally offering suggestions. "Not so much, not so much. Less, less—simple, simple, true. Don't act it, feel it; feel it, don't act it." And then, "More, more, we need more!"[88]

Sometimes after the day's filming, Griffith and certain members of the company screened the rushes from previously shot films.[89] While watching, Griffith talked to cast and crew offering his views on acting,[90] providing, one imagines, valuable opportunities to evaluate and reconsider performance style for all concerned. Only one of these sessions has been described, by Mary

Pickford, who reports that Griffith complained about her makeup in the final close-up of *Friends*. Pickford responded that "there's too much eyebrow pencil and shadowing around my eyes."[91] Griffith agreed, and presumably retook the shot. Griffith not only watched his own films but kept an eye on the competition, making the rounds of the nickelodeons every Sunday.[92] During one of these excursions, in the summer of 1908, he saw a Vitagraph film starring Florence Lawrence and decided to hire her.[93] When Griffith met his new actor, he told her, "You were very good in that—it was a good picture"[94] Griffith's filmgoing might also have had another purpose. Lillian Gish tells us that Griffith told his actors to go to movie houses and observe audience reactions. "You may be crying or having hysterics, but if you're not making the audience feel that way, you're not any use to my story. Go to a movie house and watch the audience. If they're held by what you're doing, you've succeeded as an actress."[95]

Griffith's Acting "Philosophy"

Although the recollections of associates offer glimpses of Griffith at rehearsals and filming, it is hard to extract Griffith's fully elaborated "philosophy" of acting (if such existed) from this scattered evidence. This must come from the interviews Griffith granted after his departure from Biograph. When Griffith "went public," by which time the verisimilar code was fully in place, he espoused the fundamental tenet of the literary and dramatic realists that the best art was an accurate reproduction of reality: "The motion picture technique is what technique really means, a faithful picture of life. . . . You violate the real essence of technique when you do not do it as it is . . . done in real life. The motion picture . . . should be a picture of real life . . . and emotions should be depicted as they would be in real life."[96] Griffith felt that the best actors should be instinctively capable of realistic emotions. They "just go ahead and do it as though it were a part of their really and truly experience in life."[97] Griffith actors had to know how to "feel their parts" and to "express any single feeling in the entire gamut of emotions with their muscles."[98] But the actor's face and body should be reflecting an inner feeling rather than creating feeling from the outside in. The greatest sin a Griffith actor could commit was to be caught "acting."[99] Griffith once instructed Mae Marsh, "Now feel it. Don't act. I don't want actors on my set. I want human beings. Always remember in your acting you're never to act but to feel it."[100]

Griffith did, however, believe in the external construction of a character through mannerisms and appropriate bits of business, sharing the literary and dramatic realists' opinion that accurate reproduction could be achieved by painstaking observations of people in their day-to-day activities. He often urged his actors to base their performances on the mannerisms of real people: " 'No matter where you are, watch people,' he told us. 'Watch how they walk, how they move, how they run around. If you're in a restaurant, watch them across the table or on the dance floor.' ''[101] Griffith told an interviewer in 1913 that he and Bitzer were in the habit of visiting various parts of New York City and taking photographs. By comparing these photographs with his actors' performances, Griffith hoped to ascertain "how truthfully his people had depicted various emotions."[102] Mae Marsh claimed that Griffith sent her into the slums of New York on an observation tour.[103] Lillian Gish visited a mental hospital to "learn about human nature and build our characterizations."[104] Before the filming of the death-house scenes in *Intolerance,* Griffith arranged a special tour of death row at San Quentin.[105]

Coupled with the classic realists' concern for facts and details, Griffith had a rather mystical notion of the "essence" of a good performance or performer, an intangible "something," which some possessed and others did not. Griffith once referred to this essence as "soul," that quality that enabled an actor to experience her character's emotions: "the first thing needed is 'soul.' By that I mean people of great personalities, true emotions and the ability to depict them before the camera. . . . The actor with the soul feels his part, he is living his part." It required this special quality of "soul" to face the "grim, cold-blooded, truth-in-detail telling camera lens which will register every quiver of the facial muscles, every gleam of the eye, every expression of the face, every gesture."[106]

Put simply, then, Griffith thought that actors experienced emotions, their faces and bodies reflected these emotions, and the camera captured the externalized feelings. The closer the camera, the better the chance of filming emotions: "the near view of the actors' lineaments conveys intimate thoughts and emotions better than can ever be conveyed by the crowded scene."[107]

Finally we come to the close-up, often thought to be one of Griffith's major contributions, perhaps his single most important contribution, to a "new" style of film performance. Griffith himself placed great emphasis upon the closer camera, often equating the larger-scale shot with the verisimilar code:

> We were striving for real acting. When you saw only the small, full length figures it was necessary to have exaggerated acting, which might be called "physical" acting, the waving of the hands and so on. The close-up enabled us to reach real acting, restraint, acting that is a duplicate of real life.[108]

Griffith certainly did not "invent" the close-up. Indeed, the Biographs contain very few close-ups in the modern sense of the term referring to a tight shot of the head. Though I have compiled no statistics on the Biographs, as a matter of comparison we can note that *The Birth of a Nation* in its entirety contains only eleven true close-ups and only a few more medium close-ups (head and shoulders). But Griffith did insist on bringing the camera closer to the action and apparently did so against the resistance of everybody else at

Biograph. Bitzer suggested that the actors did not want closer shots because they did not want to be recognized and have their theatrical careers jeopardized.[109] The camera itself was hard to focus at the closer range, and if the players gesticulated "too wildly" the shot would show a "displacement blur of arms, etc." "It seemed to us all except Mr. Griffith that the result [of the closer camera] would certainly seem foolish."[110] The front office at first "definitely vetoed" the closer shots, but Griffith persisted and "finally even the front office stopped griping."[111]

Though some have assumed a unidirectional causality between the closer camera and performance style, both Griffith's and Bitzer's comments indicate that the reverse may have been true. Griffith said, "we were striving for real acting," implying that the verisimilar code may have evolved during rehearsals, prior to Griffith's realization that this acting style would benefit from larger-scale shots. And Bitzer hints that the histrionic code precluded the closer camera because of the technical difficulties caused by excessive gesticulation. Modification of performance style must have preceded at least the first experiments with closer shots. Further evidence for this comes from J. Stuart Blackton, one of the founders of the Vitagraph Company, who writes in his memoirs that one of the leading matinée idols of this period, Maurice Costello, "brought something to the screen that it had lacked. He was able to convey a mood by the process of thought instead of facial contortion and pantomime. . . . It was in the scenes nearest the camera that Costello's personality was most evident. At the time the front line was twelve feet from the lens. We changed it to nine feet."[112]

We shall probably never know whether the close-up preceded the change in performance style or vice versa, but we do know that by 1913 Griffith had fully pledged himself to the verisimilar code, the new style that was to win for motion-picture acting "recognition as a genuine art." Art had not been a consideration in 1908 when Griffith strove to elicit enough action from his performers to justify the fourteen-cents-per-foot price of the Biographs. Viewing his film employment as a temporary stopgap, Griffith let economic exigencies dictate to him as he cranked out yet another reel. In the intervening five years, Griffith became more and more committed to the new film industry, no longer harboring visions of himself as a great dramatist or stage actor.

As Griffith began to see film as his life's work, his self-image as a great and inspired artist required that film be a proper medium for the embodiment of his artistic inspirations and aspirations. One method for elevating film in his own, as well as the popular, mind was to denigrate the stage. In all his claims about the "realism" of the new acting art, Griffith compared stage acting unfavorably to film acting. As we have seen, the common practice was to advocate the verisimilar code by attacking the histrionic code, but Griffith went a step further by making the histrionic code and stage acting synonymous. This strategy served the double purpose of legitimizing his new profession and making his old profession unworthy of him, so that the failure was the theatre's rather than his own.[113] Griffith fought for the employment of the verisimilar code in his films in conscious opposition to all that the stage represented for him, barely acknowledging that the new style had actually originated in the theatre. At the same time, he must have known that artistic respectability could be gained by espousing and practicing the tenets of realism, since literary and dramatic realism was the dominant movement of the late nineteenth and early twentieth centuries, already becoming passé in advanced intellectual circles by the time Griffith converted to the cause.

Let us look at two Biographs that appear to reflect Griffith's opinions about the relative merits of film and stage acting. Griffith asserted that the stage, bound by tradition and convention, was incapable of attaining the true realism that came so easily to the motion picture:

> The motion picture is an art, a distinct art, and in many ways a greater art [than the theatre] since it approaches more closely real life. . . . They [theatre people] say that we picture directors do not know the rules, the technique of the drama. We know enough of the rules and the technique to avoid them for real life is not run by "rules."[114]

Griffith repeatedly and flatly denied that film actors had anything to learn from stage actors, the former being vastly superior to the latter, who were wedded to the histrionic code.

> Moving pictures can get nothing from the so-called legitimate stage. . . . We need to depend on the stage for actors and actresses least of all. How many of them make you believe they are real human beings? No, they "act," that is they use a lot of gestures . . . such as are never seen . . . anywhere else. For range of delicacy, the development of character, the quick transition from one mood to another, I don't know an actress on the American stage . . . who can begin to touch the work of some of the motion picture actresses.[115]

Griffith claimed that stage training was a positive detriment for those hoping to act in motion pictures: "It [film acting] does not require any training in the legitimate stage for the reason that kind of acting is so bad, so far away from human life, and so unreal as to appear ridiculous in moving pictures."[116] Because stage players, unlike film actors, were incapable of studying and duplicating "real life," Griffith would not "have the average stage player in a production of mine."[117]

What was Griffith's view of the "average stage player"? To answer this question, we turn again to *A Drunkard's Reformation* (1909) and *Brutality* (1912), but it is the stage plays attended by the characters in the films that concern us here. The "real" characters in *A Drunkard's Reformation* employ the histrionic code as do the "stage actors," while in *Brutality* the "real"

A Drunkard's Reformation: The theatrical
actors.

characters use the verisimilar code and the ''actors'' the histrionic. In both
cases, however, Griffith seems to have wanted a clear distinction in performance style between the framing story and the play. The ''actors'' in the earlier film employ a more unchecked version of the histrionic code than do the
''real'' characters, while in the later film, the distinction becomes more
marked as the ''actors'' continue to employ the unchecked histrionic code
while the ''real'' characters use the verisimilar. The depiction of the ''average
stage player'' in these two films squares with Griffith's public pronounce-
ments about the outmoded nature of theatrical acting, for the ''actors'' seem
markedly retrograde compared to the ''real'' characters.

In *A Drunkard's Reformation,* Arthur Johnson takes his child to see what
appears to be a temperance melodrama set in some vague, unspecified past
time and foreign country. Twelve of the film's thirty-two shots depict action
in this play, but two examples will suffice to describe the performance style,
which shares with Griffith's own acting a self-conscious and excessive theatricality. In shots 21 and 23 the stage wife (Florence Lawrence) goes to the inn
and pleads with her husband (David Miles) to stop drinking. The wife tries to
take the drink from her husband, and they struggle, both carefully keeping
faces turned to the audience. He pushes her away, and she falls. Kneeling at
his feet, she raises her clasped hands to him and then puts her hands to her
cheeks, alternating these actions in rapid succession as she cowers before him.
Just before the husband expires, in shot 23, he staggers into his home, smashes
a bottle, clutches at his throat, struggles with his wife, and tosses his little girl
aside. Compared to his wild, frenzied, uncontrolled actions, Arthur Johnson's
drunk is a model of propriety.

In *Brutality,* Walter Miller takes Mae Marsh to a vaudeville theatre where
they see the famous murder scene from *Oliver Twist. Oliver Twist* was one of
the most popular of melodramas, and the Biograph version probably resembles the performances at the popular-priced theatres that flourished in the ear-

Brutality: The theatrical actors.

lier part of the century but faltered around the time Griffith began directing. Griffith was thus recording a vanishing performance style, the unchecked histrionic code of the full-blown popular melodrama. The presence of two performers singularly adept at the verisimilar code (Henry Walthall and Elmer Booth, the Snapper Kid of *The Musketeers of Pig Alley*) makes the use of this performance style especially interesting.

In shot 37 Fagin (Walthall) tells Sykes (Booth) that Nancy has betrayed the gang. Booth sits in his chair in aggressively macho posture, legs apart and hands folded across chest. Walthall leans over him in a theatrical pose, weight on his bent front leg, his left arm, holding a cane, extended fully behind him, as he remains motionless throughout the conversation. Walthall, playing a villain in a melodrama, seems to be deliberately mimicking the attitude-striking of the histrionic code. The one pose embodies the performance style in all five shots of the play-within-the-film.

This chapter began by asking how we might assess Griffith's involvement and influence in the transition to the verisimilar code in the films of the Biograph Company. Could one make an "auteurist" argument of sorts about the probable impact of "the real, live, tangible person," David W. Griffith, whose ideas and actions may have partially shaped the signifying practices of the films? I think we can justifiably, but guardedly, conclude that Griffith may have been one among several significant factors responsible for the shift in performance style. At least in the later years of his Biograph tenure, when Griffith had overcome his initial nervousness, when the trade press frequently lauded his films, and when the front office came more and more to depend on him, Griffith seems to have had enough authority to insist on verisimilarly coded acting.

Accepting this premise leads to another, perhaps more interesting, question. Why would a man who had been primarily exposed to the histrionic code, whose acquaintances considered him a "lousy" actor, who used the histrionic code in his own performances and initially insisted that his actors do the same, suddenly have converted to the verisimilar code? Starting with the broadest possible influence, Griffith was astute enough, as I suggested above, to realize that he could make his "new art" more respectable by allying it with the principles espoused by the literary and dramatic realists. He used the claim that film could "out-real" the theatre as part of this tactic. As we shall discuss below, most of the film industry shared Griffith's desire for respectability and believed with him that widespread acceptability could be garnered through associations with other more "legitimate" arts.

What about more direct influences in terms of day-to-day studio operations? The front office seems, for the most part, to have given Griffith carte blanche after a certain point, perhaps because his films may have saved the studio from financial disaster.[118] Hence, the money men may account for Griffith's initial adherence to the histrionic code but not for his change of heart. Scriptwriters may have made suggestions about performance style, but the historical record may never yield enough evidence to prove or disprove this hypothesis.

The historical record does, however, provide some evidence that Griffith's actors collaborated with the director in the construction of their characters, and hence in the transition in performance style. As Griffith himself said, "We developed together." In rehearsals, he would permit the actors to present their own characterizations before intervening with suggestions. He seems to have been willing enough to accept suggestions from his acting company. The older, more experienced actors, such as Claire McDowell, then, may have had frequent opportunities to contribute to the transformation in performance style. In the next chapter, we will look more closely at the work of one particular actor, Henry B. Walthall, trying to determine more precisely the nature of the mutual development of the verisimilar code.

6

Henry B. Walthall

Despite Griffith's public disdain for stage actors and his much-publicized Pygmalion-like sculpting of young, inexperienced actresses, most of his performers in fact had a theatrical background, bringing a variety of performance styles to the Biograph studio. Indeed, some had achieved greater success in the theatre than Griffith himself and may also have had more experience acting in companies that used the theatrical verisimilar code. Griffith may have been inclined to defer (albeit, quietly) to those whom he thought had superior training.

Because discounting the actor's role in the transition in Biograph performance style would be no more appropriate than discounting Griffith's, this chapter examines the Biograph career of Henry B. Walthall. But why single Walthall out from all the Biograph company to test the hypothesis of actor as "auteur"? Several factors make a focus on Walthall logical: his gender, his career pattern, his reputation among both his colleagues and the public as a fine actor who may well have influenced other actors, his statements about his craft, and, finally, his reputation even today.

The "Griffith actresses" (with the notable exception of Blanche Sweet) have already received much attention. And as mentioned in the previous chapter, the experience of Gish and the other female actors may reflect the context in which the case is strongest for Griffith as total auteur of performance style. Hence, it makes sense here to look at a male actor whom the literature has almost totally neglected but about whom there is some evidence in the historical record.[1]

Walthall's theatrical career had exposed him to a variety of acting styles. On his arrival in New York City, he was first engaged as an extra at the Murray

Hill Stock Company, a lower-priced repertory theatre that often performed public-domain material such as Shakespeare. He did more stock work with a company in Providence, Rhode Island, and on the road and then returned to New York. On Broadway, he was Captain Clay Randolph in the Civil War drama, *Winchester* and then went on to play Steve Danbury in *Under Southern Skies*. His stage career reached its height with his long-term engagement in *The Great Divide,* a Broadway play produced by prominent actor-manager and strong proponent of theatrical realism, Henry Miller.[2]

One day at the Players Club a producer approached Walthall with a job offer for him and his friend James Kirkwood, who was by then working at Biograph. Walthall went to 11 East 14th Street and discovered his friend in convict's stripes:

> Kirkwood introduced me to Griffith. I had never heard of him but he had seen me in *Under Southern Skies* and *The Great Divide.* "You are just the man I want," said Griffith. "Get on these old clothes, take this shovel and come on out in the street. There's a nice little sewer trench out there that will just fit you and bye and bye your sweet little daughter will bring papa his lunch." Well, I did it, or rather Griffith did it. My debut made in a sewer trench: *A Convict's Sacrifice. . . .* It wasn't very hard work and after that first experience I came to the conclusion that I might as well be knocking down five a day that way as loafing about.[3]

A Convict's Sacrifice was made in June 1909. Walthall appeared in seventeen Biographs before rejoining Henry Miller's company in August for a ten-week London production of *The Great Divide.* Upon his return to the States, he went to Biograph again, his first role this time as the wheat king's henchman in *A Corner in Wheat.* He remained with Biograph until September 1910, this time making forty-seven films, the last of which was *The Banker's Daughters.* For almost two years after this, he shuttled back and forth between the Pathé and Reliance studios, coming back to Biograph in June 1912 to play the lead in *A Change of Spirit* and remaining with Griffith through *The Birth of a Nation,* in which he played the lead role of "the little colonel."

Between 1909 and 1913, Walthall appeared in 102 Biographs. Walthall in his time played many parts, not only the soldier "seeking the bubble reputation even in the cannon's mouth" but society swells, discontented laborers, drunks, madmen, Mexicans, Indians, Italians, French revolutionaries, and medieval troubadours, among others.

Whether using the histrionic or verisimilar code, Walthall's work led to his being unanimously perceived as one of the best, if not the best, of the male actors at Biograph. Edwin August flatly stated that Walthall was "the best actor at Biograph."[4] Blanche Sweet concurred: "Henry Walthall was one of the best in both film and stage."[5] Linda Arvidson's praise was only slightly more guarded: "Wally's acting proved to be the most convincing of its type so far."[6] Arvidson probably was referring to Walthall's romantic costume dramas in which he employed the histrionic code, but Bitzer hinted that Walthall was seen as one of the primary exponents of the verisimilar code: "His performances were well ahead of his time."[7] George Blaisdell of *The Moving Picture World* lauded Walthall for his verisimilar performance style. "His work is so natural, so lifelike, that illusion is established on his original appearance in a picture."[8] Reviewing one of Walthall's Reliance films, *Clouds and Sunshine* (1911), the *World* identified what made Walthall's work "natural" and "lifelike." Walthall "shows his intelligence by his carefulness all through the picture for the little unnoticeable things, the hand to the hat, the slight gesture."[9]

After *The Birth of a Nation,* the critics became positively adulatory: "Walthall is a rare creation of God, that mankind should appreciate and respect. Henry Walthall, as a photoplayer, is inimitable."[10] Two years later a *Photoplay* writer was ready to award him the highest accolade of all: ". . . Henry B. Walthall, the greatest of all screen emotional stars of the sterner sex—and some think, of either sex."[11] Fans, too, appreciated Walthall's "splendid acting."[12] A piano player in a California theatre wrote to Frank Woods about Walthall, calling him "the most wonderful actor in the moving picture age." She went on to assert that Walthall was a "perfect actor. He portrays every thought, and each and every movement to perfection."[13]

Griffith, in common with everybody else, had only public praise for the actor, claiming in the 1940s that Walthall's Little Colonel was "the greatest male performance in the history of film."[14] After Walthall's death in 1936, Griffith said, "I don't know whether you could call him a great actor, but of this I am certain—he had a great soul. . . . It is given to only a few to be able to express a [great] soul to the entire world by means of an expressive face and body."[15]

It is not unreasonable to assume that the success of *The Birth of a Nation,* coupled with the extensive publicity that the male lead received, may have elevated Walthall to a preeminent position among his peers, a position that inspired both established and aspiring actors to learn from and perhaps emulate his style. Though arguing this point would require another chapter and perhaps another book, one can safely assert that close analysis of Walthall's performance may illuminate not only his acting style but that of his contemporaries and successors as well. The Biograph Company was perceived as the leading exemplar of good acting among the film studios, and Walthall occupied a similar place of esteem amongst actors.

Walthall's ideas about his craft owe more to Griffith's actual practice than to the director's on-the-record advice and opinions. Griffith, you will remember, claimed to value "real emotions" over technique, believing that if actors "felt" their parts, their inner feelings would produce the appropriate external manifestations. As Griffith told Mae Marsh, "Now feel it. Don't act." But as we have seen, Griffith devoted countless rehearsal hours to constructing characters through "bits of business," a process that certainly required his actors to act.

Walthall, adding a third step to Griffith's instructions, once summed up his acting philosophy as "Think it, feel it, do it." [16] In interviews, Walthall placed far greater stress on preparation and technique than did Griffith but professed to follow the latter's methods.

> That's what I call Lillian [Gish]—the most skilled technician the screen has ever had. I don't place much confidence in actors who rely on feeling and emotion for expression. Inspiration is undependable. Our way, Lillian's and mine, is Griffith's method: to build systematically and tediously a structure complete in every detail that the mind can conceive and that tiresome repetition can perfect. Thoughtful analysis of a character and concentration on minute ways of expressing it produce a more logical and sustained interpretation. . . . We don't depend on inspiration but we build. And the more carefully your foundation is laid, the more conscientious your attention to every detail, the more solid will be your edifice. [17]

Walthall, not given to Griffith's mystical musings about "soul," presents a more articulate summation of the verisimilar code than the director ever did. "Thoughtful analysis of character and concentration on minute ways of expressing it" developed through Griffith's endless rehearsals enabled the actors to bring to the screen the complex, individuated characters of the psychologized narrative.

Walthall was equally articulate on the matter of character, expressing in almost every interview a strong preference for the psychologized individual over the melodramatic stock figure. Recalling the Biograph years, the actor said: "I was everything good and bad together, brave and a coward, a dreamer and a bit of a cad, which is to say that I played my hero as a human being." [18] Rejecting a conventional approach to his interpretations, he preferred playing the villain: "I liked the villains best of all. . . . He has originality. He is not bound by the conventions which put a fence around the juveniles and heroes." [19] In Walthall's view, playing the villain was infinitely preferable to "the mushy, matinée idol roles, always trying to keep some villain from stealing your sweetheart and getting plotted against, etc. I'd rather play the villain, especially when he turns out to be alright in the end." [20]

Even today among devotees of the early silent cinema, Walthall retains a reputation as one of the preeminent stars of the period, whose performances seem, to those convinced of the teleological inevitability of the verisimilar code, "ahead of his time." Kalton C. Lahue, in his book about male stars of the silent cinema, *Gentlemen to the Rescue: The Heroes of the Silent Screen,* states that "few actors on the silent screen possessed the capabilities of Henry B. Walthall" and goes on to speak of his "restrained and sensitive portrayals" and of his enactment of the Little Colonel as "one of the outstanding performances in the history of the screen.''[21] A few years earlier, Joe Franklin, in a book ghosted by William K. Everson, had used much the same language to describe Walthall, ''one of the finest . . . of silent screen stars,'' who had an acting style memorable ''in those early years when there was so much broad pantomime on the screen, for its restraint and sensitive underplaying.''[22] Among an earlier generation of silent film ''historians,'' then, Walthall may have been the male star whose performances provided evidence for crediting Griffith with the development of a new and better acting style.

How much of the creation of Walthall's Biograph characters should we attribute to the actor and how much to the director? We do know that Griffith directed the majority of Walthall's Biographs. Although by 1913 Biograph had six production units in addition to the one headed by Griffith, Walthall (along with Sweet, Pickford, and Wilfred Lucas) was usually not available to any other director.[23] Unfortunately, we know very little about on-the-set interactions between director and actor. Walthall's own recollections, related in a 1926 interview, credited the director with absolute control over his performers and concurred with Griffith's image of the great artist: ''That shy child of sixteen [Lillian Gish] wouldn't have dared talk back to Griffith. It wouldn't have occurred to any of us for that matter, for he was the master instructing us. . . . The Griffith tradition . . . makes of his actors mere automatons reflecting his masterly genius.''[24] Yet Walthall's thoughtful articulation of the technique of the verisimilar code makes it doubtful that he would have functioned as a mere automaton.

An interview with Blanche Sweet confirms this: ''He [Griffith] loved Wally. He thought he was a fine actor, and he never really had much to say about Wally's acting. He showed him very little. He just said, 'Well, here's the situation' . . . or 'a little less, Wally,' or 'a little more, Wally.' He respected and depended on Wally as an actor.''[25]

An anecdote related by Bitzer perhaps best conveys the tone of the Griffith-Walthall relationship. On one occasion, Griffith, losing patience with the actor's repeated tardiness, fined Walthall fifty dollars.

> He [Walthall] enacted his rehearsal so well that the director came over to him and said, ''That's a great touch you put in. Now could you work up the transition into an even higher climax.'' Wally . . . said, ''If I do it lots better will you take a few dollars off that fine? I can't get into the part much thinking of that fifty.'' After the final take the director went to Wally and threw his arms around him, something he seldom did. (He would generally say after a good bit anyone would do well, ''We'll see what it looks like on the screen.'') The director said there can be no fine in the face of such splendid acting.[26]

Here we see that the actor put in a ''great touch'' of his own and that the director's instructions were limited to ''could you work up the transition into an even higher climax?'' This, together with the other scattered evidence, indicates that Griffith respected Walthall, who may well have been one of those actors whom Griffith felt no great need to instruct.

The above constitutes the scanty extratextual evidence about Griffith and Walthall, though, given evidence about the Biograph rehearsal process, it seems reasonable to assume that the two may have collaborated in the construction of the actor's characters. The primary evidence for the actor as collaborator must, however, come from close textual analysis. Knowledge of Walthall's theatrical career encourages us to look for signs of his theatrical training in his early Biographs. His relatively long Biograph employment permits comparing the largely histrionically coded films of his earlier period with the largely verisimilarly coded films of his later period, while also accounting for the deployment of other signifying practices. His wide range of Biograph roles permits further comparisons among the different character types and genres which his performances encompass.

Walthall arrived at Biograph with broader theatrical experience than Griffith. He had played with second-rate stock companies but also with Miller on Broadway, and he had most likely mastered both the histrionic and verisimilar codes before appearing in film. Walthall's earliest Biographs show that his theatrical experiences had indeed trained him in a wide range of performance styles.

In his first film, *A Convict's Sacrifice,* the neophyte film player uses few of the conventional gestures of the histrionic code, and his performance, by 1909 standards, is more verisimilarly than histrionically coded. Walthall plays a laborer who befriends an ex-convict (James Kirkwood), whom he persuades his employer to hire. Later, Walthall gets laid off and is unable to find work, while Kirkwood has escaped from the prison to which he has been unjustly returned.

Two examples will suffice to show Walthall's style in this film. In the first, he returns home having found no employment. He walks up to the shack that is his home, head bowed, shoulders slumped, and pauses at the foot of the stairs to smell the flowers that he carries. In the next shot, in the interior, his wife holds out her hand to him palm up, and he slowly shakes his head "no." He kneels at the bed and shows his little girl the flowers. Getting up, he turns in a semi-circle away from his wife and stops with his back to the camera, clutching the back of his neck in frustration. He then sits motionless in a chair next to a table, left hand on left knee, right elbow on right knee, head bowed. His wife gives him a piece of bread, which he picks up and looks at, then stops with the bread halfway to his mouth. His wife touches his arm, and he makes a slight gesture to the child as if to say, "Give it to her." Walthall's gestural economy, the use of a few simple movements such as clutching the back of the neck, embodies the father's quiet desperation at being unable to provide for his family.

Left: *The Convict's Sacrifice:* Walthall smells the flowers. Right: *The Convict's Sacrifice:* Walthall prays.

During this shot, Kirkwood arrives. Seeing his friend's family so badly off, he determines to surrender and allow Walthall to obtain the reward for his capture. After his apprehension, presumably on the assumption that Walthall has already gotten the reward, he tries to escape from the prison guards and is shot down outside the shack. Walthall kneels by his side, puts an arm around his shoulders and a hand on his chest and raises him slightly. Kirkwood collapses and dies, and Walthall leans forward, staring at his face. His daughter stands by him, and he takes the flowers gently from her hand. Holding the flowers in front of him, he tilts his head back, eyes closed, and mutters a prayer. He then folds the convict's hands around the flowers, encloses Kirkwood's hands in his own and slumps forward, his head on his raised forearm, the only conventional gesture in the scene.

Walthall's performance in this film shows that his stage training had prepared him to give a relatively verisimilar performance. Though there is a moment in the first scene in which he looks briefly at the camera (and Griffith?) as if seeking direction, Walthall's style required little modification to suit him to the fully developed verisimilar code of 1912 and 1913. His next film, *The Sealed Room,* in which he played one of the three principals, shows that he also had command of the histrionic code. The film is a costume melodrama set in an unspecified medieval country. Arthur Johnson is the king, Marion Leonard the queen, and Walthall the court musician and the queen's illicit lover. The king, whose suspicions are aroused, pretends to leave his castle but actually remains to catch his wife and lover in flagrante delicto. Understandably annoyed, he orders that they be walled up in the chamber where Walthall sits at Leonard's feet playing the lute. When the lovers finally notice their entombment, they portray their panic and horror with the fully extended, heavily stressed, and repeated conventional gestures of the histrionic code. Walthall falls to his knees and begins flailing wildly at the wall. Standing

The Sealed Room: The doomed lovers react
histrionically.

again, he extends his arm to the queen, finger pointed as if accusing her of
something (carelessness, complicity?). Next, he raises both arms, bent at the
elbow, to either side of his head before slumping over the back of a chair,
which he clutches. For a few moments, he staggers around, hand at his throat,
and then both sink to their knees, as Walthall fans Leonard with the lute and
then collapses.

Despite his initial capacity for both verisimilarly and histrionically coded
performance, there is an overall movement in Walthall's work toward the fully
developed verisimilar code, which a comparison of his enactment of similar
roles from his first and second Biograph periods illustrates. In *A Summer Idyl,
Thou Shalt Not* (both 1910), *Love in an Apartment Hotel* (1912), and *Death's
Marathon* (1913), Walthall plays a middle- to upper-middle-class gentleman
who proposes (or in *Love* has just proposed) to his beloved. In the earlier films,
setting and costume primarily establish his character, while in the later films
Walthall employs the byplay of the verisimilar code to convey the easy self-
confidence of the society gentleman.

In the first shot of *A Summer Idyl,* set at a society soirée, Walthall, dressed
in evening clothes, proposes to Stephanie Longfellow. He leans close to her,
hand on chest, then extends his hand to her palm up, then holds her hand in
both of his. She says no, and he pleads with right hand extended and other
hand on his chest. She remains adamant, and after she leaves, his hands sink
slowly to his sides in despair. He then raises a hand and brings it down across
his chest in a gesture of resolve. In the second shot of the film, Walthall, at
home, decides to go for a country walking tour. He brushes the hair back from
his forehead, his hand lingering in his hair while he thinks. He looks down at
his clothes and moves his hands downward from his neck to his sides indicating the discarding of the evening dress that symbolizes his present life. He
then makes a sweeping gesture of rejection with his left arm, which moves

A Summer Idyl: Walthall rejects his current life-
style in a sweeping, downward gesture.

from close to his side out perpendicular to his body. In these two shots, costume and setting construct character, while Walthall's histrionically coded
gestures serve to advance the narrative but contribute little to his character's
individuation. So much do "clothes make the man" in this instance that the
evening dress embodies a whole way of life, which Walthall rejects in his
gestural soliloquy.

In the first shot of *Thou Shalt Not,* Walthall relies less on histrionically
coded gestures but still does not individuate his character to any significant
degree. Meeting his beloved at a garden party (setting once again indicating
social class), he holds hands with her and gestures toward the garden. As they
walk, she stops to pick a flower and hands it to Walthall, who kisses it. He
then takes a ring from his pocket and hands it to her, while gesturing to his
chest and to her. She accepts, and after she exits, he walks off looking at the
flower. The props (flower and ring) make histrionically coded gestures superfluous by conveying the narrative information, but as general symbols they
lack any emotional resonance that might psychologize the characters.

In *Love in an Apartment Hotel* and *Death's Marathon,* Walthall's characters also handle props, but rather than serving as general symbols of a man in
love they aid the actor in the construction of a particular character in a particular situation. In *Death's Marathon,* Walthall is a successful and self-assured
businessman. An intertitle, "Each in Turn Seeks Her Hand" precedes a
seven-shot sequence in which Walthall and his partner (Walter Miller) both
propose to Blanche Sweet. In the first shot of the sequence, Walthall and
Miller sit on a park bench, Walthall smoking a cigar, one hand resting casually
in his lap. Miller gestures in Sweet's direction as if asking, "Can I go first?"
Walthall smiles and points at his cigar, as if saying, "Go ahead. I want to
finish this." The film intercuts shots of Miller proposing and being rejected
with shots of a perfectly composed Walthall awaiting his turn. In the first, he

Death's Marathon: Walthall awaits his turn to
propose, brushing the ash from his cigar.

brushes the ash off his cigar with his fingers, and in the second, he stands,
throws away the cigar and straightens his jacket and waistcoat. Walthall's
complacency, revealed through the byplay with the cigar, almost borders on
arrogance, an impression that his minimal wooing of Sweet strengthens. In his
proposal, Walthall uses neither histrionic gestures nor props, for his character
does not deem it necessary to make a grand declaration. He simply removes
his hat and leans over Sweet until she notices him, then sits next to her. He
points to her in a small, throwaway gesture, takes her hand and puts his other
arm around her. She acquiesces immediately, burying her head in his shoulder.

In *Love in an Apartment Hotel,* Walthall portrays a sophisticated man-
about-town engaged (once more) to Blanche Sweet. The intertitle before his
first appearance states ''The Morning After the Proposal.'' Just awakened, he
walks into the frame yawning, his hand on the back of his head. He tightens
the belt of his robe and shakes his head at his valet who asks him a question.
He moistens his lips and picks up a pitcher of water but notices his tailcoat
hanging over the back of a chair and puts the pitcher down. Picking the coat
up, he flicks some (invisible) dust off the sleeve, showing the character's fas-
tidiousness, then sniffs the coat's shoulder, enjoying the lingering perfume
where *she* had rested her head, and extends his right palm out toward Sweet's
picture on a nearby table. He picks up the picture, smiles at it, carries it to the
phone with him, and calls his beloved.

In this shot, and throughout the film, Walthall's gestures and use of props
combine to create the picture of an elegant ''toff'' in a romantic daze. Before
leaving ''for the club,'' he pauses before Sweet's picture, takes his hat off,
bends down, and smiles at it. He walks into the next shot blowing the (again
invisible) dust off the crown of his topper. Before leaving his apartment, he

Left: *Love in an Apartment Hotel:* Walthall as debonair man-about-town. Right: *Love in an Apartment Hotel:* Walthall thinks of "her," tapping his cane on his hand.

adjusts his tie and straightens his scarf. Outside in the hall, he pauses by his door and swings his cane in two or three very short arcs. Halfway down the hall to the elevator, he pauses, turns profile to camera, and smacks the handle of the cane lightly into his other hand as he thinks of *her.* While waiting for the elevator, he stands with feet slightly apart, holding the cane in both hands perpendicular to the floor. Though top hat and cane are standard accessories for this character type, Walthall uses the props to show his character's fastidious habits and elegant affectation interrupted by contemplation of his new-found love and happiness. In *A Summer Idyl,* the evening dress was a stereotypical indicator of station, and in *Thou Shalt Not,* the ring and flowers were stereotypical indicators of love, but in *Love in an Apartment Hotel* Walthall uses tailcoat, top hat, and cane for psychological individuation, rendering them expressions of his character's personality and particular situation.

Of the characters in all four films, the "toff" in *Love in an Apartment Hotel* is perhaps the most clearly individuated through verisimilar byplay. Given Walthall's penchant, often expressed in interviews, for portraying those "perplex'd in the extreme," however, he may have found greater satisfaction playing the doomed heroes of *Thou Shalt Not* and *Death's Marathon.* In both films the main character's comfortable bourgeois existence is shattered, in the earlier film by tuberculosis and in the later, in keeping with the trend toward increasing psychologization, by moral weakness leading to dissolution and suicide. Walthall's performance style in these films exhibits both continuities and differences.

In *Thou Shalt Not,* as his character deals with the emotional consequences of his illness, Walthall selects from a characteristic repertoire of gestures he habitually used when portraying his "hero as a human being." Often, when showing a character in emotional crisis, Walthall puts his hand to his mouth,

Thou Shalt Not: Walthall learns of his illness,
nervously fingering his jacket.

rubs or fingers his clothing, interlaces his fingers, clenches and unclenches his
hands, and runs a hand through his hair, all these gestures unemphasized and
integrated into the overall flow of his movements.

At the moment of the revelation of his illness, Walthall clenches his right
hand slightly and raises his left slowly in the air, before putting a hand on the
doctor's arm. He turns his head from the doctor, and his right hand plays with
the skirt of his jacket. Later, when his fiancée pleads with him to damn the
consequences and marry her, he shows his distress through clenched hands
and raises the back of his hand to his mouth in indecision. After he has, against
his better judgment, promised to marry her, the doctor sees them together. The
fiancée leaves and Walthall coughs, puts a hand to his chest, and fingers his
tie while glancing uneasily at the doctor. Walthall mixes these little "realistic" details with histrionically coded gestures, such as outward and downward
movements of rejection, but the verisimilar code predominates.

In *Death's Marathon,* Walthall's character, a gambler and a wastrel, loses
the money he has "borrowed" from his company and commits suicide.
Again, the actor uses his characteristic gestures of emotional turmoil, putting
his hand to his mouth when his partner almost discovers him taking the
money, raising a hand to his chin when he encounters his partner after the
theft, and rubbing his hands on his jacket after losing at poker. At the film's
climax, Walthall, contemplating suicide, talks to his wife on the phone as his
partner drives madly to the rescue. Walthall talks on the phone and toys with
his gun for fourteen shots, all but the first in medium, externalizing the character's changing emotions largely through props and facial expression rather
than through his characteristic little gestures. Phone in one hand, he gestures
upward with the gun, smiling as if to say, "That's where I'm going." Refus-
ing to be dissuaded, he shakes his head, and in the next shot smiles again,
looking closely at the gun. Putting phone and gun down, he takes out paper

Death's Marathon: Walthall indicates his suicidal intentions, pointing the gun to his presumed destination.

and pen, then looks almost directly at the camera as if thinking. As he writes, his mouth tightens slightly, and his eyes narrow. Holding the phone again, he toys with the gun, letting it fall slowly from his hand so that it points almost at the camera. He looks at the camera with a slight smile. After further talk and byplay with the gun, Walthall smiles, says goodbye, looks down at the gun, and raises it to his temple.

The fact that Walthall, though portraying emotionally distressed characters in both films, mixed the histrionic and verisimilar codes in *Thou Shalt Not* and used the histrionic code not at all in the climax of *Death's Marathon* may tempt us to conclude that chronology is the best predictor of Walthall's acting, that he "progressed" in linear fashion toward an increasingly verisimilar style. But such a conclusion ignores the interaction of the closer camera, editing, and props with the performance of the suicide sequence in the later film. In Chapter 4, we investigated the relationship between the deployment of other signifying practices and performance style, and hypothesized a complicated and dialectical process relating the shift from the histrionic to the verisimilar codes, the transition to the psychological narrative, and the use of character-centered signifiers. The differences between *Thou Shalt Not* and *Death's Marathon* confirm this hypothesis.

The Griffith feature *The Avenging Conscience* (1914) shows that, even within the same film, Walthall varied his style with regard to the deployment of signifying practices. In this film, Walthall's character dreams that he has killed his uncle and is pursued by hallucinatory phantoms and a flesh-and-blood justice-seeking detective. His performance style ranges from the unchecked histrionic code to the fully developed verisimilar code, with its emphasis on byplay, props, and facial expression.

The main hallucination sequence occurs primarily in long shot, with inter-

Above left: *The Avenging Conscience:* Walthall reacts to a vision. Above: *The Avenging Conscience:* Close-up of Walthall's hand stilling the detective's. Left: *The Avenging Conscience:* Walthall expresses nervousness by twiddling his thumbs.

cutting between Walthall and his "visions." Walthall spends eleven of his fourteen shots in this sequence on his knees, in a praying attitude, clasping his hands, stretching his arms out wide, and making gestures of rejection. In two shots, he lies full length on the ground writhing and shaking. The other three shots are close-ups, as Walthall either smiles or shakes his head.

Contrast this with the detective's breaking down of the suspected murderer. In this sixty-one shot sequence, the film cuts between the detective's interrogation and police activities outside the nephew's home. The interior scene is broken down into long shots of the two characters together, medium shots of each character, and close-ups of faces, hands, and other telling details. Walthall's performance is constructed through his characteristic little details and facial expressions. His hands tug at his collar, rub his knees, thrust themselves into his pockets, unsteadily reach out to still the detective's tapping pencil, or slap the edge of the table. His thumbs repeatedly twiddle nervously. Anxious glances at the detective and at a clock convey his increasing stress, which his facial expressions reinforce. He grimaces, smiles, licks and purses his lips, and narrows his eyes.

Walthall's performance style and the nature of the other signifying practices differ vastly between the vision scene and the interrogation scene. The un-

The Oath and the Man: Walthall vows vengeance.

checked histrionically coded acting of the former might almost be from a 1908 Biograph, while the latter scene represents the culmination of the verisimilar code that Griffith and his actors developed throughout the Biograph years.

Close analysis of Walthall's films has shown that both chronology and the deployment of other signifying practices significantly affect the actor's performance style. Now let us consider the variations in Walthall's acting in relationship to genre and character type.[27] We have seen that Walthall employed elements of the verisimilar code in his first film, *A Convict's Sacrifice,* while in the costume drama *The Sealed Room* he used the unchecked histrionic code. Overall, the Biograph costume dramas feature the most histrionically coded acting, as we would expect, given this genre's reliance on the external motivation and unmediated causality of the "pure" melodrama. Walthall's performances conform to this general rule, though he was one of the few actors equally adept at both codes. A film set during the French Revolution, *The Oath and the Man,* tells the story of a petit bourgeois perfumer (Walthall), his wife (Florence Barker), and their noble landlord (Francis Grandon). The landlord exercises his droit du seigneur, and the wife willingly consents, much to Walthall's distress. Come the revolution, Walthall leads the uprising of the tenantry, while wife and nobleman seek refuge in Walthall's shop. True to his religious convictions, he shields them from the mob and engineers their escape.

The film was made in September 1910, six months after *Thou Shalt Not,* in which Walthall had already employed many of those characteristic little touches with which he created psychologized and individuated characters. In this later film, however, Walthall employs the histrionic code almost exclusively. In the shot in which he confronts the wife and nobleman in the latter's palace, he points at the lord, grabs his own lapel, holds both hands out to his wife, and then puts one hand on his heart and raises the other in the air. Upon returning home, he grabs his chest with his hands, then spreads his hands out

The Face at the Window: Histrionic intoxication
with a verisimilar touch.

in front of him, palms up. Taking a knife, he raises it above his head in a
stabbing gesture, which he repeats. Lowering the knife, he points offscreen,
shakes his fist, and turns around, hiding the knife in his jacket. A priest enters
and shows him a crucifix. After looking from knife to crucifix, he drops to his
knees before the priest. Like the consumptive in *Thou Shalt Not,* this character
experiences great emotional distress, but in this film Walthall externalizes the
emotional turmoil through heavily stressed, fully extended gestures instead of
little individualizing details.

The difference in performance style in the costume melodrama and the contemporary drama of internal motivation and mediated causality becomes clear
by contrasting Walthall's portrayal of drunks in two genres and three films:
the contemporary melodrama *The Face at the Window* (1910); another contemporary melodrama from two years later, *The Burglar's Dilemma* (1912);
and the Civil War costume melodrama *The House with Closed Shutters*
(1910).

In *The Face at the Window,* Walthall portrays a college graduate whose
father disowns him after he marries an artist's model. Falling into drunken
dissolution, he abandons wife and child. The wife dies, and the grandfather
adopts the child. Years later the son is initiated into his father's and grandfather's fraternity. Walthall appears (at the window), and the fraternity boys, as
a lark, take him in and give him a drink. He meets his son, reconciles with his
father, and, of course, dies. Walthall plays his drunk scenes with much staggering and arm-waving, and the climactic scene with much shrinking back in
his chair and many appeals to heaven, but he also injects verisimilar touches,
clutching his jacket lapel, putting hand to mouth, and wiping his eyes with his
sleeve.

In *The Burglar's Dilemma,* Walthall plays Lionel Barrymore's "weakling
brother." During an argument, Walthall hits Barrymore and, in his drunken

The Burglar's Dilemma: Verisimilar intoxication:
holding onto the chair for support.

confusion, believes he has killed him. In this film, Walthall substitutes a controlled drunkenness for his earlier arm-waving and staggering, indicating his character's intoxication through his inability to remain vertical, as he wavers slightly, clutching at a chair back for support. His gestures become looser and bigger, but he retains the byplay of the verisimilar code, playing with his drinking glass, for example, fingering it and lifting it slightly from the table while talking to his brother. When the police arrive to arrest the burglar whom Walthall has accused of the "murder," he uses his typical gestures of agitation, rubbing the knees of his trousers, putting his hand to his mouth, clasping his hands at the back of his head, etc.

In *The House with Closed Shutters* (1910), Walthall is a "drink mad coward" whom Robert E. Lee entrusts with the delivery of important papers. Terrified by being shot at, Walthall flees to his home and drinks himself into a stupor. His sister dons his uniform and delivers the papers in his stead but is killed, leading everyone to assume that Walthall has died a hero's death. His mother does not correct the assumption but rather forces her son to spend the rest of his life behind "closed shutters," giving out that the recluse is actually the sister, mad with grief over her brother's death.

When Walthall first bursts into his house seeking refuge, he leans against the door with a crazed smile, his hands raised over his head. He puts both hands to his head, sees his sister, pushes her aside, and grabs the bottle. Staggering, he drinks from the bottle and collapses in a chair, laughing wildly before passing out. When his mother informs him that his sister has taken the papers, he puts both hands on top of his head and again collapses. Years later, he opens the shutters, starts back with arms spread wide, reaches out to the window, then puts his hands to his head. In portraying this character, Walthall uses none of his usual little details, maintaining the unchecked histrionic code almost throughout the film.

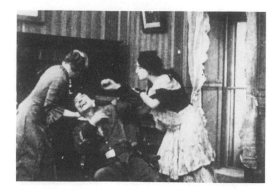

The House with Closed Shutters: Histrionic
intoxication.

In the costume melodrama, Walthall generally employed the histrionic
code. In the contemporary melodrama, as we have seen, the deployment of
other signifying practices, including the narrative structure, seems to have crucially inflected performance style. But close analysis also reveals that, in these
films, Walthall altered his performance style to establish the identity of characters with respect to such factors as nationality and social class.

Often cast as a middle- or upper-middle-class gentleman, he occasionally
played one of the "lower orders." In *The Iconoclast* (1910), Walthall is a
surly workman with a penchant for the bottle. Fired by his employer for in-
subordination, the workman plans to kill his boss, but relents after seeing the
boss's crippled child. The film ends happily as Walthall renounces the bottle
(and radical politics) and is rehired.

In the first scene, Walthall establishes his character's roughness and trucu-
lence as he sits at a table drinking with a friend. Left arm resting on table, he
passes the bottle to his friend and hits the table with his fist. His wife approaches, and he shakes his head, waving her away. At work, his employer's
friends tour the plant, and he glares at a society woman, one hand on his hip
as he looks her up and down. When the visitors reenter, he has one thumb
tucked in his waistband as he gestures with the other hand and eavesdrops on
their conversation. After he is fired, his wife asks him to go back to work. He
responds with a graceful, mocking salute, sweeping his hand down from his
head and bowing slightly in a parody of refined, "upper-class" manners.

Playing an Italian laborer in the 1909 film *In Little Italy,* Walthall's gestures signify stereotypical "Italianicity," to borrow Roland Barthes's term.[28]
Drinking wine with his sweetheart, he looks at the glass and kisses his
bunched fingertips to indicate approval. In conversation, he moves his right
hand in circular motions and opens and closes his fingers while holding his
palm up, gestures that derive from the stereotype of the Italian immigrant.

Above left: *The Iconoclast:* Walthall as surly workman, hitting the table. Above: *In Little Italy:* Walthall as an Italian, kissing his fingers. Left: *Ramona:* Walthall as an "Indian," head bowed and immobile.

In *Ramona* (1910), playing a Native American, Walthall spends much of the film with arms folded across his chest in the stereotypical pose of "Indian" impassivity. This containment becomes a hallmark of the performance, as even in moments of intense emotion he eschews the fully extended movements of the unchecked histrionic code, instead modifying the conventional gestures to suit his character's stoicism. Watching the whites burn his village, he turns his back to the camera, folds his arms, raises his hands high above his head, fists clenched, but in a slow and weighty gesture, then puts his fist on top of his head but with both elbows close to his chest. After the whites throw him and his wife (Mary Pickford) out of their house, he stands with one arm around Pickford, his face buried in her hair and his hand at his side, unmoving in silent resignation. Only when the character goes mad does he use the unchecked histrionic code.

Does the above close analysis of Henry Walthall's Biographs shed any light on the issue of the actor as collaborator in the move to the verisimilar code? The answer is a qualified yes. First-time viewers of Walthall's Biographs, surprised by the fact that he could be so "subtly effective" in some films and yet so "hammy" and "over the top" in others, conclude that Walthall was a "good" actor subject to bad days and bad performances. Accustomed to the dominance of the verisimilar code and unaware that earlier actors had available a wider range of stylistic options, these naive viewers tend to characterize any departure from verisimilitude as "bad." In the terms established in this book, however, Walthall's performances range from the unchecked histrionic code to the smallest nuances of the verisimilar. These extreme variations in style depended, I believe, neither on happenstance nor inspiration, but on a range of factors, some more susceptible than others to the actor's control.

As we have seen, Walthall arrived at the Biograph studio well versed in both the histrionic and the verisimilar codes. We can reasonably conclude that Griffith did not entirely mold Walthall as he may have his inexperienced young female actors. Walthall's Biograph performances exhibit an overall movement toward the verisimilar code, a movement common to the rest of the Biograph Company and the other film studios. One may infer that Walthall's work with Griffith and the Biograph Company encouraged the further development of a performance style that he had already learned. One might also speculate that Walthall may have influenced both Griffith and his fellow actors in their adoption of the verisimilar code.

Though no hard data illuminate the matter, it can be assumed that Griffith and his actors made conscious decisions about performance style in relation to the deployment of other signifying practices. Consider *The Avenging Conscience* again. Since Griffith and Walthall had available the options of both codes, they may well have decided that the unchecked histrionic code could better express the character's intense anguish in the vision scene and that the verisimilar code would add to the suspense of the character's breakdown in the interrogation scene. At the same time, Griffith must have felt, as we know from his recorded comments on the matter, that the unedited long shot better suited the histrionic acting of the former, while the closer camera and analytical editing worked better with the verisimilar acting of the latter. Hence, Walthall may have tailored his performance to the deployment of signifying practices, or Griffith may have tailored the deployment of signifying practices to Walthall's performance.

Walthall may have experienced the most freedom in constructing characters across genres and in establishing characters' class and nationality. Perhaps conforming to contemporary perceptions of the "correct" performance style, Walthall used the histrionic code in the costume melodrama. In the contemporary melodrama, he seems to have been more adept than many other Biograph actors at the crafting of the individuated characters linked to the emerging dominance of psychological narratives. His skillful use of props, combined with the byplay of his characteristic gestures (hand to mouth, rubbing his knee, etc.), sets Walthall's performances apart from those actors who used the verisimilar code less successfully. Moreover, his use of distinct postures, movement patterns, and "national" gestures distinguished his various characters from one another.

Close analysis of Walthall's performances provides more evidence to dispute the teleological inevitability and "naturalness" of the emergence of the verisimilar code. Here we have an actor of preeminent reputation among his contemporaries who clearly thought about his craft and yet who, nonetheless, exhibits no clear "progression" toward the verisimilar code. Rather, Walthall alternates between the old style and the new according to the film's narrative structure and other signifying practices, as well as according to his character type. Examination of Walthall's films permits us to see in microcosm the residual traces of the early cinema and the emerging conventions of the classical Hollywood cinema in the transitional period during which the Biographs were made.

The historical record will probably never yield enough hard data to determine conclusively the exact contribution that Henry B. Walthall or any other actor made to the emergence of the verisimilar code. Even were more evidence available, however, the complexity of the transformation from the histrionic to the verisimilar codes prevents easy generalizations about the contributions of individual actors or directors. Both Walthall and Griffith should be seen as strands in a complex web of determinants.

7

Trade Press Discourse

As Sherlock Holmes suggested, the press is a most valuable institution. The discourse of the film-industry trade press can illuminate the transformation in cinematic acting style between 1908 and 1913 in three ways. First, trade press discourse serves as a marker of both industry reception of performance style and of the industry's perception of audience reception of performance style. The trade press enables us to trace the shifting norms of performance style: What was considered appropriate cinematic acting at what time? The writers of the trade press rapidly developed a consensus that verisimilitude was the desideratum, as early as 1908 characterizing as verisimilar performances that, in the terms developed here, seem clearly histrionically coded. By 1913, the trade press itself spoke of the 1908 performance style as false, theatrical, and stagy, or, in other words, as histrionic. Trade press discourse thus serves to generalize the findings of this book beyond the films made by D. W. Griffith at the Biograph Company to the industry as a whole.

Second, in the absence of studio records, trade press discourse sometimes provides the only information about industry practices, which journals such as *The Moving Picture World* and *The New York Dramatic Mirror* both reflected and inflected. As Kristin Thompson suggests, "The growth of a trade press after 1907 . . . contributed to making . . . norms uniform across the industry. Almost from the beginning trade papers and instruction books emphasized a specific conception of what constitutes a good film."[1] The trade press reporters not only watched films but visited the studios, conducted interviews and gave advice in their columns that producers often heeded.[2]

Third, the trade press can locate the transformation in performance style within the larger culture. Trade press discourse about the class associations of signifying practices relates changes in performance style to the contemporary debate about socially acceptable entertainments. Evidence from the trade press shows that the film industry, at a moment of crisis, attempted to distance itself from the "cheap amusements" condemned by cultural arbiters and adopted signifying practices associated with what were perceived as respectable cultural products. The verisimilar code, associated with the "legitimate" Broadway stage, seemed clearly preferable to the histrionic, associated with the "cheap" melodrama.

The Transformation in Performance Style as Reflected in Trade Press Discourse

In what follows, I trace the *New York Dramatic Mirror*'s and *The Moving Picture World*'s views on performance, starting in May 1908 with the *Mirror* and January 1907 with the *World*.[3] We will begin with the histrionic code, pro and con, and proceed to the verisimilar code, pro and con, though the fact that a writer praising the histrionic code by implication denigrates the verisimilar and vice versa, complicates organizational strategy. As was the case with theatrical performance, appropriate acting was defined mostly by opposition to inappropriate acting, so that the two codes are always opposed, even if only implicitly.

Until 1909, by which time the consensus on the desirability of verisimilitude was forming, writing about acting was infrequent, though one can unearth defenses of the histrionic code, or at least statements of the position of those who advocated histrionically coded performance. The earliest comment found contrasts the histrionic code appropriate for film with the verisimilar code employed on the legitimate stage: "The actor who is too reposeful on the stage and expresses his meaning and feeling merely . . . in subtle movements is utterly worthless for the moving picture. Sometimes the actor who has risen no higher than to scrub parts or the chorus can be made good use of for the moving pictures because of his proneness to gesture and motion."[4] A year later, the *World* again voiced the same argument: "The expression on the face of the actor may help him . . . but his pose is even more important. He must throw his hat into the air to express joy, snap his fingers to show contempt, and droop his shoulders to indicate sorrow."[5]

Occasionally, the wording of reviews seems to imply that the acting was insufficiently histrionic. A review of Selig's *East Lynne* complained that the acting was "tediously slow," and Biograph's *A Night of Terror* was "partly spoiled . . . by the slow acting of the principals."[6] *Napoleon and the English Sailor* was "not very well acted" because "the figures moved as though they were made of wood." The reviewer complained that the actor "moves with as calm a demeanor as though nothing of importance depended upon it,'' when he should have been showing ''feverish haste.''[7]

The nonindustry press tended to be pro-histrionic, assuming, with an undercurrent of condescension, the inevitability of histrionic performance given the quality of the actors and the nature of the medium. Claiming that film employed actors who ''have failed in the legitimate,'' a theatrical journalist said that ''as everything is done in pantomime, the players must be acting all the time. This may account for the acute exaggerations noticeable in some films.''[8] The Spectator quoted an article from the Philadelphia *Saturday Post* expressing the same sentiments: ''Repose, an admirable device for obtaining dramatic effect in the spoken drama, is not only useless, but positively out of place in the moving picture play. Gestures must be made quickly. If the actor is not gesturing, his eyes, his lips or his face must twitch.''[9]

Woods disagreed with this statement, advocating ''effective repose.'' But overall, the Spectator's columns provide perhaps the most articulate statements of the pro-histrionic position, because Woods, while championing verisimilitude, nonetheless gave a platform to the opposition. As a nickelodeon owner wrote to Woods, ''Acting is a delightful luxury . . . but action is a prime necessity.''[10] According to Woods, many film exchanges and exhibitors demanded histrionic acting, in the belief that their patrons preferred it:

> Probably the most marked change that has taken place in the style of picture acting in the last year or two has been in the matter of tempo. In the old days the pictures were literally ''moving'' pictures, and lively moving pictures at that. Everything had to be done on the jump. The more action that could be crowded into each foot of film the more perfect the picture was supposed to be. Some of this manner of picture acting still survives . . . but, generally speaking, it has given place to more deliberation. People in the pictures now move somewhat after the style of human beings, instead of jumping jacks.[11]

Writing in June 1910, Woods placed the transition to the verisimilar code as early as the middle of 1908, around the time when he himself began campaigning against the old style of acting. Though I would date the transition to 1910–1911 at Biograph, and perhaps a little later at other companies, the trade press championed verisimilitude and attacked the histrionic code long before most studios adopted the new style. In November 1908, an anonymous ''Rules for Moving Picture Actors'' appeared in the *Mirror,* anticipating so many of Wood's ideas that he is almost certainly the author. Taking an ironic tone, the writer instructed actors self-consciously to act, that is, to use the histrionic code: ''Always bear in mind that you are acting. There is nothing the moving picture maker dislikes so much as to have his pictures appear like events in real life.''[12] Writing in a more serious tone, Woods objected to ''violent gestures such as no human being would indulge in real life.''[13]

As early as 1908, writers in the *World* complained of the same thing. Contrasting a French and American film, a reviewer praised the French actors: "The acting is as unconscious as life . . . whereas the American drama was full of stagy poses and punk heroism."[14] Later the same year, the *World* once more compared American acting unfavorably to French, speaking of films that had turned into "orgies of gesticulation."[15] By 1910, critics began to cite the specific behavior and gestures they wished abolished: "Why, oh! why is it necessary for the actor, every time he goes forth, to stick out his arm and point the index finger in the direction he is going?" asked an exhibitor writing to the *World*.[16] C. H. Claudy, a regular columnist for the *World*, devoted an entire column to a discussion of acting, providing an unusually detailed description of gesture. Stating that there was a "growing cry against poor acting before the camera," Claudy concluded that the problem was not "poor acting" but "too much acting," "the overdoing of a part," by which he seems to mean the use of the histrionic code. Claudy takes to task Kalem's *Big Elk's Turndown,* which told of a girl kidnapped by "Indians":

> But no . . . kind of Indians . . . ever gesticulated so violently, so rapidly, so much. They lose all dignity, all realism, when they spend most of their time with their arms in the air. . . . The father and lover, when starting for the rescue, exhibit the same characteristics. Lover examines tracks, raises hands to heaven and flies. Father shakes gun in air, waves arms violently about head, loses several seconds in, apparently, calling to heaven to witness what he's going to do to 'em, and then, he flies. The Indians . . . also gather together, point, raise arms to heaven, and then run. They do too much acting.

From Claudy's recounting, the Kalem actors clearly employed the unchecked histrionic code more typical of 1908 than 1911. Claudy himself made the connection between this style of performance and the acting of the previous century when he concluded, "Desperate Desmond barnstorming fifty years ago had the same motions."[17]

Toward the end of Griffith's tenure at Biograph, the verisimilar code had triumphed, at least in principle, and the trade press engaged in a mopping-up action against the histrionic code. Frank Woods's successor at the *Mirror,* the Reviewer, could say in 1912 that "the day when the actor pointed to the door to inform the spectator that he was going in has virtually disappeared." But unnecessary gesticulation, had not completely disappeared, continued the Reviewer, citing "the group of players, plotting to do some unknown thing which the spectator cannot fathom, or the actor inferring [sic] what he will do in the future and has done in the past."[18]

In 1913, Louis Reeves Harrison of the *World* attacked the very foundation of the histrionic code, denying a one-to-one correspondence between emotions and standardized gestures:

One of the greatest mistakes made by actors is in supposing expression of feeling to be a purely physical manifestation, that there are twists of the face and movements of the hands which will be accepted as depicting this or that phase of mind. Anger, indignation or any of the affections may be shown in a hundred different ways, according to the character of the individual. There are no universal methods in exhibiting emotion.[19]

From the first, writers critical of the histrionic code used words such as "real life," "naturally," and "realism," all of which disclose their allegiance to the fundamental principle of nineteenth-century literary, dramatic, and theatrical realism that artistic representation should reflect extratextual reality. Whether attacking the histrionic code or advocating the verisimilar, the majority of the trade press journalists assumed that verisimilitude was the primary goal. From 1908 to 1913, pleas for verisimilarly coded performance asserted that film acting should approximate real-life behavior. Once again, Frank Woods most forcefully stated this argument, with respect not only to acting but to all aspects of film:

Any art is the most perfectly developed in which the artificial and even the art itself is concealed . . . [and] motion pictures, by reason of the natural surroundings that can be employed or simulated and the absence of all appearances of stage artificiality that can be easily attained, can be made to seem records of the absolutely real. . . . The director . . . who earnestly strives to get the most commanding effect with a powerful story will not fail to see that every action and scene shall appear to be as if it were an actual happening in life.[20]

Woods wrote this in March 1912, shortly before leaving the *Mirror* to work with Griffith at Biograph, but he had been calling for verisimilar performance since the start of the paper's film section in 1908. In an unsigned article, from November 1908, the author, undoubtedly Woods, urged Americans to emulate foreign acting standards. Whereas American actors "cannot conceal" themselves and their "theatrical training," "when a foreign picture . . . shows a farmer or a peasant, the character appears to be real and genuine, not the work of an actor at all."[21] In 1909, Woods equated good acting with verisimilar acting: "The better and more real the work of the players, the closer they come to approximating actual life."[22] By 1910, he boldly stated that "realism" is "the chief end of motion picture acting."[23] A week later he praised the actors in *The Unchanging Sea* (Biograph) for "conveying not one hint of acting at all" and performing "with scarcely a gesture and with perfect naturalness."[24] Later that same month he summed up his philosophy of film acting in two words: "Be natural!"[25]

Now, as we have seen with the nineteenth-century theatre, it is all very well to tell an actor to be natural, but how is she to achieve this end? As did their theatrical counterparts, proponents of cinematic verisimilitude told actors to refrain from excessive gesticulation, to dispense with the quick and broad movements of the histrionic code and substitute byplay—small movements of head, hands, and face that would accumulate to reveal emotion and delineate character. In 1908, the French seemed to epitomize byplay and restraint, since they expressed themselves through "an arch of the eyebrows, a shrug of the shoulders, a gesture of the hands."[26] By 1911, most writers held the opinion that Americans had outstripped the French in the matter of restrained acting.

> It is the very infrequency and simplicity of the gesture that gives it its effectiveness. When we see two Frenchmen or Italians gesticulate we take small note, because we are accustomed to see the Latin races go through a perfect fury of gesticulation over nothing in particular. The gestures of Americans . . . are . . . pregnant with meaning because the whole man has to be charged with the . . . emotion before he seeks to give it utterance in gesture. This is especially true of some of the good Western pictures. A wave of the hand, a turn of the body, a swinging of the arms means more than a hundred thousand excited gestures of a company of Frenchmen, Italians or South Americans.[27]

If gestures were to be few and small, actors had to give each movement enough emphasis for the audience to grasp its significance. Epes Winthrop Sergent, who wrote the weekly "Technique of the Photoplay" for the *World,* said, "the picture player must convey his emphasis by making prominent the vital actions. This should be done not by violent ranting, but by pointing up the action; by dwelling upon it, until the spectator assimilates the point." Sergent gives an example: a girl at a dance has two admirers, A and B. She is chatting with A, whom she prefers, but B has the right to the next dance and she leaves A with "a lingering glance of regret." This glance should be emphasized: "if the girl hesitates for a moment, half turns back to the man she cares for and yields only to the pressure of the second man, the deliberate action points up the situation."[28]

By 1912, writers pointed to instances of verisimilar byplay and restraint as proof that the verisimilar code had defeated the histrionic. As Claudy put it, "Every month sees less and less meaningless gesticulation, more and more restraint." There was "an increasing demand for natural, sincere, unmelodramatic acting." Claudy goes on to describe the portrayal of a drunk by a Mr. Johnston in Eclair's *The Awakening:*

> Instead of coming in and staggering around the room and knocking things over and generally behaving as only a very, very drunken beast would behave. . . . Mr. Johnston "carries his liquor" like a gentleman. He doesn't stagger. He doesn't knock things over. He doesn't lurch and stutter. Instead he "gets over" his condition by a very simple and artistic copying of the actions of a man who has had a little too much—his mouth is dry—and he moistens his lips; his head is confused and he winks a couple of times as he passes his hand over his forehead—he moves slowly and carefully—he shows impatience at being petted [by his mother.] The

little touch of his involuntary movement away while patting his arm is very well done.[29]

One of Claudy's colleagues at the *World* agreed with him about the advent of acting that was "natural and convincing and intelligible" and contrasted the old and new styles' approach to the same situation: "The photoplay actor no longer finds it necessary to point to his stomach to show that he is hungry. He can get his hunger to the screen by the manner in which he looks at a chunk of bread."[30] Just as a woman can signal love by looking at a man, a man can signal hunger by looking at a piece of bread.

Trade press writers believed that the details and restraint of the verisimilar code depended a great deal on use of the eyes and face. While film scholars have often connected emphasis of facial expression with the close-up, the trade press began to discuss its significance even when the long-shot tableau style still dominated. It seems as though actual film practice lagged behind the trade-press discourse, that the desire to see the actors' faces predated cinematic techniques particularly tailored to highlight facial expression.[31]

Comparing film and stage acting, a *World* writer stated in 1908 that "the power of good pictures to convey the phases of emotion by the facial expression of the actor is greater than that of the actual stage."[32] Reviewing *A Fool's Revenge* (Biograph, 1909) the *Mirror* praised the "clear facial expressions" and the "natural but intensely suggestive gestures and poses."[33] Similarly, the *World*'s review of *Compassion* (Eclair, 1909) stated that the "facial expressions of the actors . . . are good and the entire film seems natural,"[34] while in *The Eavesdropper* (Biograph, 1909), "the facial expressions . . . are excellent."[35] Not only reviewers responded to the use of the face and eyes. A correspondent to the *World* wrote a "Biograph Appreciation," in which he lauded the Biograph actors and their facial expressions. In Biograph films, because of "the clearness of the features . . . every little change of expression is noticeable." The writer relates this to the verisimilar code: "the Biograph people are such masters of facial expression and they so 'look the part' that it doesn't seem like acting."[36]

By 1911, Louis Harrison could claim that the use of the face and eyes was transforming the very nature of acting: "An entirely new art is coming into existence through facial expression in the photoplay."[37] By the time Griffith left Biograph, facial expression was seen as a crucial, perhaps the crucial, component of the verisimilar code. A writer of advice to would-be actors stated, "Facial expression is perhaps the most important part of photoplaying. . . . [and] the eyes are really the focus of one's personality in photoplaying. With the aid of the other facial features they can express almost all the emotions and passions felt by a human soul."[38]

By this time reviewers were criticizing filmmakers for not bringing players close enough to the camera. Reviewing Edwin Porter's adaptation of James

Hackett's stage version of *The Prisoner of Zenda,* the *World* questioned the efficacy of Porter's long-shot style:

> The question of bringing the actors well to the foreground is open to debate, though it seems that . . . a little closer camera work would have brought better results. Facial expressions . . . were sacrificed to . . . get depth to scenes, necessary when many characters enter into the action, but of less obvious value when only two or three players are concerned in an incident where much may be communicated by varying expression.[39]

As E. H. Southern, a leading theatrical actor of the period, discovered while starring in a 1916 Vitagraph feature, filmmakers rapidly adapted to the verisimilar code's emphasis on facial expression, making film acting different from stage acting:

> We do our acting before the moving camera . . . with . . . our gestures limited, with our space for moving about cut to the narrowest allowance . . . Everything is limited for the actor except his facial expressions . . . That is why every expression must be intensified in moving pictures, because through the expression alone [the audience members] receive an impression of the picture you are trying to convey.[40]

Because the face and eyes presumably most directly reflected a character's thoughts and emotions, the trade press considered facial expression an indispensable component of the verisimilar code's construction of a psychologized individual. From the first, writers linked close shots with thinking: "The characters . . . appear in heroic size on the screen, thus making facial expression clear to the spectator. . . . People prefer to see characters . . . close enough to see what they are thinking about."[41] In 1909, a *World* writer, the pseudonymous Lux Graphicus, complimented the anonymous Biograph cameraman (Billy Bitzer) for his work in *The Way of Man:* "He puts his camera near the subject and the lens, and you see what is passing in the minds of the actors and actresses." In doing so he produced "actual photographs of thinking men and women" that had "a psychological as well as a photographic interest." For Lux Graphicus the "best moving pictures of the time" were those in which the actors "perceptibly think and let the audience see what they are thinking."[42]

As understood by the trade press, the verisimilar code created individuated characters through the use of small, realistic details, facial expression, and the eyes. Accepting the new style, critics responded by equating good acting with individuated characters: "the acting in this film [*Lady Helen's Escapade* (Biograph, 1909)] is superb. Each character stands out individually and distinctly."[43] By 1911, trade press writers began to sound as if they had just discovered Henry James's "The Art of Fiction" and wholeheartedly embraced his belief that character and incident are all but indistinguishable. Complaining that "there is entirely too much sameness in heroes," Claudy commended a Selig actor who illustrated a nervous disposition by the way "he continually jerked at his collar and 'perked' his chin . . . he gave his character with his actions, before he had those actions to perform."[44] Harrison also saw characterization as an essential part of verisimilitude:

> Plot and action simply give opportunity for the development of character. . . . Many [directors] honestly believe in the pre-eminence of action and plot, with characterization a poor second if it appears at all and that is the principal cause of failure on the part of those in front to feel a deep interest in what is going on. Intensified character is the source of action.[45]

Claudy and Harrison advocated the conflation of character and narrative that became a fundamental component of the classical Hollywood cinema; in Woods's words, "the manner of the action . . . may be strongly expressive of character and emotions."[46] By 1913, film had rejected the unmediated causality and external motivation of the melodrama, which clearly revealed characters as plot functions, substituting the mediated causality and internal motivation of the realist novel and drama, which rendered plot and character indistinguishable. Cinematic conformance to "realist" signifying practices may have been, as we shall see in the next section, part of a deliberate strategy to ally film with more respectable cultural products.

Performance Style and the Debate over Cheap Amusements as Reflected in Trade Press Discourse

The transformation of performance style was related to the position of the film medium in turn-of-the-century American society. Full understanding of the transition from the histrionic to the verisimilar codes requires situating the film industry with regard to efforts to regulate the leisure hours of the working classes. Situating the trade press's assessment of the link between performance style and both the "respectable" and "disreputable" theatre, in the context of a larger cultural debate over cheap amusements—e.g., penny arcades, dance halls, saloons, and, especially, the "cheap" melodrama—necessitates the adducing of evidence concerning cultural arbiters' struggles against cheap amusements and their policy of offering what they perceived as equally entertaining alternatives. As a report of the Russell Sage Foundation put it: "recreation within the modern city has become a matter of public concern; *laissez faire,* in recreation as in industry, can no longer be the policy of the state."[47] This chapter thus shifts methodological gears, as it were, from intertextuality to "contextuality."

For the film industry, the year 1908 constituted a moment of crisis with regard to representational strategies, industry organization and, perhaps most seriously, the medium's relation to the larger society. As the storefront moving picture shows proliferated at a remarkable rate, the nickelodeons and the films they showed came under increasing attack from state and civic organizations. The film industry used several strategies to respond to these criticisms, among them choosing to ally itself with cultural arbiters (e.g., urban reform organizations, schools, churches, and libraries), and the respectable entertainments they endorsed, while distancing itself from the cheap amusements they abhorred.[48] As part of this strategy, the industry began to emulate the signifying practices of respectable entertainments, the Broadway stage among them. The verisimilar code had, by the turn of the century, become the dominant performance style in the "legitimate" theatre. Trade press discourse reveals that film's adoption of the verisimilar code and its rejection of the histrionic accords with the strategy of emulating respectable entertainments.

The New York City nickelodeon closings contributed to the aura of crisis surrounding the film industry circa 1908. When the dominant cinematic exhibition site shifted, circa 1905, from the solidly middle-class vaudeville houses to the disreputable storefront moving picture shows frequented by immigrants and the working classes,[49] neither public nor private interests controlled film content, while the dark, crowded, firetrap nickelodeons remained largely unregulated. Many respectable citizens came to believe that the "moving picture dens" blighted the urban landscape and the lives of its inhabitants. Alarmed by the almost total lack of state supervision, reform-minded civic groups suddenly began demanding government investigation and control of the new medium.

Early in December of 1908, responding to pressure from concerned clerics and civic organizations, New York's Mayor McClellan convened hearings on the moving picture shows. Members of the clergy, representatives of children's aid societies, and other "public spirited" citizens denounced the nickelodeons as dens of iniquity fostering everything from pickpockets to prostitutes. The atmosphere was also said to encourage lascivious behavior on the part of the more respectable clientele: "the darkened rooms combined with the influence of pictures projected on the screen have given opportunities for a new form of degeneracy."[50] On Christmas Eve, the mayor revoked the common show licenses of some 550 nickelodeons.

Only a week before the nickelodeon closings, the most powerful elements of the film industry, headed by the Edison and Biograph studios, had formed the Motion Picture Patents Company, an economic organization intended to regulate distribution and exhibition and, not incidentally, ensure that the majority of profits accrued to the film producers.[51] Shortly after its formation, the Trust sent an announcement to exhibitors setting forth its goals. Among them: "To encourage in all possible ways the commendation and support of the moving picture business by the better class of the community.''[52] Clearly, the better class of the community would hardly frequent dirty, crowded, smelly storefronts charging a mere five cents for admission, and the Trust sought to bring exhibition sites more in line with the expectations of the "better classes." Nor did the Trust believe that these desirable patrons could be expected to enjoy the same (often "immoral") fare that thrilled the uneducated and ignorant foreigner or laborer. Films would now be "Moral, Educational and Cleanly Amusing."[53]

In order to ensure that films were indeed moral, educational, and cleanly amusing, the Trust cooperated with the National Board of Censorship, a private review board to which the manufacturers voluntarily submitted their films. The board had been formed at the initiative of the Association of Motion Picture Exhibitors of New York shortly after the Christmas Eve shutdown. The New York exhibitors asked a number of civic organizations to participate, but when the board transformed itself into a national agency in May 1909, the People's Institute of New York City began to play a dominant role.[54]

The People's Institute, a progressive reform organization that attempted to involve "the masses" in the political process, epitomizes the cultural arbiters valorizing those respectable entertainments the film industry began to emulate. Founded by Charles Sprague Smith in 1897, the People's Institute's interest in the theatre made the organization the perfect candidate to lead the new Board of Censorship.[55] Smith championed the drama as a source of uplift, believing that it "contained a great power of inspiration and instruction."[56] A circular from the People's Institute, if not actually written by Smith, certainly reflected his sentiments: "The Institute believes that good drama is educative in the best sense, developing taste, social sense and human sympathy."[57]

The Institute, selecting acceptable plays for a reduced-price ticket program for teachers, students, and wage-earners, provided a model for the constraints voluntarily acceded to by the film industry, as the acceptance of censorship constituted one strategy for warding off further attacks from the private sector and regulation from the public. But the Institute's definitions of the culturally acceptable and nonacceptable may have indirectly influenced the film industry's adoption of the emulation of respectable entertainment strategies. The Institute offered the reduced-price tickets, as well as other cultural fare such as free lectures, not merely to uplift and enlighten the masses but to lure them away from the cheap amusements that Smith and others believed pandered to the baser instincts. Rather than simply constraining cheap amusements through censorship, reform organizations, such as the Institute, attempted to provide equally appealing, but uplifting, substitutes, proffering their cultural activities as "counter-attraction," to borrow a period term.[58] Smith asserted that, through the reduced-price ticket program, the People's Institute was "gradually substituting for the cheap, often meretricious, melodrama and vaudeville, commonly accessible to those of limited means, the best that the theatre affords, thus making good drama a source of pleasure and uplift to a multitude of lives.''[59]

The film industry took the hint, emulating respectable entertainments while distancing itself from precisely the kinds of cheap amusements to which the reformers objected. Said Stephen Bush of *The Moving Picture World,* ''The motion picture, the greatest factor in the future instruction and amusement of mankind, must range itself with the forces that make for good, that mean progress and spell advancement.''[60] The motion picture, asserted those within or sympathetic to the film industry, constituted as valuable a source of uplift as any cultural or educational institution. As the well-known pundit Elbert Hubbard put it, the moving picture ''is one of the things that is helping to make this old world over into a better and happier place.''[61] In 1908, the *World* asserted that the moving picture could out-reform the reformers in providing educational benefits: ''No university settlement or extension work can do more for the education and amusement of the masses than the moving picture theatre.''[62]

According to the trade press, the motion picture itself now offered a powerful counter-attraction, as those cheap amusements pandering to the worst instincts of the masses gave way before the salubrious influence of the nickelodeon. *The Nickelodeon* reported that, ''Saloon keepers have protested excitedly against its [the nickelodeon's] permanent establishment as a menace to their trade. The saloon has lost its hypocritical and pious cloak as the workingman's club. The nickelodeon now beckons to the saloon's former patron with arguments too strong to be withstood.''[63] *The Views and Film Index* summarized the results of a People's Institute survey of cheap amusements, arguing that the nickelodeon would replace the penny arcades as well as the saloons.

> They [the penny arcades] were found to be places of an entirely distinct character and not always a pleasant one. Attended largely by children, they showed in numerous cases a tendency to offer vicious pictures. It was the only way, apparently, in which they could compete with the larger, more extensive pictures of the cinematograph shows. Even so, it was found, the penny arcades were not holding their own. Their numbers are diminishing; their owners are in many cases making them over into the more desirable nickelodeons.[64]

While the nickelodeon may have drawn patrons from both saloons and penny arcades, the non-filmgoing public perhaps most closely associated the moving picture with low-priced theatres offering lurid melodramatic fare, such as those that had clustered around New York City's Bowery. ''Respectable'' sorts believed this melodrama, along with other ''sensationalist'' media, such as dime novels, to be a deeply corrupting influence, inciting both impure thoughts and improper actions. Just as late-twentieth-century media critics can seem obsessed with ''harmful'' television, their late-nineteenth-century counterparts spoke endlessly of "harmful" theatre. In 1887, for example, the Reverend Otto Peltzer, author of the biblical play "Moses and Pharaoh," wrote an impassioned defense of the theatre, attempting to persuade his fellow Christians of the stage's moral potential. The popular melodrama, by contrast, came in for resounding condemnation:

> There is much room for argument against a certain class of production on the stage to-day. . . . It is to be regretted that, like the sensational scandal-and-criminal columns of the daily papers, these exhibitions are intensely gratifying to a certain class of patrons of the theatre. . . . The jargon of the swamp, the debasing lingo of the police reporter, the abounding epithets of tap-room frequenters, the colloquialisms of the street arab will come trippingly from the pens of these play-makers. Horrors intensified, grossness exaggerated, modern barbarity, the doings of swindlers, drunkards, beggars, thieves, the lowest form of degradation, scenes in the gambling halls and prisons . . . accidents, explosions and mangled limbs, are their leading features. . . . Plays with convicts for heroes; with plots made up of impossibilities and exaggerations . . . give no instruction—they are monstrosities that teach no lessons. They positively poison the minds of a young generation.[65]

When Peltzer wrote, the "pure" melodrama, from which film would borrow so much, still thrived, performed nightly by stock companies in the larger cities and touring companies in smaller cities and towns. But the first decade of the twentieth century relegated this "ten, twenty, thirt' melodrama" (as opposed to the elaborately mounted Broadway productions of Belasco and Boucicault) to the margins of American popular culture, firmly associating it in the minds of the "respectable" classes with the low, the tawdry, and the unseemly. Thirty years after Peltzer's diatribe, H. J. Smith, writing in *The Atlantic Monthly,* made clear the status of the popular-priced melodrama.

> The majority of us scoff at the melodrama as a matter of course, and, as a matter of course, we know nothing about it, except perhaps what we may have inferred from certain lurid bill-boards. It seems to occupy precisely the same place in the dramatic world that the hurdy-gurdy occupies in the world of music, and the old-fashioned camp meeting in the world of religion.[66]

Some empirical evidence from the period shows that *The Atlantic Monthly*'s readers, if they went to the theatre at all, probably did not patronize the melodrama, being much more likely to attend "legitimate" productions. The Russell Sage Foundation's 1911 survey of cheap amusements found sixteen "low-priced" theatres in New York City occasionally presenting melodramas—"now nearly driven out by vaudeville so that no Manhattan theatres are now confined to it."[67] The average price for these theatres was 45 cents, as opposed to $1.20 for the "standard theatre" and 7 cents for the nickelodeons.[68] What does this mean in terms of the probable class composition of these theatres' respective audiences? In this period, wage-earners such as porters and elevator operators earned from $8 to $10 a week. A 1907 survey of two hundred Greenwich Village wage-earners' families found a range of annual incomes from $250 to $2,556 with an average for the district of $851.38.[69]

These figures indicate that all but the very poorest could occasionally attend the nickelodeons, while the better-off workingmen's families could attend the "low-priced" theatres, which included vaudeville. The admission price of the "standard theatres" however, constituting as it did a large portion of many families' weekly incomes, would have made attendance a considerable financial sacrifice.[70] Indeed, the Russell Sage survey found that the class composition of the nickelodeon audience was "working, 72%," "clerical, 25%," and "leisured, 3%," while that of the high-priced theatres was "leisured, 51%," "clerical or business, 47%," and "working, 2%."[71] Though the survey provides no breakdown of the audiences at the popular-priced melodramas, we may safely infer that their patrons came from the same class as those attending the nickelodeons, and not from the class that read *The Atlantic Monthly* and patronized the high-priced theatres.

Indeed, the general consensus was that the moving picture had driven the popular priced melodrama out of existence by successfully competing for patrons. The 1908 People's Institute survey of cheap amusements remarked that "the old-time crass melodrama has been in large measure dethroned, crowded out by the cheap vaudeville and the nickelodeon."[72] The *Mirror* ran a series of articles exploring the various reasons for the decline of melodrama. Jules Murray, a manager of a theatrical circuit, described the situation in detail and made a prediction for the future:

> The medium class of companies and the small fellows and the popular price houses have been hit very hard by the moving picture. . . . It is really astounding, the number of these little show houses there are in every city and town my companies have visited. . . . Eight, ten and fifteen are common in the good one-night stand cities—that is to say, one-night stands that used to be called good.
>
> I am inclined to believe that . . . the first-class two-dollar and dollar-and-a-half attractions on the one side and the five-cent houses on the other, will get practically all the money. There will be no middle ground to speak of.[73]

Trade press evidence indicates that members of the moving picture industry wanted to close the gap, in the public perception at least, between the "two-dollar and dollar-and-a-half attractions" and the "five-cent houses." Yet both the scanty empirical evidence available and period discourse indicate a strong relationship between the melodrama and the moving picture, not only in terms of narrative structure but in terms of audiences. Given incomes and admission prices, one could infer that the melodrama was primarily patronized by members of the "working classes." Given period discourse, one could further infer that these patrons deserted their "blood and thunder" theatrical productions for the moving-picture equivalent.

At first, during the reign of the histrionic code, the trade press happily gave credit to the nickelodeons for putting the cheap theatres out of business, claiming that the motion picture not only resembled the melodrama but could actually surpass the stage's melodramatic emotions and effects. In April 1908, the *World* claimed that "the nickelodeon has the ten, twenty, thirt' repertoire companies pushed against the plaster."[74] A theatre manager asserted that film lured away the popular-price audience by going the pure melodrama one better: "With the coming of the moving picture show the rapid-fire melodrama has become the imitation, the moving picture the real thing. . . . The public that demanded a quick succession of pictures—that is, scenes—have gone over to the moving picture houses."[75]

But, later, as the verisimilar code gained ascendancy, the trade press reviled the melodrama, stating that film was infinitely superior. *The Edison Kinetogram* happily reported a lecture by G. P. Baker, professor of dramatic literature at Harvard. Said Professor Baker: "Motion pictures are taking the place of melodramas. There is less tendency toward crime and immorality in the picture show."[76] In 1911, Stephen Bush clearly articulated industry strategy. To "gain the sympathy and recognition of the best and highest elements in our civilization" filmmakers must reject "cheap comedy and cheap melodrama."[77] In the same issue of the *World* an anonymous author remarked, "Public intelligence and education . . . have laughed and scorned the melodrama to death, and it can scarcely be revived via the moving picture route. It is altogether too unreal to please this wise and inquisitive generation."[78] A year earlier, H. F. Hoffmann had accused melodramatic films of driving away the respectable audiences that had viewed the actualities shown in the vaudeville houses. At Keith's Union Square Theatre, according to Hoffmann, films drew "society people, professional people of all branches, interesting the financiers, the merchants and all others of the most desirable class until . . . somebody thought of the punk melodrama." But when audiences of this desirable class felt that they were "having 10–20–30 melodrama stuffed down their throats" they "quietly withdrew," realizing that "instead of brains catering to brains, it was a case of class [the manufacturers] catering to class [the audience], and that let them out."[79]

As the film industry and the trade press disassociated film from the déclassé melodrama, they tried to persuade cultural arbiters and potential "respectable" patrons to associate the moving picture with the legitimate Broadway stage instead. In an "official communique," the Motion Picture Patents Company declared that it wished to "put the motion picture show on a basis with the very highest class of theatrical performances from every standpoint."[80] The same week, the *Mirror* reported the formation of the National Board of Censorship that would restore "the confidence of the great public" and cause the motion picture to "assume its rightful position on a level with the very highest grade of theatrical endeavor." To achieve this goal the manufacturers had to cease "pandering to the inferior minds" that were "content with very ordinary subjects" and "take a leaf out of the book of the late Richard Mansfield, and play up to the highest form of intelligence . . . rather than down to a comparatively low one."[81] Assuming "its rightful position" as the equal of the "very highest grade of theatrical endeavor" meant that the film industry had to employ the conventions of these theatrical endeavors, including the star system and the valorization of the playwright/scenariast.

Standard film histories have often credited Carl Laemmle, an independent producer, with importing the star system into the film industry in 1911 as a means of fighting the Motion Picture Patents Company. Richard deCordova has corrected this misconception, dating the development of the star system to late 1909 and early 1910. At this time, according to deCordova, a discourse about the "picture personality," such as Florence Lawrence and Mary Pickford, began to appear in the trade press. In addition, members of the MPPC began to hire well-known theatrical actors to appear in their films. Vitagraph began the trend in May 1909, hiring Elita Proctor Otis and prominently advertising her appearance in *Oliver Twist* as "Nancy Sykes, the role which this eminent actress has made famous throughout the world." Edison, later that year, engaged the French pantomimist Pilar-Morin for a series of films.[82] By 1911, the discourse on the "picture personality" included a listing of actors' prior credits, both cinematic and theatrical, a tactic that deCordova states served to "legitimize film acting, *in general,* by associating it with the acting of the legitimate stage."[83]

The trade press urged the motion picture industry to legitimize itself through association with the writing of the legitimate stage as well, calling for scenarios penned by well-known writers of fiction and drama, and hailing their employment when it occurred. In 1908, for example, the *Mirror* ran an article by a "moving picture enthusiast," who strenuously advised the use of "a higher class of authorship in the construction of plots or stories." As opposed to the "crudest kind of drama" and "the lowest kind of slapstick comedy" that had hitherto dominated, higher-class authors would produce stories that would appeal to the "more intelligent class of spectators."[84] As Kristin Thompson has shown, the studios soon followed this advice, obtaining scenarios from the numerous free-lance writers of novels and short stories as well as from the less numerous free-lance playwrights.[85]

The association with the legitimate stage strategy may have succeeded. In 1911, the *Mirror* reported that "attendance at the better picture theatres does not wholly include people in search of cheap amusements. In the audience at these theatres will be seen persons of the class that also patronizes the regular theatre."[86] By 1913, George Blaisdell of the *World* told of a "woman . . . of means" who had totally forsaken the theatre: "Why, we used to go to the theatre one night a week. Now we go to the pictures nearly every night. We don't think of the theatre anymore."[87]

This "woman . . . of means" may not have been an isolated instance. In 1912, the entire theatrical industry suffered a severe economic decline, attributed by many, as had been the case earlier when the melodramatic stage declined, directly to the burgeoning film industry. Summing up the situation in March 1912, Robert Grau reported that many first-rank players were "forced to abandon tours started in the fall of 1911''; he added that twenty traveling combinations closed in December, and that in New York City, "fully a third" of theatres converted to moving pictures; more than fifty towns within a 150-mile radius of New York were for the first time without theatres for touring companies.[88] In fact, as Robert McLaughlin has shown, between 1910 and 1920, the estimated number of companies on tour during an average week fell from 236 to 34.[89] Finding themselves unemployed as a result of the faltering theatre, many actors turned to film: "Scores of them [stage actors] are applying daily at the studios . . . and among them are some of the most popular and best people in the business."[90]

Rejection of the melodrama, the adoption of the conventions of the "standard" theatre, and the inclusion of new spectators who had formerly patronized the "respectable" stage would not, however, necessarily entail rejection of those spectators who had formerly patronized the cheap theatres along the Bowery. Perhaps this latter group simply did not know any better and could be encouraged to acquire more cultivated tastes: "Take the veriest dyed-in-the-wool lover of tank melodrama, who never saw a real play in his life—make him attend a motion picture theatre daily and see capable companies doing faithful, honest work, and it would be a good safe bet that the next time he saw a heroine rant or a hero clutch at his vitals and roll his eyes, he would laugh instead of applaud."[91]

This statement shows the film industry's conformance to the counter-attraction strategy of reform-minded cultural arbiters. Note the implication that the correspondence between film and real plays would wean the "veriest dyed-in-the-wool lover of tank melodrama" from his cheap amusements by introducing him to better things. This weaning from cheap amusements entailed teaching the former lover of tank melodrama to laugh at the histrionic code, and thus, one assumes, to applaud the verisimilar code. Here we clearly see that the film industry's alliance with cultural arbiters through dissociation from the melodrama and association with the legitimate stage involved not only borrowing conventions such as the star system but also abandoning the signifying practices of the cheap theatres for those of the high-priced. Chief among these signifying practices were narrative structure and performance style.

The trade press urged, in addition to the hiring of "real writers," the writing of "realist" narratives, featuring individuated characters with internal motivation and mediated causality. As we saw earlier, trade press writers had, by 1911, wholeheartedly adopted the Jamesean principle that character was as important as plot. The consensus among the trade press seems to have been that scenarists should take the well-made realist play as their exemplar. The Spectator pointed out that "mere action without some effort to give the action meaning" gave the industry a bad reputation among "people of intelligence."

Films could only achieve "a wider and better patronage" by "getting away from action and nothing but action."[92] Unlike some of his brethren, Woods did not demand the absolute abolition of such "cheap" action genres as the slapstick comedy and the melodrama but he did demand their reformation: "they must be well and carefully conceived and played, there must be logical reason for the thrilling incidents . . . if they are to interest and amuse the more intelligent class of picture spectator."[93]

Logical reasons depended on internal motivation: "the moving picture drama requires as strictly as does the acted drama that adequate motivation be presented for the actions of the characters."[94] With adequate motivation contributing to characterization, the film industry might indeed equal "the very highest class of theatrical performances." Reviewing *Lady Helen's Escapade* (Biograph, 1909), the *World* noted that by "cultivating . . . the delineation of character in the moving picture, the Biograph Company can contribute much towards the 'uplift' about which the self-constituted oracles of the daily press are talking and writing so much."[95]

Lux Graphicus of the *World* made a direct connection between the psychologized individual and film's becoming a respectable entertainment like the theatre. Stating that Biograph films feature "actual photographs of thinking men and women" and therefore have a "psychological . . . interest," he claimed that "people all over the city are as familiar with . . . Biograph pictures as they are with that of a Belasco masterpiece." If this trend were to continue, said Graphicus, the film industry's greatest desire might be realized: "If the more wealthy classes of this city were aware of the fine dramatic stuff that the Biograph Company is making, a moving picture theatre de luxe, on upper Broadway, between Forty-second and Fifty-ninth streets, would become a permanent feature of the theatrical world."[96]

"Actual photographs of thinking men and women" required, most likely, that these men and women convey their thought processes through the verisimilar code. Although consensus as to the superiority of the verisimilar code emerged fairly rapidly, some advocates of the histrionic code dissented from majority opinion, and the debate over performance style formed part of a larger debate over the film industry's association with cheap amusements versus respectable entertainments, and thus, by implication, over the class composition of the audience.

A 1909 article in the *World* indicates the terms of the debate:

> A good many of the Biograph pictures depend too much on the acting. . . . It must be remembered that a considerable portion of the public have no appreciation for fine art. . . . [Biograph] plays to the intelligent, discriminating public, and is prone to forget the masses which are not discriminating.[97]

As usual, however, Frank Woods most clearly articulated the debate. The same week that these comments appeared in the *World* an exhibitor wrote to the *Mirror* voicing similar sentiments about Biograph films. Frank Woods paraphrased: "In commenting specifically on Biograph pictures from the standpoint of the average picture spectator, the writer . . . expresses dissatisfaction with certain pictures from this company [Biograph] which he thinks go too far in the direction of fine acting without action." According to Woods, Biograph was attempting to strike a balance between acting and action: "the Biograph producers . . . understand . . . that too much art is undesirable. All of the [film producers] have . . . come dangerously near to shooting over the heads of their audience. . . . Their aim is to give as much fine art in acting as it is possible to employ and at the same time have an action story that would hold the interest."[98]

Other "unenlightened" manufacturers tenaciously clung to the histrionic code and the melodrama despite the best efforts of the other studios to "improve" performance style:

> Some producers who apparently held to the idea that sensational melodrama was the thing most wanted by motion picture spectators and that melodrama could only be expressed in picture pantomime of the furiously athletic style of acting, have argued that repose and subtle finesse must be wasted when presented to the average public as found in motion pictures.[99]

Woods even explicitly linked the histrionic code with the cheap melodrama and the verisimilar code with the Broadway stage:

> The kind of acting that appears not to be acting is the kind that is best appreciated by patrons of the pictures. This is the same quality of acting that we see in Broadway theatres as compared with the acting that used to be seen in cheap melodrama. . . . Intelligence and genuine realism count in directing and acting picture pantomime to a greater degree than stage work. A stage performance with stagy people overacting . . . may get by in the theatre, especially the popular price theatre, but in picture pantomime the thing that is demanded by all classes is . . . that highest quality of acting that appears not to be acting.[100]

The phrase "demanded by all classes" indicates that Woods, conforming to the reformers' counter-attractions strategy, did not feel that the adoption of the verisimilar code would drive the old patrons out of the nickelodeons. Woods repeatedly claimed that "good acting" was "appreciated . . . by all classes of patrons, the uncultured included." The adoption of the verisimilar code would not only make film a respectable entertainment, it would turn it into a respectable "mass" medium that would include all classes in the audience:

> The fact that the classes that made up the audience of the popular priced theatre used to accept mock heroics and applaud them is beside the question. It does not indicate that they would not have applauded good acting to a greater degree had

they ever had the opportunity. The moment that motion picture dramas were offered to them showing natural surroundings instead of painted scenes the popular priced public deserted the melodrama theatre and put it out of business. And they did not necessarily come to the pictures because they liked the cheap theatrical style of acting formerly deemed essential but more probably because they saw in the picture scenes that more nearly represented nature and real life. Having never seen anything but bad acting, they possibly supposed that no actor could do anything else. . . . When . . . the motion picture business . . . commenced to introduce a little art into their pantomime, the effect was astonishing. The uncultured were quick to applaud . . . [and] the cultured, who had hitherto looked on the motion picture drama as a joke . . . began to sit up and take notice.[101]

Our examination of trade press discourse in this chapter reveals that one can fully understand the transition from the histrionic to the verisimilar code only within the context of the debate over cheap amusements. Although both the textual analysis of Chapter 4 and the modified auteurist perspectives of Chapters 5 and 6 contributed to our understanding of the shift in performance style, this chapter underscores the necessity for film historians to situate both textual signifying practices and industry practices within a particular social, historical, and cultural moment. Clearly, both the transition from the apsychological narrative of external motivation and unmediated causality to the psychological narrative of internal motivation and mediated causality, as well as Griffith's desire to emulate and then outstrip the legitimate stage, must be understood as responses to the debate over film's position within society. The shift in performance style can then be seen as part of the cinema's transition from the cheap amusement of the ''lower orders'' to mainstream mass medium appealing to patrons of all classes.

8

Conclusion

This book has taken a pluralistic methodological approach, conceiving of the transformation of performance style in the Griffith Biographs as resulting from a complexly overdetermined interaction among text, intertext, and context. Now, in the hope of narrative resolution, let us return to where we began—with the two Biograph films, *A Drunkard's Reformation* and *Brutality*. This time, however, we shall look at them not through the eyes of our imaginary New Yorker, Josiah Evans, but through the insights gained from the analyses of the preceding seven chapters. A brief further discussion of these two films will illustrate how the methodological approaches developed in these pages can, in fact, work together to illuminate not only the workings of specific texts but the overall transition in performance style and the implications of this transition for the cultural position of the moving picture.

Both films, you may remember, relate the tale of an abusive drunk's reformation through a visit to the theatre. The parallel scenes that Josiah noticed in his viewings showed the wives' despairing reactions to their husbands' harsh treatment. In *A Drunkard's Reformation,* the wife (Linda Arvidson) collapses into her chair and rests her head on her arms, which are extended straight out in front of her on the table. Then she sinks to her knees and prays, her arms fully extended upward at about a forty-five degree angle to her body. In *Brutality,* the wife (Mae Marsh) sits down, bows her head, and begins to collect the dishes. She looks up, compresses her lips, pauses, then begins to gather the dishes once again. Once more she pauses, raises her hand to her mouth, glances down to her side, and slumps a little in her chair. Slumping a little more, she begins to cry.

Josiah had associated *A Drunkard's Reformation* with the cheap stage melodramas of his youth and *Brutality* with the legitimate Broadway productions of Gillette and Belasco. The intertextual frame we have constructed permits us now to understand why he would have drawn these connections and how they would have informed his evaluation of the two performance styles. As a member of the "cultivated" middle classes, now accustomed to the verisimilar code of the uptown theatres, he would undoubtedly have appraised Linda Arvidson's performance as "bad" and Mae Marsh's as "good." While our intertextual frame permits us to understand his evaluations, it does not demand that we share them; nonjudgmentally, we can now characterize Arvidson's performance as histrionic and Marsh's as verisimilar. Our close analysis of the deployment of gestural practices in these films situates them within the Biograph Company's gradual abandonment of the histrionic code and adoption of the verisimilar. The close analysis also leads us to recognize that Arvidson is performing a gestural soliloquy, accounting for her employment of the unchecked histrionic code, and that props—the dishes that Marsh first collects and then ignores—aid Marsh's verisimilar performance.

It is also possible now to relate Josiah's assessment of the two performance styles to his probable opinion in the cultural debate over the moving picture. As someone whose friends belonged to the People's Institute and whose wife served on the National Board of Censorship, he would have considered the change in performance style a promising sign of the moving picture's increasing distance from cheap amusements and emerging closeness to "respectable" entertainments with the potential for uplift. In our discussion of these two scenes, then, the intertextually derived descriptive language that we have developed, in conjunction with close analysis and contextual analysis, permits the articulation of the specifics of a representational change that had profound implications for the motion picture's position within the larger culture.

Although neither Josiah nor this book examined the narrative structures of *A Drunkard's Reformation* and *Brutality,* considering the differences between them again illustrates the mutual inflection of the text/intertext/context methodologies. By examining the determinant properties of the text in terms of the shift from the pure melodrama to the "realist" psychological drama, we may further account for the differences between the two films Josiah viewed. Paralleling *After Many Years* and *Enoch Arden, A Drunkard's Reformation* begins in media res, while *Brutality* first establishes internal motivation and mediated causality. The first shot of *A Drunkard's Reformation* shows the wife and daughter at home awaiting the arrival of the wayward husband. The film then cuts to the husband carousing at a saloon. These shots establish narrative tension but not character psychology. Was this respectably dressed family man an alcoholic at the time of his marriage, or has some recent crisis precipitated his alcoholism?

By contrast, the first ten shots of the fifty-six shot *Brutality* take the form of character exposition, establishing both the husband's loving nature, as he courts his future bride, and his fiery temper, as he almost comes to blows with a passerby who accidentally bumps into him. The next few shots show the marriage's gradual decline as drink exacerbates the husband's bad qualities. Hence, this drunkard's reformation can be seen in psychological terms, as the triumph of his good side over his bad side, rather than as a convention of melodramatic narrative structure.

Investigation of narrative structure was predicated on the close connection in the theatre between the emergence of the verisimilar code and the increasing importance of the psychologized character. The narrative structure of the later film can be related to nineteenth-century "realist" literature and drama, and then by exploring the class associations of these forms as well as those of the cheap melodrama, we can situate the linked changes in narrative structure and performance style within the overall transformation of the film industry from cheap amusement to mass entertainment. Again, the text/intertext/context methods work in concert.

Josiah might also have noticed the differences in performance style between the "real people" in each film and the stage actors in the plays-within-the-films. The "real" characters in *A Drunkard's Reformation* employ the checked histrionic code, but the "actors" in the film's staged temperance melodrama employ the unchecked version. In *Brutality* the "real" characters employ the verisimilar code, while the "actors" in the scene from a performance of *Oliver Twist* continue to employ the unchecked histrionic code. As I remarked earlier, in both films the "actors" seem markedly retrograde compared to the "real" characters, reflecting contrasts in performance style that apparently resulted from Griffith's desire to valorize the verisimilar potential of cinematic acting over that of theatrical acting. Now I shall argue that these internal contrasts are, in fact, complexly overdetermined, and that this overdetermination again illustrates the mutual inflection of the text/intertext/context methodologies.

The reader may remember the description of Henry Walthall's enactment of Fagin in *Brutality* that seemed deliberately to mimic the attitude-striking of the histrionic code. His strategy recalls the primary insight of the analysis of Henry Walthall's films: Biograph actors seemed to vary performance styles to correspond to a film's narrative structure and other signifying practices. This textual evidence of variation between the histrionic and verisimilar codes, which close analysis of *A Drunkard's Reformation* and *Brutality* substantiates, argues against an inevitable "progression" toward the new style, an argument reinforced by the evidence regarding production context. Although the Biograph front office may have recognized the contrast between the relative repose of the "real people" and the "actors" in *A Drunkard's Reformation,* the money men seem at first to have resisted any change in performance style that might have threatened their revenues. Our survey of the trade press lends credibility to the front office's fears that exhibitors, and, by implication, their audiences, would not wholeheartedly embrace a transformation of performance style.

Most important, the play-within-the-film scenes in both *A Drunkard's Reformation* and *Brutality* directly connect to our discussion of the film industry's forging of alliances with influential cultural arbiters through emphasizing the medium's uplifting potential. Both films draw an implicit parallel between the theatre's effect upon the spectator within the film and the films' probable effect upon their spectators. In fact, the *Biograph Bulletin*'s copy for *A Drunkard's Reformation* makes this parallel explicit: "The whole construction of the picture is most novel, showing . . . a play within a play. . . . The play depicts to the leading actor in the picture the calamitous result of drink, while the whole presents to the spectator the most powerful temperance lesson ever propounded."[1] *A Drunkard's Reformation* could be taken, by those so inclined, as evidence of the industry's good faith in aiming to disassociate itself from vicious and degrading cheap amusements.

Both Griffith's desire to mold a cinematic acting style that would appear to have greater verisimilitude than the theatre's and the front office's initial resistance to and ultimate embrace of the verisimilar code can be more fully understood in terms of the connection between transformations in cinematic signifying practices and the cultural debate about the status of moving pictures. Griffith, a man of great "artistic" aspirations, failed miserably as both stage actor and playwright. His contemptuous references to his early films as "sausages" does not disguise his need to build a reputation in an "artistic" medium that could match the theatre's cultural prestige. Hence, he would willingly have allied with those seeking to emulate the signifying practices of respectable entertainments. While the Biograph front office may initially have feared that the verisimilar code would drive away their old audience, they may eventually have been willing to trade potential short-range losses for a higher cultural status that might ultimately entail a greater profit potential. The money men must have been savvy enough to gauge the prevailing trend toward the emulation of "respectable" entertainments, and the trade press's lauding of the new performance style would certainly have alerted them to its probable public-relations benefits.

This book has linked textual analysis to intertextual analysis within the specificity of a historical moment that saw the triumph of the "realist" mode of representation in most respectable cultural forms. But this by no means indicates that the verisimilar code resulted from an inevitable progression toward an essentially cinematic acting style synonymous with the "realistic" representation of everyday behavior. While this book's mutually inflecting methodologies certainly do not establish a definitive "theory" of performance studies, they do point to the value of considering cinematic signifying practices as well as textual conditions of production and reception within the larger historical context. This approach reveals the conflict between different social formations that contextualizes the transformation in performance style, precluding the conception of any one mode of representation as "natural" or "inevitable."

Such full consideration of specific historical circumstances should also preclude the assertion of essentialist class associations. In other words, while a "realist" mode of representation in literature and stage drama does seem to have become dominant in the United States circa the turn of the century, labeling realism as inherently bourgeois or "middle class" reintroduces that teleological perspective against which this book has strongly argued. It has been asserted that realism, by which is meant in this context any artistic strategy that claims to represent an external reality, naturalizes the status quo by reproducing the dominant order, thus making it seem familiar, acceptable, and inevitable. Stephen Heath said of "vraisemblance": "It is the naturalization of that reality articulated by a society as the 'reality,' and its success is the degree to which it remains unknown as a form, to which it is received as a mirror of 'Reality.' "[2] The implication is that realism under capitalism serves the interests of the dominant class, the bourgeoisie. Catherine Belsey forcefully articulated this position, labeling the nineteenth-century classical realist text as "predominantly conservative." "The experience of reading a realist text is ultimately reassuring . . . because the world evoked in the fiction, its patterns of cause and effect, of social relationships and moral values, largely confirm the patterns of the world we seem to know."[3]

But the postulation of the ideological essentiality of any particular mode of representation (as in the blanket assertions of Heath and Belsey and others) ignores history, and history must be seen as representing, to use Fredric Jameson's felicitous phrase, the "untranscendable horizon." Raymond Williams—who warns us that "realism" is a "difficult word"—argues that some of the characteristics of late-eighteenth- and nineteenth-century realism, such as contemporaneity, secularity, and social inclusiveness, though initially associated with the bourgeoisie's rise to power, could be appropriated by others in the class struggle. Only the sort of detailed historical analyses that Williams has undertaken in his studies of the English stage can reveal the shifts in the associations of particular realist conventions with certain social formations.[4]

Thus, this book has not only failed to construct a definitive theory for the study of cinematic performance but it has proposed an argument the whole thrust of which mitigates against such a construction, since any particular performance mode must be studied within the context of the specific historical and cultural conditions that gave rise to it. The various methods used in this book nonetheless do have some general applicability beyond the study of the transformation of performance style in the Griffith Biograph films between 1908 and 1913. As I observed at the outset, the study of cinematic performance has thus far been conducted primarily through ahistorical textual analyses predicated on the personal preferences of the analyst. Such studies do much inadvertently to illuminate the analyst's subjectivity, but they seldom do much to cast light on the object of study.

In this postmodern age one cannot claim to separate the subject from the object, for to do so replicates the worst excesses of social-science positivism. But we have seen that a sympathetic understanding of a particular period's "reality" and of the precise elements that then connoted verisimilitude has enabled us to understand the period's own judgments about good and bad acting without imposing our own. The mutually inflecting text/intertext/context methods temper to some degree the analyst's personal preferences. Given the increasingly pervasive recognition among film scholars of the importance of historical context, no one should find this conclusion particularly startling.

Notes

1. Introduction

1. The details of the imaginary Josiah's imaginary excursions accord with the numerous descriptions of moving picture theatres that I have encountered in the trade press. Particularly interesting is a report written by New York City's Commissioner of Accounts Raymond B. Fosdick for Mayor William J. Gaynor (see "Report on New York Picture Theatres," *Motography,* April 1911, pp. 27–30).

2. The term *performance* has multiple and varied uses/meanings outside the discipline of cinema studies. In " 'All the World's a Stage': Performance as Interdisciplinary Tool," a paper presented at the 1989 meeting of the International Communications Association, San Francisco, Barbie Zelizer outlines three usual meanings of the term in academic research: (1) "*Performance qua performance* offers the most defined frame for academic research interests, with the most identifiable boundaries. It is a performance of *Les Misérables* or a Jackson Pollock painting"; (2) "*Performance as social interaction* is a less-defined spatial and temporal frame, as in . . . street-performative activity." Here Zelizer refers to the early work of Erving Goffman (*Behavior in Public Places* [Garden City, N.Y.: Doubleday, 1959] and *The Presentation of Self in Everyday Life* [Garden City, N.Y.: Doubleday, 1959]); (3) "*Performance as sociocultural structure* becomes even more spatially and temporally diffuse." Here Zelizer refers to the "social dramas" of Victor Turner (*The Ritual Process* [Ithaca: Cornell University Press, 1969] and *Dramas, Fields, Metaphors* [Ithaca: Cornell University Press, 1974]), to the "definitional ceremonies of anthropologists" such as Barbara Myerhoff (*Number Our Days* [New York: Simon and Schuster, 1980]), and to "the wide-ranging, and potentially amorphous, culture-in-action" of Clifford Geertz (*The Interpretation of Cultures* [New York: Basic Books, 1973] and *Local Knowledge* [New York: Basic Books, 1983). Obviously, the second and third categories are not unrelated to the first, and discussions of cinematic acting may indeed benefit from broadening the scope of inquiry to include such uses of the term. In this book, however, I shall,

for pragmatic purposes, use the term *performance* interchangeably with the term *acting*, thus skirting the theoretical quagmires and endless qualifications that would result from the broader usage.

3. Dyer, *Stars*, p. 151.

4. One cannot, of course, ignore V. I. Pudovkin's classic treatise, *Film Technique and Film Acting*. But Pudovkin's work remains of limited use for film historians and theoreticians because it is primarily addressed to practitioners. He was concerned not with a general theory of performance but with teaching actors and directors to emulate a distinct style of performance in a distinct style of film, that is, with adapting Stanislavski's principles to the Soviet cinema of montage. For those concerned with the history of performance style in the Soviet cinema, however, Pudovkin's work would prove invaluable. Similarly, books such as Edward Dmytryk and Jean Porter Dmytryk's *On Screen Acting* constitute valuable evidence for investigating performance style in the classical Hollywood cinema. My discussion in this book draws on both theatrical and cinematic period instruction manuals.

5. One manifestation of this interest is the ever-lengthening list of books, which includes Eileen Bowser, *The Transformation of Cinema, 1907–1915* (New York: Scribner's Sons, 1990); Richard deCordova, *Picture Personalities: The Emergence of the Star System in America* (Urbana: University of Illinois Press, 1990); Thomas Elsaesser and Adam Barker, eds., *Early Cinema: Space, Frame, Narrative* (London: British Film Institute, 1990); Tom Gunning, *D. W. Griffith and the Origins of American Narrative Film* (Urbana: University of Illinois Press, 1991); Miriam Hansen, *Babel and Babylon: Spectatorship in American Silent Film* (Cambridge: Harvard University Press, 1990); Charles Musser, *The Emergence of Cinema: The American Screen to 1907* (New York: Scribner's Sons, 1990), *High-Class Moving Pictures: Lyman H. Howe and the Forgotten Era of Traveling Exhibition, 1880–1920* (Princeton: Princeton University Press, 1991), *Before the Nickelodeon: Edwin S. Porter and the Edison Manufacturing Company* (Berkeley and Los Angeles: University of California Press, 1991); Charles Musser and Paolo Cherchi-Usai, eds., *American Vitagraph* (Washington, D.C.: Smithsonian Institution Press, forthcoming); and William Uricchio and Roberta E. Pearson, *Cultural Crisis, Cultural Cure? The Case of the Vitagraph "High-Art" Moving Pictures* (Princeton: Princeton University Press, forthcoming).

6. While few have written about film performance as Dyer narrowly defined it, the field of performance/acting, broadly defined to encompass such subjects as stars, the institution of stardom and audience reception, embraces a bewildering variety of concerns. During the 1980s several articles appeared that relate to actors, stars, and performance/acting. Two respected film journals, *Wide Angle* and *Screen*, have devoted entire issues to the theme, including articles on Joan Crawford's sleeves and Jimmy Stewart's publicity photographs (Charles Wolfe, "The Return of Jimmy Stewart: The Publicity Photograph as Text," and Charlotte Cornelia Herzog and Jane Gaines, "Puffed Sleeves Before Teatime," both in *Wide Angle* 6:4 (1985): 44–53 and 24–33); and on sexual politics in the films of Katherine Hepburn (Simon Watney, "Katherine Hepburn and the Cinema of Chastisement," *Screen* 26:5 [September–October 1985]: 52–63). A similarly eclectic collection can be found in Bisplinghoff, "On Acting: A Selected Bibliography." More recently, *CineAction!*, the Canadian film

journal of avowedly leftist goals, published an issue on stardom (No. 7, December 1988).

7. Affron, *Star Acting*, pp. 7, 9.

8. Ibid., p. 9.

9. Dyer, *Stars*, p. 152.

10. See Gunning, "D. W. Griffith and the Narrator System."

11. Ibid., p. 162.

12. Ibid., p. 745.

13. Lewis Carroll, *Through the Looking Glass* (New York: New American Library, 1960), p. 186.

14. On the misuse of *melodrama*, see Merritt, "Melodrama: Postmortem for a Phantom Genre."

15. Thompson, "Beyond Commutation," 74.

16. Frank Woods, "Spectator's Comments," *The New York Dramatic Mirror*, December 28, 1910, pp. 28–29.

17. Advertisement, ibid., December 13, 1913, p. 36.

18. Colgate Baker, "David W. Griffith: The Genius of the Movies," in D. W. Griffith Clipping Files, New York Public Library for the Performing Arts at Lincoln Center (henceforth, DWG Clipping Files).

19. Hettie Grey Baker, "The Man Who Made the Movies," in DWG Clipping Files.

20. Denig, "Watching the Screen."

21. Kristin Thompson, in Bordwell, Staiger, and Thompson, eds., *The Classical Hollywood Cinema*, p. 190.

22. "Notable Films of the Week," *Moving Picture World*, April 24, 1909, p. 515.

23. Ibid., May 29, 1909, p. 712.

24. "High Art in Picture Making," *New York Dramatic Mirror*, May 1, 1909, p. 38. At almost the same time, the *Mirror* negatively characterized much of the acting in pre-1909 Vitagraph films; reviewing Vitagraph's new *The Life Drama of Napoleon Bonaparte and the Empress Josephine of France*, the *Mirror* said, "There is none of the hasty action which has marred so many previous Vitagraph subjects, but each character moves with natural feeling and effective restraint that distinguishes the high-class actor from the melodramatic" (April 17, 1909, p. 13). This review provides further evidence that, though other studios quickly began to move toward the new style, Biograph may have led the way.

25. Lux Graphicus, "On the Screen," *Moving Picture World*, July 3, 1909, p. 11.

26. See Graham, Higgins, Mancini, and Vieira, *Griffith and the Biograph*, pp. 6–7.

27. Further research into this period for another project has convinced me that Biograph did indeed play a leading role in the transformation of acting style. Briefly, my impression is that Biograph was among the first, if not the first, American studio to switch to the new style. But European films, particularly those of Pathé, which the trade press touted as an exemplar of performance style, may also have been influential.

28. The 1987 Vitagraph retrospective at the Giornate del Cinema Muto, in Pordenone, Italy, has proved something of a corrective, initiating the focus of scholarly

attention on the output of another studio. Two books, at least, had their origin at the retrospective. See Musser and Cherchi-Usai, eds., *American Vitagraph,* and Uricchio and Pearson, *Cultural Crisis, Cultural Cure?*

29. Eileen Bowser, ed., *Biograph Bulletins, 1908–1912.*

30. See, for example, Linda Arvidson, *When the Movies Were Young;* Pickford, *Sunshine and Shadow;* Gish, *The Movies, Mr. Griffith, and Me;* and Brown, *Adventures with Griffith.*

31. See Gunning, *D. W. Griffith and the Narrator System,* and Graham, Higgins, Mancini, and Vieira, eds., *Griffith and the Biograph.*

32. Allen, *Vaudeville and Film,* p. 212.

33. Ibid., p. 213. The increase in dramatic films, as opposed to actualities (early documentaries) or comedies, is of particular significance because this project focuses only on acting in dramatic films. An investigation of comic performance style during this period would require another monograph, given the profound differences between comic and dramatic performance styles. On this point see Naremore, *Acting in the Cinema,* pp. 76–77.

34. Musser, "Another Look at the Chaser Theory," p. 49.

35. Ibid., p. 40.

36. Allen, "Looking at 'Another Look at the Chaser Theory,' " p. 49.

37. Gunning, *D. W. Griffith and the Narrator System,* pp. 126–27.

38. Musser, "Nickelodeon," pp. 4–11.

39. Ibid., p. 6.

40. Ibid., p. 10.

41. Gunning, *D. W. Griffith and the Narrator System,* p. 59.

42. deCordova, "The Emergence of the Star System in America," *Wide Angle* 6:4 (1985): 5.

43. deCordova, "The Emergence of the Star System in America: An Examination of the Institutional and Ideological Function of the Star" (Diss., University of California, 1986), p. 88.

44. deCordova, "Emergence of the Star System," 5.

45. Musser, "The Changing Status of the Film Actor," pp. 57–62.

46. On this point, see Staiger, "Blueprints for Feature Films," pp. 173–94.

47. Bordwell, Staiger, and Thompson, *The Classical Hollywood Cinema,* p. 190.

48. deCordova, "Emergence of the Star System," diss., p. 168.

49. Ibid., p. 185.

2. The Theatrical Heritage

1. Schickel, *D. W. Griffith,* p. 110.

2. Ibid., p. 154.

3. Ibid., p. 151, quoting a review by Frank Woods.

4. As more and more film scholars become fascinated with this early period, the literature is proliferating rapidly. A good introduction to the pre-1908 period is Fell, ed., *Film Before Griffith.*

5. Staiger, "The Eyes Are Really the Focus," 15.

6. Bennett and Woollacott, *Bond and Beyond,* pp. 6–7.

7. Culler, *The Pursuit of Signs,* p. 103.

8. Bennett and others would argue, correctly I believe, that the reader has no more independent existence than the text and that a true investigation of the production and reception of meaning must account for texts, intertexts, readers, and the context of a particular historical moment. In this book, however, I cannot deal in detail with the reception of performance style by the original audiences for these films. The lack of historical data and the theoretical difficulties entailed renders the investigation of the reception of the early silent cinema, or, indeed, any cinema, extremely problematic. In Chapter 7 of this book, I shall use evidence from the trade press to suggest how performance in the Griffith Biographs may have been received by a particular segment of the audience. In another project, I am attempting to develop a preliminary methodology that permits discussion of the conditions of reception for the early American cinema; see Uricchio and Pearson, *Cultural Crisis, Cultural Cure?*

9. On the process of encoding and decoding, see Stuart Hall, "Encoding and Decoding," in Stuart Hall, Dorothy Hobson, Andrew Lowe, and Paul Willis, eds., *Culture, Media, Language: Working Papers in Cultural Studies, 1972–79* (London: Hutchinson Education, 1980), pp. 128–38. Because I am defining the codes here as shared intertextual frameworks, I am ruling out investigating the kinds of preferred, negotiated, or oppositional readings theorized by Hall and others such as John Fiske. Again, I cannot fully investigate the reception of performance style.

10. For recent discussions of this highly codified performance style see Dyer, *Stars,* 155–56; Naremore, *Acting in the Cinema,* pp. 51–60, and Susan Roberts, "Melodramatic Performance Signs," *Framework* nos. 32/33 (1986): 68–74. For the best historical surveys of nineteenth-century acting, see Downer, "Players and Painted Stage," and West, "The London Stage." For an attempt to apply a semiotic model to the performance of Shakespearean plays see Marvin Rosenberg, "Sign Theory and Shakespeare," *Shakespeare Survey Annual* 40 (1987): 33–40.

11. Downer, "Players and Painted Stage," 574.

12. Anonymous, *The Art of Acting, or, Guide to the Stage: In Which the Dramatic Passions are Defined, Analyzed, and Made Easy of Acquirement* (New York: Samuel French, 1855), p. 16.

13. Stebbins, *Delsarte's System of Expression,* p. 429.

14. Ibid.

15. Morgan, *An Hour with Delsarte,* p. 91.

16. Eco, *A Theory of Semiotics,* p. 231.

17. Metz, *Language and Cinema,* p. 131.

18. The concept of an idiolect is a vexed one among linguists. See Roland Barthes, *Elements of Semiology,* pp. 21–22.

19. Steele MacKaye, unpublished lecture, quoted in Morris, "The Influence of Delsarte in America," p. 35.

20. The New York publishing firm of Edgar S. Werne specialized in Delsartism, flooding the market with instruction books. See, for example, Elsie N. Wilbor, ed., *Delsarte Recitation Book and Directory,* 2nd edition, 1883.

21. Zorn, *The Essential Delsarte,* p. 164.

22. Bill Nichols, "Glossary," in Nichols, ed., *Movies and Methods,* p. 629.

23. Barthes, *Elements of Semiology,* p. 529.

24. Nichols, *Movies and Methods,* p. 629.

25. Pavis, "Problems of a Semiology of Theatrical Gesture," p. 71.

26. A. J. Greimas, quoted in Brooks, *The Melodramatic Imagination,* p. 70.

27. Brooks, ibid., p. 71.

28. Barthes, *Elements of Semiology,* p. 64. Eco, however, disputes the primacy of the verbal. "It is true that every content expressed by a verbal unit can be translated into another verbal unit; it is true that the greater part of the content expressed in non-verbal units can also be translated into verbal units; but it is likewise true that there are many contents expressed by complex non-verbal units which cannot be translated into one or more verbal units (other than by a very weak approximation) (Eco, *A Theory of Semiotics,* p. 173). I suspect that gestures can be much more readily translated into words than such other semiotic systems as music or painting. Interestingly enough, however, Eco supports his point by referring to Wittgenstein's realization of the inadequacy of words to convey the "meaning" of a "certain Neapolitan gesture" (p. 173). It is, of course, possible that Wittgenstein was simply being overly polite.

29. I am *not* arguing that the histrionic code is actually a digital "language." Clearly, the gestures of the histrionic code, unlike the basic elements of digital forms of communication, do not derive their meaning from their opposition to other elements within a series. Nonetheless, the resemblance of the histrionic code to such digital forms facilitates the development of the analytic model that I present here.

30. Fowle Adams, *Gesture and Pantomimic Action,* p. 43.

31. Smith, "The Melodrama," p. 321.

32. Boucicault made this remark in a lecture delivered July 29, 1882, which is included in his *Art of Acting,* p. 35.

33. Ibid., p. 33.

34. On opposition in natural language, see Barthes, *Elements of Semiology,* pp. 78–86.

35. Garcia, *The Actor's Art,* p. 51.

36. Boucicault, *Art of Acting,* p. 31 (brackets and emphasis in the original).

37. Garcia, *The Actor's Art,* p. 60.

38. Fredericks, *The Stage and Histrionic Education,* p. 1.

39. T. S. Eliot, "Gus the Theatre Cat," in Eliot, *Old Possum's Book of Practical Cats,* p. 42.

40. Todorov, *The Poetics of Prose,* p. 83.

41. Barthes, "The Realistic Effect," p. 134.

42. Fredric Jameson, *The Political Unconscious* (Ithaca: Cornell University Press, 1981), p. 82 (emphasis in original).

43. Heath, *The Nouveau Roman,* p. 20.

44. Charlton Andrews, "Stage Realism," *The New York Dramatic Mirror,* May 29, 1912, p. 5.

45. James, "The Real Thing," in *The Portable Henry James,* pp. 102–36.

46. James, "The Art of Fiction," in ibid., p. 397.

47. Williams, *The Long Revolution,* p. 48.

48. See Auerbach, *Mimesis,* for a discussion of various aspects of the emergence of literary realism.

49. The secondary sources on literary realism I have consulted include George J. Becker, "Modern Realism as a Literary Movement," in Becker, ed., *Documents of*

Literary Realism; Pizer, *Realism and Naturalism;* Kolb, *The Illusion of Life;* and D. A. Williams, *The Monster in the Mirror.*

For good discussions of the various meanings of realism see the entry in Raymond Williams, *Keywords,* and his "A Lecture on Realism."

50. W. D. Howells, "The Editor's Study," *Harper's Monthly* 72 (May 1886), p. 972.

51. James, "The Author of Beltraffio," in *Eight Tales From the Major Phase,* p. 60.

52. Ibid., p. 229.

53. James, "Art of Fiction," in *Portable Henry James,* p. 389.

54. Benson, "Realism in Fiction," p. 605.

55. Perry, *A Study in Prose Fiction,* pp. 222–23.

56. Barthes, "The Realistic Effect," p. 133.

57. Ibid., p. 134 (emphasis in original).

58. Howells, "The Editor's Study," p. 972.

59. James, "Art of Fiction," in *Portable Henry James,* p. 401 (emphasis in original).

60. I am distinguishing between dramatic and theatrical realism. *Dramatic* refers to the play text and *theatrical* refers to the production/performance. The two are not necessarily synonymous. A realist text could have a non-realist production, and, as was often the case with the melodrama, a non-realist text could have a realist production.

61. Walkley, *Drama and Life,* p. 36.

62. Calder, "What's Wrong with the American Stage?" p. 80.

63. Ibid., p. 81.

64. August Strindberg, "Naturalism in the Theatre," preface to 1888 edition of *Miss Julie,* in Becker, *Documents,* p. 398.

65. Calder, "What's Wrong," p. 80.

66. McArthur, *Actors and American Culture: 1880–1920,* p. 172.

67. Chaney, "The Failure of the American Producer," p. 6.

68. Ibid.

69. Andrews, "Stage Realism," p. 5.

70. West, "The London Stage," p. 33.

71. Albert Goldie, "Subtlety in Acting," *The New York Dramatic Mirror,* November 13, 1912, p. 4.

72. Downer, "Players and Painted Stage," p. 562.

73. Henry Irving, "The Art of Acting," in Cole and Chinoy, eds., *Actors on Acting,* pp. 358 and 359.

74. "Irving as Becket," *New York Daily Tribune,* November 9, 1893, reprinted in Young, *Famous Actors and Actresses of the American Stage,* p. 556.

75. Irving, "Art," in Cole and Chinoy, eds., *Actors on Acting,* p. 359.

76. Edward Gordon Craig, *Sir Henry Irving* (New York: Longmans, Green & Co., 1930), pp. 56–57.

77. André Antoine, *Le Théâtre Libre,* excerpted in Cole and Chinoy, eds., *Actors on Acting,* p. 214.

78. Ibid., pp. 213–14.

79. Tommaso Salvini, *Leaves from the Autobiography of Tommaso Salvini*, excerpted in Cole and Chinoy, ibid., p. 455.

80. Charlton Andrews, "The Decline of Acting," *The Theatre*, July 1913, p. 36.

81. William Gillette, "The Illusion of the First Time in Acting," in Matthews, ed., *Papers on Acting*, p. 131.

82. Mukarovsky, *Structure, Sign, and Function*, p. 52.

83. Roman Jakobson, "Realism in Art," in Matejka and Pomorska, *Readings in Russian Poetics*, p. 41.

84. Goldie, "Subtlety in Acting," p. 4.

85. Hammerton, *The Actor's Art*, pp. 48–49.

86. Gillette, "Illusions," in Matthews, *Papers*, p. 132.

87. Williams's characterization of Strindberg appears in *The Politics of Modernism: Against the New Conformists* (London: Verso, 1989), p. 65. For Strindberg's remarks, see Preface to *Miss Julie*, in *Pre-Inferno Plays*, translated by Walter Johnson (Seattle: University of Washington Press, 1970), p. 85.

88. Belasco, "Belasco Attacks Stage Tradition," p. 166.

3. The Histrionic and Verisimilar Codes in the Biograph Films

1. Bennett and Woollacott, *Bond and Beyond*, p. 65.

2. Tom Gunning also uses the term "gestural soliloquy" for this performance device in his dissertation, "D. W. Griffith and the Narrator System," and his book *D. W. Griffith and the Origins of American Narrative Film*.

3. Cross, *Next Week East Lynne*, p. 135.

4. On the use of props, see also Naremore, *Acting in the Cinema*, pp. 84–87.

5. Elam, *The Semiotics of Theatre and Drama*, pp. 72–75.

6. See Gunning, "D. W. Griffith and the Narrator System," p. 747; Bordwell, Thompson, and Staiger, *The Classical Hollywood Cinema*, pp. 189–91, and Staiger, "The Eyes Are Really the Focus," pp. 18–20. Chapter 7 of this book will look at trade press discourse on the verisimilar code, which also emphasizes the extreme importance of the face and eyes.

This footnote seems a good point to enumerate my disagreements with the Staiger article. I must first dispute Staiger's assertion that "the employment of theatre workers in filmmaking provides one of the strongest explanations for the appearance of a particular acting style" (p. 19). One cannot, when discussing this period, simply refer to the theatre. One must specify which theatre: the "first class" Broadway house; the popular-priced theatre largely given over to the melodrama; the resident stock companies; or the touring combinations sent out by the theatrical syndicates. Without further investigation, the fact that many film directors had theatrical backgrounds proves nothing. In which theatre, employing what performance style, did they work? Griffith's theatrical experiences, as I will show in a later chapter, exposed him mainly to the histrionic code, though he may, of course, have seen performances employing the verisimilar code.

Of course, Griffith's attitudes, and those of his colleagues, toward acting constitute another issue, but here again Staiger oversimplifies. In the period in question, the film industry's perceptions of the relation of film to theatrical acting underwent several shifts. In 1907–1908 some critics rejected theatrical acting as unsuitable by virtue of its "repose," presumably believing that the new style would fail to "get it across." In the next few years the film industry sought, as Staiger says, to emulate the "first class theatre" but also, as she omits to mention, to distance itself from the popular-priced theatre, where the histrionic code still reigned. By 1912 the film industry had developed a consensus as to what constituted appropriate film acting, convincing itself that it could not only outdo the popular-priced theatre but could surpass the verisimilar code as seen on the legitimate stage. It is true that "by 1912, companies were filming popular stage successes with current theatrical stars" (p. 19), but the reaction of the trade press was far from laudatory as suggested by a review of Nat Goodwin's Fagin in *Oliver Twist:* "The well defined action of the best motion picture actor is missing throughout" ("Nat Goodwin Disappointing," *The New York Dramatic Mirror,* June 5, 1912, p. 27). It should teach that if players of note are to enter film production it is necessary that they study to employ the art and technique of the picture, which at its best is decidedly removed from the stage.

7. Two methodological caveats, with which I did not wish to clutter the text, may be relevant here. The fact that most gesture is analogic rather than digital under normal circumstances prevents the analyst from segmenting gestural signification. The analyst armed with a Steenbeck flat-bed editing table can stop the flow of gesture at will. Although the technology enables us to note each small gesture, the reader should realize that this segmentation is an artificial process, and that one of the essential features of the verisimilar code is its analogical nature.

Although with the Steenbeck it becomes possible to annotate movement, assigning a specific meaning to each gesture or combination of gestures is much more difficult with the verisimilar than with the histrionic code, partly, of course, because the former is not predicated on a one-to-one correspondence between gesture and meaning. In the absence of a lexicon restricted by convention, gesture and especially a combination of gestures can take on an infinity of meaning, with the narrative context alone limiting the connotations. For this reason, the analyst's personal judgment becomes a greater factor with the verisimilar than the histrionic code. Suppose that an old man enters a shot, head bowed, shoulders sagging, arms hanging limply at sides. Does this signify defeat, despair, resignation, sadness, or simply momentary weariness? The problem becomes intensified with facial expression: two people can debate the meaning of a particular close-up for hours, as in the often-cited instance of Garbo's expression in the closing shot of *Queen Christina.* Even facial expression combined with posture can defeat attempts at quick and facile interpretations. Certainly no one would dare to impose a single, precise meaning on the final shot of *Vertigo* as Jimmy Stewart, having witnessed the second death of his beloved, teeters on the brink of oblivion.

8. Marsh, *Screen Acting,* p. 54.

9. Bowser, ed., *Biograph Bulletins,* p. 428.

10. Throughout the Biographs, actors use diectic gestures, leading me to include them in the histrionic code. However, I have no evidence that the diectic gesture was frequently employed in the theatrical histrionic code. Because theatrical performers could have used verbal shifters and might not have needed diectic gestures, it may be the case that the standardized and conventional use of diectic gestures originates with

silent film. If so, it would be inaccurate to label conversational gestures as either histrionic or verisimilar. However, between 1908 and 1913, while actors continued to point, their pointing movements became smaller, less emphasized, and more flowing.

11. The importance of the face and eyes to the verisimilar code may tempt one to conclude that the increasing closeness of the camera between 1908 and 1913 accounts for the transformation of performance style. The reverse could just as well be true, however: the new performance style may have brought about the closer camera, a possibility we will consider in Chapter 4.

12. Metz, *Language and Cinema*, p. 103. Some data about changes in signifying practices during Griffith's Biograph years, particularly those practices most often associated with performance, editing, and camera distance, may be helpful. In "D. W. Griffith and the Narrator System," Gunning tells us that the average number of shots per thousand feet of film was 16.6 in 1908 and 87.8 in 1913 (p. 761). As for scale, the long shot, with space above and below the characters' heads and feet, was standard in 1908. By 1910 the characters were framed at the ankle, and by 1911 characters were framed in three-quarter shot, which became the predominant scale of the classical Hollywood cinema. As Gunning points out, however, beginning in 1909 characters increasingly step forward to be framed between ankle and knee, so that camera distance does not remain a constant even in the earlier films.

Intertitles do not survive for many films. Because the earliest Biograph with intertitles at the Library of Congress is *A Change of Heart* (September 1909), there has been confusion about the presence of intertitles in the earlier Biographs, our knowledge of which derives primarily from the Paper Print Collection. Gunning has concluded that most, and probably all, of the Griffith Biographs originally had titles. We do know that dialogue titles became increasingly frequent, a factor bearing directly on the construction of character.

For further information about film style in this period see Bordwell, Staiger, and Thompson, *The Classical Hollywood Cinema*, pp. 155–240, and Barry Salt, "The Early Development of Film Form," in Fell, ed., *Film Before Griffith*, pp. 284–89.

4. Performance Style and the Interaction of Signifying Practices

1. Despite the slipperiness of the word *melodrama*, a provisional definition is in order here. I define *melodrama* as the nineteenth-century theatrical genre characterized by stock one-dimensional characters, verbal hyperbole, episodic narratives motivated by coincidence, heightened emotional situations, and spectacular staging. Because none of these criteria necessarily separates melodrama from comedy it is necessary to include other distinguishing characteristics. In comedy, the humor often depends on the spectators' perceived superiority to the protagonists, while melodrama encourages spectator identification. Pathos, from which much of the identification stems, is often missing from comedy. Working together, identification and pathos can engender an emotional catharsis for the spectator, especially as the dualistic moral structure of the plays, pitting pure good against pure evil, always ends in a "poetically just" resolution. These criteria, while in no sense definitive, can at least serve as a basis for judging how closely Biograph narratives adhere to what we shall for convenience

refer to as "pure melodrama." (I thank Robert Stam for helping me to refine this definition.)

2. Bordwell, Staiger, and Thompson, *The Classical Hollywood Cinema*, p. 13.

3. Ibid., p. 17.

4. Gerould, "Russian Formalist Theories of Melodrama," p. 160.

5. One might wish to take issue with Balukhatyi's assertion that melodramatic characters interested the spectator solely because of their importance to the plot. Evidence suggests that melodrama audiences certainly responded passionately to the characters, cheering the hero and hissing the villain. We should not, however, be so condescending as to think these reactions totally naive: there may well have been an element of self-conscious awareness in the audience's participation. Douglas Reid, in a study of the popular theatre in Victorian Birmingham, writes: "the simple-minded proletarian audience stereotype understates, indeed ignores the common sense of the common people. . . . There is a hidden assumption . . . that because many melodramas . . . were *written* as though their audiences were simpletons, therefore they all were simpletons" (Reid, "Popular Theatre in Victorian Birmingham," in Bradby, James, and Sharratt, *Performance and Politics in Popular Drama*, p. 80; emphasis in original).

6. Culler, *Structuralist Poetics*, p. 230.

7. Todorov, *The Poetics of Prose*, p. 66.

8. Ibid., p. 68.

9. Chatman, *Story and Discourse*, p. 114.

10. Quoted in James L. Smith, *Melodrama*, p. 7.

11. Ibid., p. 8.

12. Barthes, *Elements of Semiology*, p. 64, and *The Fashion System*, p. xi.

13. Bordwell, Staiger, and Thompson, *The Classical Hollywood Cinema*, p. 15.

14. Barthes, *The Fashion System*, p. 13. I suspect that Barthes, were he alive today, would wish to reconsider the claim that "words determine a single certainty" in light of recent assertions of verbal and textual indeterminacy. But for the sake of argument, we might perhaps agree that, in any society at any particular moment, gestures are *relatively more* polysemic than words.

15. Hanford C. Judson, "What Gets Over," *The Moving Picture World*, April 15, 1911, p. 816.

16. Frank Woods, "Spectator's Comments," *New York Dramatic Mirror*, November 13, 1909, p. 15.

17. The Kuleshov experiment, the probably apocryphal staple of Film 101 courses, involves Lev Kuleshov, one of the most important directors of the Soviet silent cinema, who was said to have intercut the expressionless face of actor Mozhukhin with various objects, such as a coffin, food, and a child. Audiences reportedly remarked on Mozhukhin's subtlety of response, suggesting the effectiveness of film editing for closing off possibilities of meaning.

18. David Alan Black, "Genette and Film: Narrative Level in the Fiction Cinema," *Wide Angle* 8:3 and 8:4 (Fall 1986), p. 20.

19. Ibid., p. 22.

20. A hypothetical example of the intrinsic narrator's ceding of authority through the employment of character-centered signifiers may aid clarification. A film begins

with a long shot of an anonymous prisoner sitting on a bunk looking sad. Suppose that a camera movement shows the posters of Marx and Lenin adorning the cell walls. Then suppose that the character picks up a snapshot. Now presume a cut to a close-up, followed by a cut to a picture of two small children, followed by a reaction shot of the prisoner crying.

In this hypothetical scene, signifiers from four signifying practices—performance, mise-en-scène, camera work, and editing—convey narrative information. The long shot of the prisoner reveals little about the character's mental processes except the general affect of sadness. The camera's move to the political posters reveals her political predispositions. The prisoner's handling of the prop in conjunction with her point-of-view shot and her crying give insights into the character's emotions at that particular moment.

21. Bowser, ed., *Biograph Bulletins*, p. 156.

22. Ibid., p. 134.

23. Gunning discusses *After Many Years* in terms of the narrator system; see "D. W. Griffith and the Narrator System," pp. 172–81).

24. Bowser, ed., *Biograph Bulletins*, p. 33.

25. Linda Arvidson's account of Griffith's dispute with the front office over "the first picture to have a dramatic close-up" (Linda Arvidson, *When the Movies Were Young*, p. 66) has led people to believe that the shot of Annie is a close-up in the modern sense, that is, a shot of her head and face, or what in 1908 would have been termed a bust shot. The shot is, in modern terms, a medium close-up.

As for the intercutting between Annie and Enoch, the idea was not entirely original with Griffith. An 1869 production of *Enoch Arden* had included, in a separate scene, "The Vision of Enoch in the Tropical Land," while twenty years later, the actor-manager Newton Beers produced a seven-act, sixteen-scene version complete with special scenery and revolving stage, which approximated cross-cutting. Wendy Dozoretz, "Toward an Understanding of Griffith's Growth as a Film Director: A Comparison between *After Many Years* and *Enoch Arden*," manuscript, November 1976).

26. David Bordwell discusses the cross-cutting between Annie and Enoch in terms of the transitional cinema's not having standardized the eyeline-match cut. See his "Textual Analysis, Etc.," *Enclitic* (Fall 1981/Spring 1982), p. 128.

5. D. W. Griffith and the Biograph Company

1. Crofts, "Authorship and Hollywood," p. 17.

2. Ibid.

3. Griffith, "Pictures vs. One-Night Stands," p. 447.

4. Letter from Marshall Neilan to Barnett Braverman, April 19, 1944, in the Barnett Braverman Research Collection of the David W. Griffith Papers at the Museum of Modern Art (henceforth, Braverman-DWG Papers). Braverman was a journalist who devoted many years of his life to researching a never-completed biography of Griffith. His notes, deposited in the Griffith collection at the Museum of Modern Art, contain many letters from and interviews with those associated with Griffith during the Biograph years. The notes are disorganized, making accurate attribution of quotes diffi-

cult. In addition, it is hard to be sure whether Braverman is quoting verbatim or paraphrasing, and whether the quotations are from interview notes or written correspondence. I have nonetheless relied heavily on Braverman's notes, since they constitute much of the surviving evidence about Griffith at Biograph.

5. Merritt, "Rescued from a Perilous Nest," pp. 2–30. George Pratt contributed to a chronology of Griffith's career, which appears as an appendix.

6. Ibid., p. 3.

7. *Boston Transcript,* May 8, 1906, in the Nance O'Neil Clipping File, New York Public Library for the Performing Arts at Lincoln Center (henceforth, O'Neil-NYPLPA).

8. *Boston Transcript,* 1904, O'Neil-NYPLPA.

9. Review of *Magda,* an English translation of the German playwright Hermann Suderman's *Heimat. Evening Sun,* May 23, 1904, in O'Neil-NYPLPA.

10. *San Francisco Bulletin,* September 20, 1898, in O'Neil-NYPLPA.

11. Goddard, "Some Players I Have Known," p. 238.

12. *Boston Transcript,* May 8, 1906, in O'Neil-NYPLPA.

13. David W. Griffith, "A Fool and a Girl," playscript in DWG Papers.

14. Publicity stills from "A Fool and a Girl," NYPLPA.

15. Griffith may not, however, have employed precisely the same style in film as he did on the stage, especially since he always seems to have made a clear distinction between the two media.

16. Graham, et al., *D. W. Griffith and the Biograph Company,* pp. 13–20.

17. Interview with Eddie Dillon, Braverman-DWG Papers.

18. Billy Bitzer, unpublished memoirs, in the DWG papers (henceforth, Bitzer-DWG Papers). A condensed version was eventually published as *Billy Bitzer: His Story.* Higgins, et al., list no film in which Griffith appeared as a bartender, providing us with another salutary warning about the accuracy of memoirs written decades after the event.

19. Bitzer, *His Story,* p. 69.

20. Bordwell, Staiger, and Thompson, *The Classical Hollywood Cinema,* pp. 116–21.

21. Gunning, "D. W. Griffith and the Narrator System," pp. 93, 95.

22. Graham, et al., *D. W. Griffith and the Biograph Company,* pp. 1–2.

23. Charles Musser, "Early Cinema and Its Modes of Production," paper presented at conference of the Society for Cinema Studies, Iowa City, Iowa, 1989, p. 3.

24. Ibid., p. 7.

25. Ibid., p. 8.

26. Ibid., pp. 10–11.

27. Lawrence, "Growing Up with the Movies," p. 96.

28. Henderson, *David W. Griffith: The Years at Biograph,* p. 34.

29. Linda Arvidson, *When the Movies Were Young,* pp. 108–9.

30. Gish, *The Movies, Mr. Griffith, and Me,* pp. 35–37.

31. Arvidson, *When the Movies Were Young,* pp. 66–67.

32. Interview with Stanner E. V. Taylor, Braverman-DWG Papers.

33. Frederick Jones Smith, "The Evolution of the Motion Picture: From the Stand-

point of the Scenario Editor,'' *The New York Dramatic Mirror* (henceforth, *NYDM*), January 4, 1913, p. 25.

34. Arvidson, *When the Movies Were Young*, p. 218. Griffith married Linda Arvidson, an actress, before he began working at Biograph; she joined the Biograph troupe shortly after he did, before he had become a director. Reportedly, Griffith initially told her not to reveal their marriage, and she continued to use her birth name for professional purposes. They separated in 1911 and were formally divorced in 1936.

35. Pickford, *Sunshine and Shadow*, p. 119.

36. Stanner E. V. Taylor interview, Braverman-DWG papers.

37. Patrick Loughney, untitled presentation, University Interdisciplinary Seminar on Cinema and Interdisciplinary Interpretation in Columbia University, The Museum of Modern Art, May 12, 1982.

38. Patrick G. Loughney, ''In The Beginning Was the Word: Six Pre-Griffith Motion Picture Scenarios,'' *Iris* 2:1 (1984), p. 18.

39. Gunning, ''D. W. Griffith and the Narrator System,'' p. 631.

40. Tom Gunning agrees with this analysis and indicates that Jay Leyda had reached the same conclusion. Gunning, private communication.

41. Frank J. Marion and Wallace McCutcheon, *The Nihilists* (shot February 28, 1905), photocopy in possession of Patrick Loughney.

42. Edward W. Townsend, ''Picture Plays,'' *The Outlook,* November 27, 1909, p. 706.

43. J. Sidney McSween, ''Players of the Film Drama,'' *The Theatre,* October 1912, p. 113.

44. Townsend, ''Picture Plays,'' p. 706.

45. Epes Winthrop Sergent, ''The Technique of the Photoplay,'' *The Moving Picture World,* July 22, 1911, p. 108.

46. Arvidson, *When the Movies Were Young,* p. 31.

47. Ibid., pp. 92–93.

48. Gish, *The Movies, Mr. Griffith, and Me,* p. 85.

49. Interview with Edwin August, Braverman-DWG Papers.

50. Interview with Lionel Barrymore, Braverman-DWG Papers.

51. In Bitzer-DWG Papers.

52. In a private communication, James Naremore has pointed out that Griffith's rehearsal methods bear a resemblance to Stanislavski's. But because Stanislavski, according to Naremore, was ''not conscientiously studied in America until the late twenties'' (Naremore, *Acting in the Cinema,* p. 52), there is no question of direct influence. Speculation about such parallel but unrelated developments, which requires greater knowledge of the Russian theatre than I possess, would be a fascinating research project for someone familiar with both Griffith and Stanislavski.

53. In Bitzer-DWG Papers.

54. Lawrence, ''Growing Up with the Movies,'' p. 107.

55. Pickford, *Sunshine and Shadow,* pp. 114–15.

56. Frank Woods, ''Spectator's Comments,'' *NYDM,* June 4, 1910, p. 12.

57. Interview with Mary Pickford, ''Daily Talks,'' *Philadelphia Telegraph,* June 6, 1912, in Mary Pickford Clipping Files-NYPLPA.

58. Arvidson, *When the Movies Were Young,* p. 92.

59. Ibid.

60. Pickford, *Sunshine and Shadow*, pp. 143–44.

61. Edwin August interview, in Braverman-DWG Papers.

62. Karl Brown, *Adventures with David W. Griffith*, pp. 27–28.

63. Gish, *The Movies, Mr. Griffith, and Me*, p. 85.

64. Letter from Mary Pickford to Barnett Braverman, June 18, 1943, Braverman-DWG Papers.

65. Marsh, *Screen Acting*, p. 115.

66. Interview with Claire McDowell, Braverman-DWG Papers.

67. Gish, *The Movies, Mr. Griffith, and Me*, pp. 95–96.

68. Interview with Blanche Sweet, in Rosenberg and Silverstein, eds., *The Real Tinsel*, p. 195.

69. Ibid.

70. Letter from Dorothy Bernard Van Buren to Barnett Braverman, October 10, 1944, in Braverman-DWG Papers.

71. Barrymore interview, in Braverman-DWG Papers.

72. Gish, *The Movies, Mr. Griffith, and Me*, p. 85.

73. Bitzer, *His Story*, p. 75.

74. Gish, *The Movies, Mr. Griffith, and Me*, p. 37.

75. Arvidson, *When the Movies Were Young*, p. 217.

76. McDowell interview, in Braverman-DWG Papers.

77. Loos, *A Girl Like I*, p. 80. I must remark that, having had the pleasure of seeing Blanche Sweet both on film and in person, I find it hard to imagine her being anyone's "passive instrument," even at the age of sixteen.

78. Interview with Christy Cabanne, Braverman-DWG Papers.

79. Mary Pickford to Samuel Goldwyn, *Pictorial Review*, March 1923, p. 7, quoted in Braverman-DWG papers.

80. Interview with Mae Marsh, in Rosenberg and Silverstein, *The Real Tinsel*, p. 211.

81. Colgate Baker, "David W. Griffith."

82. McDowell interview in Braverman-DWG Papers.

83. Henderson, *David W. Griffith*, pp. 73–74.

84. Interview with Lillian Gish, *Reel I* (Winter 1971), p. 10.

85. Marsh, *Screen Acting*, p. 117.

86. Brown, *Adventures with Griffith*, p. 15.

87. Gish interview, *Reel I*, p. 10.

88. Gish, *The Movies, Mr. Griffith, and Me*, p. 87.

89. Blanche Sweet, personal conversation, April 12, 1983.

90. Gish, *The Movies, Mr. Griffith, and Me*, p. 97.

91. Pickford, *Sunshine and Shadow*, pp. 124–25.

92. Interview with Raoul Walsh, Braverman-DWG Papers.

93. Linda Arvidson claims that the film was called *The Dispatch Bearer* (*When the Movies Were Young*, pp. 58–59). The Vitagraph filmography in *The Vitagraph Company of America: Il Cinema prima di Hollywood* (Pordenone, Italy: Edizioni Studio Tesi, 1987) lists no film of that name made in 1908.

94. Lawrence, "Growing Up with the Movies," p. 99.

95. Gish, *The Movies, Mr. Griffith, and Me*, pp. 100–101.

96. Colgate Baker, "David W. Griffith."

97. Griffith, "What I Demand of Movie Stars," p. 40.

98. Ibid.

99. Gish, *The Movies, Mr. Griffith, and Me,* p. 87.

100. Interview with Mae Marsh, in Braverman-DWG Papers.

101. Gish, *The Movies, Mr. Griffith, and Me,* p. 97.

102. Edward Martin Woolley, "The Story of David W. Griffith: The $100,000 Salary Man of the Movies," *McClure's,* September 1914, DWG Clipping Files– NYPLPA.

103. Marsh, *Screen Acting,* p. 108.

104. Gish, *The Movies, Mr. Griffith, and Me,* p. 97.

105. Brown, *Adventures with Griffith,* pp. 115–20.

106. Griffith, "Movie Stars," p. 40.

107. Griffith, "What I Demand of Photoplay Stars," p. 6.

108. Welsh, "David W. Griffith Speaks," p. 49.

109. Bitzer here is simply repeating a widespread, yet unfounded, myth that Richard deCordova disputes: "Almost all of the early actors came from provincial stock companies, not Broadway. Few had much of a reputation to lose" (deCordova, "The Emergence of the Star System in America: An Examination of the Institutional and Ideological Function of the Star" [diss.], p. 155). Certainly Biograph boasted no major theatrical actors among its company when Griffith arrived, and, unlike Edison and Vitagraph, it never did employ stage stars during Griffith's tenure.

110. Bitzer-DWG Papers.

111. Bitzer, *His Story,* p. 70.

112. J. Stuart Blackton, "Hollywood With Its Hair Down or Hollywood Memories: Forty Years of Movies," manuscript in the Margaret Herrick Library, Academy of Motion Picture Arts and Sciences, p. 112. The nine-foot line did not at all approximate the modern close-up, framing the actors instead from the ankles to the top of the head.

113. Russell Merritt offers a more psycho-sexual analysis of Griffith's rejection of the theatre. See his "Rescued from a Perilous Nest."

114. Welsh, "Griffith Speaks," p. 49.

115. "A Poet Who Writes on Motion Picture Films," *The Theatre,* June 1914, p. 312.

116. Baker, "David W. Griffith."

117. Welsh, "Griffith Speaks," p. 49.

118. Biograph's financial records for this period have not survived, but Charles Musser argues that "Biograph had been in a period of protracted crisis when Griffith took over. Although not all historians might agree, I believe that his accomplished output in 1908 did much to rescue Biograph from commercial disaster." "Early Cinema and Its Modes of Production," paper presented at conference of the Society for Cinema Studies, Iowa City, Iowa, 1989, p. 10.

6. Henry B. Walthall

1. Most of Biograph's male actors sank into a post-Griffith obscurity, making it difficult to find information about them. Others, including Bobby Harron and Arthur Johnson, died young, leaving little in the record.

2. George Blaisdell, "At the Sign of the Flaming Arcs," *The Moving Picture World,* January 10, 1914, p. 175.

3. Owen, "The Little Colonel," pp. 27, 30.

4. Interview with Edwin August, in the Barnett Braverman Research Collection, David W. Griffith Papers, the Museum of Modern Art.

5. Blanche Sweet interview, in Rosenberg and Silverstein, eds., *The Real Tinsel,* p. 197.

6. Arvidson, *When the Movies Were Young,* p. 102.

7. Bitzer, *His Story,* p. 72.

8. Blaisdell, "Sign of the Flaming Arcs," p. 175.

9. *Moving Picture World,* September 16, 1911, p. 790.

10. "Bennie Chats With the Players," p. 114.

11. Cohn, "The Reformation of Wally," p. 31.

12. "Letters and Questions Answered by the Spectator," *New York Dramatic Mirror,* August 16, 1911, p. 21.

13. Ibid., June 26, 1911, p. 28.

14. Gish, *The Movies, Mr. Griffith, and Me,* p. 150.

15. D. W. Griffith to *The Los Angeles Times,* quoted in Slide, *The Idols of Silence,* p. 63.

16. Gish, *The Movies, Mr. Griffith, and Me,* p. 286.

17. Myrtle Gebhardt, "The Unknown Quantity," *Picture Play,* July 1926, in *The Scarlet Letter* Clipping File, NYPLPA.

18. Donnell, "I Remember When," p. 40.

19. "Henry B. Walthall: A Gentleman of Hollywood," p. 26.

20. Gebhardt, "Unknown Quantity."

21. Kalton C. Lahue, *Gentlemen to the Rescue: The Heroes of the Silent Screen* (New York: Castle Books, 1972), pp. 223–24.

22. Joe Franklin, *Classics of the Silent Screen: A Pictorial Treasury* (Secaucus, N.J.: Citadel, 1959), p. 240.

23. Bitzer-DWG Papers.

24. Gebhardt, "Unknown Quantity."

25. Slide, *The Idols of Silence,* p. 59.

26. Bitzer, in DWG Papers.

27. I am aware that the concept of genre remains a vexed one among film scholars, and I am not prepared, in this chapter, to offer a fully elaborated theorization of Biograph genres. Generally, however, the costume melodrama resembles the nonpsychological narrative of external motivation and unmediated causality. As we have seen, the contemporary melodrama ranges along the continuum from psychological to nonpsychological.

28. Roland Barthes, "Rhetoric and the Image," in Barthes, *Image, Music, Text,* p. 53.

7. Trade Press Discourse

1. Bordwell, Staiger, and Thompson, *The Classical Hollywood Cinema,* p. 194.

2. Frank Woods, Spectator of the *New York Dramatic Mirror* and foremost champion of the verisimilar code, often received correspondence from industry readers sup-

porting or contesting his positions. Sometimes the opinions expressed in his columns directly influenced filmmakers' decisions, as suggested by the following anecdote: Woods told of a company filming a scene in which a son, having been reunited with his mother after a long absence, goes upstairs to bed, turning to look at his mother once before exiting. A dispute arose. "One party contended that the turn to the front at the exit should be eliminated, citing the Spectator as proof. The other party held that the turn toward the mother was, in this instance, the most natural thing . . . citing the Spectator's views on the naturalistic" (Frank Woods, "Spectator's Comments," *The New York Dramatic Mirror,* March 22, 1911, p. 28; henceforth, citations to Woods's columns in the *NYDM* will be identified as Spectator).

3. As I have discovered in my work on the Vitagraph Company (see Uricchio and Pearson, *Cultural Crisis, Cultural Cure?*) the trade press often simply reprinted, with only slight variation, studio publicity. Hence, one should not view the trade press as a completely separate and dissenting voice. The congruences between industry and trade press discourse and among the various journals themselves account for my reliance on *The Moving Picture World* and *The New York Dramatic Mirror.* Although other journals existed (*The Nickelodeon, The Views and Film Index,* and *Show World* among them), my research has revealed no significant dissenting views. Moreover, *The Moving Picture World* and *The New York Dramatic Mirror* (henceforth, *MPW* and *NYDM*) were undoubtedly the most prominent and influential of the journals.

Also, given the disjunction between the written descriptions in film reviews and the film texts themselves, one would not use the trade press alone to trace the emergence of the verisimilar code. As we shall see later in the chapter, the press had reason to valorize the verisimilar code even before it became dominant. While reviewers may have used such terms as "natural" or "true to life," they rarely detailed the expressions and gestures that led them so to characterize the performance. Even when the reviews do contain hints of description, asserting that the actor exercised restraint or that the facial expression was marvelously clear, we are certainly not dealing with absolutes but with the entire range from the histrionic to the verisimilar. For example, restraint could mean that the performers used the checked rather than the unchecked histrionic code, not that they used the verisimilar. The debate on acting (mostly one-sided) taking place in the editorials and regular columns of the trade press is more valuable than the reviews, although unclear terminology and inadequate description still remain a problem.

An example may help to illustrate this point. The performers in *The Maniac Cook,* released January 4, 1909, rely almost exclusively on the histrionic code, often in its unchecked form. Yet the *MPW* said of the film, "All of the motions are correct and natural, perhaps too realistic, as when the cook arranges the legs of the child and takes the knife to cut them. . . . It is no mere moving picture on a screen but the real art of the actor as displayed on our best stages" ("Comments on Film Subjects," January 9, 1909, p. 10).

4. *MPW,* July 13, 1907, p. 298.

5. "How Moving Pictures Are Made: A Chicago Newspaperman Gets a Peek Inside the Selig Studios," *MPW,* May 14, 1908, p. 434.

6. "The Moving Picture Field," *NYDM,* June 20, 1908, p. 6.

7. "Comments on Film Subjects," *MPW,* January 16, 1909, p. 69.

8. F. Oppenheimer, "The Moving Picture," *The Theatre*, January, 1909, p. 14.

9. Valentine Karly, "Drama by the Foot," *The Saturday Post* (Philadelphia), quoted in Spectator, May 29, 1909, p. 15.

10. Spectator, October 21, 1909, p. 32.

11. Ibid., June 4, 1910, p. 16. As we saw in Chapter 5, Griffith at first insisted on the histrionic code in the belief that exchanges and exhibitors demanded it. Woods's statement lends credence to his position.

12. "Rules for Moving Picture Actors," *NYDM*, November 14, 1908, p. 11.

13. Spectator, July 10, 1909, p. 15.

14. *MPW*, June 4, 1908, p. 5.

15. Rollin Summers, "The Moving Picture Drama and the Acted Drama," *MPW*, September 17, 1908, p. 213.

16. "The Pointer," *MPW*, September 17, 1910, p. 621.

17. C. H. Claudy, "Too Much Acting," *MPW*, February 11, 1911, p. 54.

18. "Views of the Reviewer," *NYDM*, June 19, 1912, p. 27.

19. Louis Reeves Harrison, "Dumb Eloquence," *MPW*, January 11, 1913, p. 133.

20. Spectator, March 27, 1912, p. 24.

21. "Earmarks of Makers," *NYDM*, November 14, 1908, p. 10.

22. Spectator, September 11, 1909, p. 14.

23. Ibid., May 7, 1910, p. 18.

24. Reviews of Licensed Films, *NYDM*, May 14, 1910, p. 20.

25. Spectator, May 28, 1910, p. 20.

26. Summers, "The Moving Picture Drama and the Acted Drama."

27. Louis Reeves Harrison, "The Eloquence of Gesture," *MPW*, November 4, 1911, p. 357. This quotation clearly reveals the culture-bound nature of verisimilitude: restraint has different meanings in different cultures. To this American writer, simplicity of gesture and restraint signify reality because of his conviction that this is the way Americans "naturally" behave. One infers that an actor portraying a Frenchman sans excessive gesticulation could be condemned as "unrealistic." Paradoxically, by 1911, an actor playing an American had to use the verisimilar code to be thought "natural," while an actor playing one of the "Latin races" probably had to use the histrionic.

28. Epes Winthrop Sergent, "Technique of the Photoplay," *MPW*, August 26, 1911, pp. 525–26.

29. C. H. Claudy, "The Pictures from the Public Viewpoint," *MPW*, March 23, 1912, p. 1050.

30. Bannister Merwin, "The Future of the Photoplay," *MPW*, June 1, 1912, p. 805.

31. In the long-shot tableau style, however, facial expression can be discerned in a good-quality 35mm print, even in the absence of editing. The poor-quality 16mm prints, however, to which early film scholars are so accustomed, make the discernment of facial expression particularly difficult. Moreover, a lifetime's viewing has trained me to associate the importance of facial expression with closer shots. Viewers in 1908, not accustomed to a closer camera, may well have watched facial expression even in the long shot.

32. Summers, "The Moving Picture Drama and the Acted Drama," p. 213.

33. Reviews of New Films, *NYDM*, March 13, 1909, p. 16.

34. *MPW,* May 1, 1909, p. 56.

35. Ibid., May 8, 1909, p. 72.

36. Carl Anderson, "A Biograph Appreciation," *MPW,* July 31, 1909, p. 165.

37. Louis Reeves Harrison, "Eyes and Lips," *MPW,* February 18, 1911, p. 348.

38. Agnew, *Moving Picture Acting,* p. 40.

39. "D," "Hackett on the Screen," *NYDM,* February 26, 1913, p. 28.

40. E. H. Southern, "The 'New Art' as Discovered by E. H. Southern," *The Craftsman,* September 1916, p. 579.

41. Spectator, April 21, 1909, p. 22.

42. Lux Graphicus, "On the Screen," *MPW,* July 3, 1909, p. 11.

43. "Notable Films of the Week," *MPW,* April 24, 1909, p. 515.

44. Claudy, "Too Much Acting."

45. Louis Reeves Harrison, "What is Dramatic?" *MPW,* August 3, 1912, p. 421.

46. Spectator, January 25, 1911, p. 29.

47. Michael Davis, *The Exploitation of Pleasure* (New York: Russell Sage Foundation, 1911), p. 4.

48. On the subject of cheap amusements, see Lewis Erenberg, *Steppin' Out: New York Night Life and the Transformation of American Culture, 1890–1930* (Westport, Conn.: Greenwood, 1981); John Kasson, *Amusing the Million: Coney Island at the Turn of the Century* (New York: Hill and Wang, 1978); Kathy Peiss, *Cheap Amusements: Working Women and Leisure in Turn-of-the-Century New York* (Philadelphia: Temple University Press, 1986); Roy Rosenzweig, *Eight Hours for What We Will: Workers and Leisure in an Industrial City, 1870–1920* (New York: Cambridge University Press, 1983); and Robert Sklar, *Movie-Made America: A Cultural History of American Movies* (New York: Vintage, 1975). Between 1908 and 1914, there were at least fourteen studies of the problem of leisure in several major urban centers; see Alan Havig, "The Commercial Amusement Audience in Early 20th-Century American Cities," *Journal of American Culture* 5 (Spring 1982), pp. 1–19).

49. Some scholars have disputed the view that immigrants and the working classes formed the majority of the nickelodeons' audiences. On this point, see Russell Merritt, "Nickelodeon Theaters, 1905–1914: Building an Audience for the Movies," in T. Balio, ed., *The American Film Industry* (Madison: University of Wisconsin Press, 1976), pp. 83–102; Robert Allen, "Motion Picture Exhibition in Manhattan, 1906–1912: Beyond the Nickelodeon," in Fell, ed., *Film Before Griffith.* For a response, see Robert Sklar, "Oh! Althusser!: Historiography and the Rise of Cinema Studies," *Radical History Review* 41 (Spring 1988), pp. 10–35.

50. The Reverend Fellowes Jenkins of the Society for the Prevention of Cruelty to Children, quoted in "Mayor Hears Evidence," *The New York Daily Tribune,* December 26, 1908.

51. For detailed accounts of the Motion Picture Patents Company see Gunning, "Griffith and the Narrator System," and Robert Anderson, "The Motion Picture Patents Company" (Diss., University of Wisconsin, 1983).

52. Motion Picture Patents Company, "Announcement to Exhibitors," February 1, 1909, quoted in Gunning, "Griffith and the Narrator System," p. 452.

53. Motion Picture Patents Company, "Advertisement," quoted in Gunning, ibid., p. 447.

54. Nancy J. Rosenbloom, "Between Reform and Regulation: The Struggle Over Film Censorship in Progressive America, 1909–1922," *Film History* 1 (1987), p. 309. See also Daniel Czitrom, "The Redemption of Leisure: The National Board of Censorship and the Rise of Motion Pictures in New York City, 1900–1920," *Studies in Visual Communication* 10:4 (Fall 1984), pp. 2–6.

55. For a history of the People's Institute see Robert Bruce Fisher, "The People's Institute of New York City, 1897–1934: Culture, Progressive Democracy, and the People" (Diss., New York University, 1974).

56. Letter from Charles Sprague Smith to Andrew Carnegie, May 28, 1904, in Box 3, People's Institute Records, Rare Books and Manuscripts Department, New York Public Library (henceforth, Institute Records).

57. "A People's Theatre," n.d., in ibid.

58. Davis, *The Exploitation of Pleasure*, p. 5.

59. Charles Sprague Smith, *Tenth Annual Report of the People's Institute*, in Box 3, Institute Records.

60. W. Stephen Bush, "The Film of the Future," *MPW*, September 5, 1908, p. 172.

61. "Elbert Hubbard on the Moving Pictures," *MPW*, January 10, 1910, p. 10. Reprinted from *The New York American*. Hubbard wrote the popular series "Little Journeys to the Homes of the Great," edited three journals, and gave public lectures. See Freeman Champney, *Art and Glory: The Story of Elbert Hubbard* (Kent, Ohio: Kent State University Press, 1968). Hubbard was so enamored of film that he declared himself a "moving picture fiend" (quoted in General Film Company, *Education and Entertainment in Motion Pictures: Catalogue*, New York, n.d.).

62. Bush, "The Film of the Future," pp. 172–73.

63. Lucy France Pierce, "The Nickelodeon," *The Nickelodeon*, January 1909, p. 8.

64. *Views and Film Index*, March 14, 1908, p.3.

65. Otto Peltzer, *The Moralist and the Theatre* (Chicago: Donald Fraser and Sons, 1887), p. 16.

66. Smith, "The Melodrama," p. 320.

67. Davis, *The Exploitation of Pleasure*, p. 22.

68. Ibid., p. 28.

69. Louise Bolard More, *Wage-Earners' Budgets: A Study of Standards and Cost of Living in New York City* (New York: Henry Holt and Co., 1907), p. 6.

70. Of course, not all wage-earners attended only the vaudeville theatres. There is evidence, for example, that a good many poorer New Yorkers had access to Shakespearean productions. See Pearson and Uricchio, "How many times shall Caesar bleed in sport: Shakespeare and the cultural debate about moving pictures," 243–61. Uricchio and Pearson, *Cultural Crisis, Cultural Cure?* provides detailed discussion of theatrical attendance patterns in New York City.

71. Davis, *The Exploitation of Pleasure*, p. 30. The high-priced theatres did have 50-cent and even 25-cent seats in the gallery for matinee performances, and period discourse about the patrons in this section suggests that they belonged to what the Russell Sage survey would have characterized as the "clerical" and "working" classes.

72. John Collier, "Cheap Amusements," *Charities and the Commons* 20 (April 11, 1908), p. 74.

73. "An Absorbing Problem," *NYDM*, April 25, 1908, p. 3.

74. Roy L. McCardell, "The Chorus-Girl Deplores the Moving Picture Triumph Over the Drama," *MPW*, April 11, 1908.

75. "Good and Bad Melodrama," *NYDM*, May 9, 1908, p. 2. For the rest of the *NYDM*'s 1908 series on this subject, see: "What is the Cause: A Great Falling Off of Patronage in the Popular Price Theatres," April 18, p. 5; "The Popular Price Theatre," May 16, p. 4; "The Melodrama Theatre: The Discussion as to Its Decline in Popularity and Its Needs Continued," June 6, p.4; and "Popular Price Drama Waning," November 28, p. 4.

76. "Harvard Professor Praises Pictures," *The Edison Kinetogram*, June 15, 1911, p. 15.

77. W. Stephen Bush, "Signs of a Harvest," *MPW*, August 5, 1911, p. 272.

78. "The Film Maker's Responsibilities," *MPW*, August 5, 1911, p. 271.

79. H. F. Hoffmann, "What People Want: Some Observations," *MPW*, July 9, 1910.

80. *MPW*, April 3, 1909, p. 399.

81. "Censorship of Films," *NYDM*, April 3, 1909, p. 13. Richard Mansfield was a leading actor-manager.

82. deCordova, "The Emergence of the Star System in America: An Examination of the Institutional and Ideological Function of the Star" (Diss.), pp. 104–8.

83. Ibid., p. 176.

84. "Room for Improvement," *NYDM*, August 22, 1908, p. 9.

85. Bordwell, Staiger, and Thompson, *The Classical Hollywood Cinema*, pp. 163–66.

86. Editorial, *NYDM*, January 4, 1911, p. 3.

87. George Blaisdell, "At the Sign of the Flaming Arcs," *MPW*, January 4, 1913.

88. Robert Grau, "The Moving Picture Show and the Living Drama," *The American Monthly Review of Reviews*, March 1912, p. 329.

89. McLaughlin, *Broadway and Hollywood*, p. 2. Because touring companies had previously enabled even Broadway failures to make a profit, the decline of these companies put the profit-making burden on the Broadway show, affecting, McLaughlin argues, the kinds of productions staged.

90. "Observations by Our Man About Town," *MPW*, April 27, 1912, p. 323.

91. C. H. Claudy, "The Educational Photo Play," *MPW*, June 10, 1911, p. 1300.

92. Spectator, October 2, 1909, p. 32.

93. Ibid., May 31, 1911, p. 28.

94. Summers, "The Moving Picture Drama and the Acted Drama," September 19, 1908.

95. "Notable Films of the Week," *MPW*, April 24, 1909, p. 515.

96. Lux Graphicus, "On the Screen," *MPW*, July 3, 1909, p. 11.

97. Hans Leigh, "Acting and Actors," *MPW*, October 2, 1909, p. 443.

98. Spectator, October 2, 1909, p. 32.

99. Ibid., August 21, 1909, p. 22.

100. Ibid., May 22, 1909, p. 16.
101. Ibid., June 19, 1909, p. 16.

8. Conclusion

1. Bowser, ed., *Biograph Bulletins,* p. 77.
2. Heath, *The Nouveau Roman,* p. 20.
3. Belsey, *Critical Practice,* p. 51.
4. On the term *realism,* see Raymond Williams, "Keywords," p. 216. For the historical context of "realistic" representation, see Raymond Williams, "A Lecture on Realism," and his *Problems in Materialism and Culture,* particularly the essay "Social Environment and Theatrical Environment," pp. 125–47.

Bibliography

Affron, Charles. *Star Acting*. New York: E. P. Dutton, 1977.

Agnew, Frances. *Moving Picture Acting*. New York: Reliance Newspaper Syndicate, 1911.

Allen, Robert C. "Looking at 'Another Look at the Chaser Theory,' " *Studies in Visual Communication* 10:4 (Fall 1984).

———. *Vaudeville and Film, 1895–1915: A Study in Media Interaction*. New York: Arno, 1980.

Arvidson, Linda (Mrs. D. W. Griffith). *When the Movies Were Young*. New York: Dover, 1969.

Auerbach, Erich. *Mimesis: The Representation of Reality in Western Literature*. Princeton: Princeton University Press, 1974.

Baker, Colgate. "David W. Griffith: The Genius of the Movies." *The New York Review*, December 13, 1913.

Baker, Hettie Grey. "The Man Who Made the Movies." *Leslie's Illustrated Weekly*, July 30, 1914.

Barthes, Roland. *Elements of Semiology*. New York: Hill and Wang, 1977.

———. *The Fashion System*. New York: Hill and Wang, 1977.

———. *Image, Music, Text*. New York: Hill and Wang, 1977.

———. "The Realistic Effect." *Film Reader* 3:131–35.

Becker, George J., ed. *Documents of Literary Realism*. Princeton: Princeton University Press, 1963.

Beckman, Frank J. *The Vanished Villains: An Exercise in Nostalgia*. Manuscript, New York Public Library for the Performing Arts at Lincoln Center.

Belasco, David. "David Belasco Attacks Stage Tradition." *The Theatre*, May 1911.

Belsey, Catherine. *Critical Practice*. London: Methuen, 1980.

Bennett, Tony, and Janet Woollacott. *Bond and Beyond: The Political Career of a Popular Hero*. London: Macmillan, 1987.

"Bennie Chats with the Players: Henry B. Walthall of Essanay." *Motion Picture Magazine,* October 1915.

Benson, A. C. "Realism in Fiction." *The Cornhill Magazine,* May 1912.

Bentley, Eric, ed. *The Theory of the Modern Stage.* New York: Penguin, 1968.

Birdwhistle, Raymond. *Kinesics and Context.* Philadelphia: University of Pennsylvania Press, 1970.

Bisplinghoff, Gretchen. "On Acting: A Selected Bibliography." *Cinema Journal* 20:1 (1980): 79–85.

Bitzer, Billy. *Billy Bitzer: His Story.* New York: Farrar, Straus and Giroux, 1973.

Booth, Wayne. *The Rhetoric of Fiction.* Chicago: University of Chicago Press, 1961.

Bordwell, David, Janet Staiger, and Kristin Thompson. *The Classical Hollywood Cinema: Film Style and Mode of Production to 1960.* New York: Columbia University Press, 1985.

Boucicault, Dion. *The Art of Acting.* New York: Columbia University Press, 1926.

Bowser, Eileen, ed. *Biograph Bulletins, 1908–1912.* New York: Octagon, 1973.

Bradby, David, Lewis James, and Bernard Sharratt. *Performance and Politics in Popular Drama.* Cambridge: Cambridge University Press, 1980.

Braudy, Leo. *The World in a Frame.* Garden City, N.Y.: Anchor, 1977.

Brooks, Peter. *The Melodramatic Imagination.* New Haven: Yale University Press, 1976.

Brown, Karl. *Adventures with David W. Griffith.* New York: Da Capo, 1973.

Calder, Chester, T. "What's Wrong with the American Stage?" *The Theatre,* March 1913.

Carroll, Lewis. *Through the Looking Glass.* New York: New American Library, 1960.

Chaney, Sheldon. "The Failure of the American Producer." *The Theatre,* July 1914.

Chatman, Seymour. *Story and Discourse: Narrative Structure in Fiction and Film.* Ithaca: Cornell University Press, 1978.

Cohn, Alfred A. "The Reformation of Wally." *Photoplay,* December 1917.

Cole, Toby, and Helen Krich Chinoy, eds. *Actors on Acting.* New York: Crown, 1970.

Crofts, Stephen. "Authorship and Hollywood." *Wide Angle* 5:3 (1984): 16–22.

Cross, Gilbert B. *Next Week East Lynne.* Lewisburg, Pa.: Bucknell University Press, 1977.

Culler, Jonathan. *The Pursuit of Signs: Semiotics, Literature, Deconstruction.* Ithaca: Cornell University Press, 1981.

———. *Structuralist Poetics.* Ithaca: Cornell University Press, 1975.

deCordova, Richard. "The Emergence of the Star System in America." *Wide Angle* 6:4 (1985): 4–13.

———. "The Emergence of the Star System in America: An Examination of the Institutional and Ideological Function of the Star." Diss., University of California, Los Angeles, 1986.

———. *Picture Personalities: The Emergence of the Star System in America.* Urbana: University of Illinois Press, 1990.

Denig, Lynde. "Watching the Screen." *The Theatre,* October 1914.

Dmytryk, Edward, and Jean Porter Dmytryk. *On Screen Acting.* Stoneham, Mass.: Butterworth, 1984.

Donnell, Dorothy. "I Remember When." *Motion Picture Classic,* November 1925.

Downer, Alan S. "Players and Painted Stage." *Proceedings of the Modern Language Association* 61:2 (1946): 522–76.

Dyer, Richard. *Stars*. London: British Film Institute, 1979.

Dyos, H. J., and Michael Wolff, eds. *The Victorian City*. London: Routledge and Kegan Paul, 1973.

Eco, Umberto. *A Theory of Semiotics*. Bloomington: Indiana University Press, 1979.

Elam, Kier. *The Semiotics of Theatre and Drama*. New York: Methuen, 1980.

Eliot, T. S. *Old Possum's Book of Practical Cats*. New York: Harcourt, Brace, Jovanovich, 1982.

Fell, John, ed. *Film Before Griffith*. Berkeley and Los Angeles: University of California Press, 1983.

Fowle Adams, Florence A. *Gesture and Pantomimic Action*. New York: Edgar S. Werne, 1897.

Fredericks, L. *The Stage and Histrionic Education*. 1878.

Garcia, Gustave. *The Actor's Art*. London: Messrs. Simpkin, Marshall and Co., 1888.

Gerould, Daniel. "Russian Formalist Theories of Melodrama." *Journal of Popular Culture* 1:1 (1978): 152–68.

Gish, Lillian. *The Movies, Mr. Griffith, and Me*. Englewood Cliffs, N.J.: Prentice Hall, 1969.

Goddard, Henry. "Some Players I Have Known." *The Theatre*, September 1908.

Graham, Cooper C., Steven Higgins, Elaine Mancini, and Joao Luis Vieira. *D. W. Griffith and the Biograph Company*. Metuchen, N.J.: Scarecrow, 1986.

Grau, Robert. "The Moving Picture Show and the Living Drama." *The American Monthly Review of Reviews*, March 1912.

Griffith, David W. "Pictures vs. One-Night Stands." *The Independent*, December 11, 1916.

———. "What I Demand of Movie Stars." *Motion Picture Classic*, February 1917.

———. "What I Demand of Photoplay Stars." *Photoplay*, September 5, 1915.

Gunning, Thomas. "D. W. Griffith and the Narrator System: Narrative Structure and Industry Organization in the Biograph Films, 1908–1909." Diss., New York University, 1986.

———. *D. W. Griffith and the Origins of American Narrative Film*. Urbana: University of Illinois Press, 1991.

Hamilton, Clayton. "The Art of the Moving Picture Play." *The Bookman*, January 1911.

Hammerton, J. M. *The Actor's Art*. New York: Benjamin Blom, 1897.

Heath, Stephen. "Film Performance." *Cine-tracts* 1:2 (1977): 7–17.

———. *The Nouveau Roman*. Philadelphia: Temple University Press, 1972.

Henderson, Robert M. *David W. Griffith: The Years at Biograph*. New York: Farrar, Straus and Giroux, 1970.

"Henry B. Walthall: A Gentleman of Hollywood." *Silver Screen*, October 1934.

Hollman, Larry Lee. "Florence Lawrence." *Films in Review*, August/September 1980: 385–94.

Inglis, William. "Morals and Moving Pictures." *Harper's Weekly*, July 30, 1910.

James, Henry. *Eight Tales from the Major Phase*. New York: W. W. Norton, 1969.

———. *The Portable Henry James*. New York: Viking, 1968.

Kolb, Harold H. *The Illusion of Life: American Realism as a Literary Form*. Charlottesville: University Press of Virginia, 1969.

Lawrence, Florence. "Growing Up with the Movies." *Photoplay,* January 1915.

Loos, Anita. *A Girl Like I*. New York: Viking, 1966.

Lotman, Juri. *Semantics in the Cinema*. Ann Arbor: Michigan Slavic Contributions, 1976.

Lovell, Terry. *Pictures of Reality*. London: British Film Institute, 1980.

Lusk, Norbert. "Acting in the Silent Drama." *The Theatre,* July 1914.

McArthur, Benjamin. *Actors and American Culture, 1880–1920*. Philadelphia: Temple University Press, 1983.

McLaughlin, Robert. *Broadway and Hollywood: A History of Economic Interaction*. New York: Arno, 1974.

Marsh, Mae. *Screen Acting*. Los Angeles: Photostar Publishing Company, 1922.

Matejka, T., and K. Pomorska. *Readings in Russian Poetics: Formalist and Structuralist Views*. Cambridge: MIT Press, 1971.

Matthews, Brander, ed. *Papers on Acting*. New York: Hill and Wang, 1958.

Medvedev, M. *The Formal Method in Literary Scholarship*. Cambridge: Harvard University Press, 1985.

Merritt, Russell. "Melodrama: Postmortem for a Phantom Genre." *Wide Angle* 5:3 (1984): 24–31.

———. "Rescued From a Perilous Nest: D. W. Griffith's Escape from Theatre into Film." *Cinema Journal* 21:1 (1981): 2–3.

Metz, Christian. *Language and Cinema*. The Hague: Mouton, 1974.

Miller, Henry. "Realism in Acting." *Harper's Weekly,* January 5, 1906.

Morgan, Anna. *An Hour with Delsarte*. Boston: Lee and Shepard, 1889.

Morris, Virginia Elizabeth. "The Influence of Delsarte in America as Revealed through the Lectures of Steele MacKaye." M.A. thesis, Louisiana State University, 1941.

Mukarovsky, Jan. *Structure, Sign, and Function*. New Haven: Yale University Press, 1978.

Musser, Charles. "Another Look at the Chaser Theory." *Studies in Visual Communication* 10:4 (1984): 22–44.

———. "Before The Nickelodeon: Edwin S. Porter and the Edison Company." Diss., New York University, 1986.

———. *Before the Nickelodeon: Edwin S. Porter and the Edison Manufacturing Company*. Berkeley and Los Angeles: University of California Press, 1991.

———. "The Changing Status of the Film Actor." In Jay Leyda and Charles Musser, eds., *Before Hollywood: Turn-of-the-Century Film from American Archives*. New York: American Federation of the Arts, 1986.

———. *The Emergence of Cinema: The American Screen to 1907*. New York: Scribner's Sons, 1990.

———. *High-Class Moving Pictures: Lyman H. Howe and the Forgotten Era of Traveling Exhibition, 1880–1920*. Princeton: Princeton University Press, 1991.

———. "The Nickelodeon Era Begins: Establishing the Framework for Hollywood's Mode of Representation." *Framework,* Fall 1983: 4–11.

Musser, Charles, and Paolo Cherchi-Usai, eds. *American Vitagraph*. Washington, D.C.: Smithsonian Institution Press, forthcoming.

Naremore, James. *Acting in the Cinema*. Berkeley and Los Angeles: University of California Press, 1988.

Nichols, Bill, ed. *Movies and Methods*. Berkeley and Los Angeles: University of California Press, 1976.

O'Brien, Mary Ellen. *Film Acting: The Technique and History of Acting for the Cinema*. New York: Arno, 1983.

Oppenheimer, F. "The Moving Picture." *The Theatre*, January 1909.

Owen, Kenneth. "The Little Colonel." *Photoplay Magazine*, August 1915.

Pavis, Patrice. "Problems of a Semiology of Theatrical Gesture." *Poetics Today* 2:3 (1983): 65–93.

Pearson, Roberta E., and William Uricchio. "How Many Times Shall Caesar Bleed in Sport: Shakespeare and the Cultural Debate About Moving Pictures." *Screen* 31:3 (Fall 1990): 243–61.

———. " 'How to Be a Stage Napoleon': Vitagraph's Vision of History." *Persistence of Vision* 9 (1991): 75–89.

Peltret, Elizabeth. "Walthall and the Little Colonel." *Motion Picture Classic*, November 1918.

Perry, Bliss. *A Study in Prose Fiction*. Boston: Houghton Mifflin, 1904.

Pickford, Mary. *Sunshine and Shadow*. Garden City, N.Y.: Doubleday, 1955.

Pizer, Donald. *Realism and Naturalism in Nineteenth Century American Literature*. Carbondale: Southern Illinois University Press, 1984.

"A Poet Who Writes on Motion Picture Films." *The Theatre*, June 1914.

Poggi, Jack. *Theatre in America: The Impact of Economic Forces, 1870–1967*. Ithaca: Cornell University Press, 1968.

Pudovkin, V. I. *Film Technique and Film Acting*. New York: Grove, 1970.

Rahill, Frank. *The World of Melodrama*. University Park: Pennsylvania State University Press, 1967.

Rosenberg, Bernard, and Harry Silverstein. *The Real Tinsel*. New York: Macmillan, 1970.

Schickel, Richard. *D. W. Griffith: An American Life*. New York: Simon and Schuster, 1984.

Slide, Anthony. *The Idols of Silence*. Cranbury, N.J.: A. S. Barnes, 1976.

Smith, H. J. "The Melodrama." *Atlantic Monthly*, March 1907.

Smith, James L. *Melodrama*. London: Methuen, 1973.

Southern, E. H. "The 'New Art' as Discovered by E. H. Southern." *The Craftsman*, September 1916.

Staiger, Janet. "Blueprints for Feature Films: Hollywood's Continuity Scripts." In Tino Balio, ed., *The American Film Industry*. Madison: University of Wisconsin Press, rev. ed., 1985.

———. "The Eyes Are Really the Focus: Photoplay Acting and Film Form and Style." *Wide Angle* 6:4 (1985): 14–23.

Stebbins, Geneviève. *Delsarte's System of Expression*. New York: Dance Horizons, 1977.

Thompson, Grahame F. "Approaches to Performance." *Screen* 26:5 (1985): 78–90.

Thompson, John. "Beyond Commutation: A Reconsideration of Screen Acting." *Screen* 26:5 (1985): 64–76.

Thompson, John. "Screen Acting and the Commutation Test." *Screen* 19:2 (1978): 55–69.

Todorov, Tzvetan. *The Poetics of Prose*. Ithaca: Cornell University Press, 1977.

Uricchio, William, and Roberta E. Pearson. "Dante's Inferno and Caesar's Ghost: Intertextuality and Conditions of Reception in Early American Cinema." *Journal of Communication Inquiry* 14:2 (Summer 1990): 81–97.

———. " 'Films of Quality,' 'High Art Films,' and 'Films de Luxe': Intertextuality and Reading Positions in the Vitagraph Films." *Journal of Film and Video* 44:1 (Winter 1989): 15–31.

———. *Cultural Crisis, Cultural Cure? The Case of the Vitagraph "High-Art" Moving Pictures*. Princeton: Princeton University Press, forthcoming.

Walkley, A. B. *Drama and Life*. Freeport, N.Y.: Books for Libraries, 1908.

Welsh, Robert E. "David W. Griffith Speaks." *The New York Dramatic Mirror*, January 14, 1914.

West, E. J. "The London Stage, 1870–1890: A Study in the Conflict of the Old and New Styles of Acting." University of Colorado Studies, Series B, Studies in the Humanities 2:1 (1943): 31–84.

Wexman, Virginia Wright. "Kinesics and Film Acting: Humphrey Bogart in *The Maltese Falcon* and *The Big Sleep*." *Journal of Popular Film and Television* 7:1 (1978): 42–55.

Williams, D. A. *The Monster in the Mirror: Studies in Nineteenth Century Realism*. Oxford: Oxford University Press, 1976.

Williams, Raymond. *Keywords: A Vocabulary of Culture and Society*. New York: Oxford University Press, 1976.

———. "A Lecture on Realism." *Screen* 18:1 (1977): 62–74.

———. *The Long Revolution*. Westport, Conn.: Greenwood, 1961.

———. *Marxism and Literature*. Oxford: Oxford University Press, 1977.

———. *Problems in Materialism and Culture*. London: Verso, 1980.

Young, William C. *Famous Actors and Actresses of the American Stage*. New York: Bowker, 1975.

Zorn, John W. *The Essential Delsarte*. Metuchen, N.J.: Scarecrow, 1968.

Index

Peltzer, Otto, 132
Penny arcades, 1, 128, 131
People's Institute, 1, 3, 130, 131, 133, 141
Performance: Dyer's definition of, 4–5; interdisciplinary meaning of, 147–48n2
Performance style: and Delsarte system, 22–
25; everyday life distinguished from, 6, 22;
everyday life represented by, 28, 30, 35;
and externalized mental process, 42, 45,
48–50, 55, 59, 65, 66, 137; Griffith's
views on, 89–93, 99, 101–2; historical
context of, 5, 6, 9; and interaction of signifying practices, 38, 69–70, 113, 116, 118,
158n20; intertextual analysis of, 7, 9; melodramatic, 7–8, 9, 20, 41, 42, 55, 78, 97,
114; naturalistic, 7–8, 9, 20; neglected by
film theory, 5; realistic, 7–8, 20, 30, 31–
33, 92–93, 94–95, 124; textual analysis of,
5, 7, 9; Walthall's views on, 101–2. See
also Histrionic code; Verisimilar code
Performance style, transition in: and character-centered signifiers, 52, 57, 63, 111; and
closer camera, 94; documented in trade
press, 11–12, 120–28, 134–39; film actors'
influence on, 99; and film scholarship, 4–5,
7; gradualism of, 75; Griffith's responsibility for, 5, 10–13, 75, 94, 97–98; and interaction of signifying practices, 51, 52, 59;
intertextual analysis of, 19–20, 140, 141,
142; mixing of codes in, 50, 51, 59, 64,
111; and narrative structure, 52, 57, 63,
111, 139, 141–42; and psychologized character, 14, 16, 52, 57, 63, 111, 139, 141–
42; and rehearsals, 86; teleological interpretation of, 18–20, 119, 142, 143–44;
Walthall as example of, 99, 103, 106, 111,
118–19
Personal, 85
Photoplay, 87, 101
Pickford, Mary: and development of star system, 135; and relations with Griffith, 84,
87–92 passim, 103; verisimilar code mas-
tered by, 50; roles played: in *Friends*, 46–
47, 48; in *His Lost Love*, 58–62; in *The
New York Hat*, 43–45, 50; in *Ramona*, 117
Pilar-Morin (French pantomimist), 135
Pluralism, methodological, 9, 16, 140
The Poetics (Aristotle), 27
Point-of-view shots, 56, 158n20
Porter, Edwin, 126
Posture, body, 5, 7, 18, 155n7; in Delsarte
system, 22, 23–24; in verisimilar code, 46,
47, 118
Powell, Frank, 57, 84
Pratt, George, 77
The Prisoner of Zenda, 127
Production, film: director's role in, 76, 82–

83; economics of, 14–15, 94, 129; organization of labor in, 7, 82–83; and rehearsals, 85–89; and script development, 84–85
Props: characters' thought processes revealed
by, 59, 61, 62, 65, 67, 71; in histrionic
code, 39, 43, 51, 70; and interaction of
signifying practices, 65, 70, 158n20; in
verisimilar code, 33–34, 43, 47, 48, 61,
111, 141; Walthall's use of, 107–8, 109,
118
Psychoanalysis, 19, 77
Psychologization, of character: and cultural
legitimation of film, 137; and narrative
causality, 52–55, 57, 58, 59, 63; and realist aesthetics, 31–32, 35, 52–53, 57, 58,
136, 141; and transition in performance
style, 14, 16, 52, 57, 63, 111, 139, 141–
42; and Walthall's performance style, 107,
109, 113, 118

Queen Elizabeth, 16
Quo Vadis, 16

Ramona, 117
Reaction shots, 50, 74, 158n20
Realism: and Barthes's realistic effect theory,
31, 32, 33, 45; as bourgeois ideology, 144;
and character construction, 31–32, 35, 52,
57, 127–28; and cultural legitimation of
film, 128, 136; dramatic, 31–33, 36, 52,
92, 95, 98, 124, 128, 142, 144, 153n60;
literary, 4, 8, 29–31, 32, 33, 36, 52, 92,
95, 98, 124, 128, 142, 144; and narrative
structure, 31–32, 36, 52–53, 57, 58, 128;
and performance style, 7–8, 20, 30, 31–33,
92–93, 94–95, 124; and psychologization,
31–32, 35, 52–53, 57, 58, 136, 141; theatrical, 5, 8, 28–29, 32–33, 98, 100, 124,
153n60; and theories of verisimilitude, 27–
31
Reception theory, 19, 151n8
Reflection shots, 49–50
Reformism, 1, 15, 129–32
Rehearsals, 85–89, 101, 102, 104, 160n52
Representation: in cinema, 5, 13–14, 129,
141; in realist aesthetics, 29–30, 144,
169n4
Rescued from an Eagle's Nest, 79, 80
Reviews. *See* Trade press
Robertson, T. W., 31, 32, 33
The Rocky Road, 57–62
Rosmersholm (Ibsen), 77, 78
Russell Sage Foundation, 128, 132, 133
Russian formalism, 53

Saloons, 128, 131
Salvini, Tommaso, 35

Compositor:	Princeton University Press/Printing
Text:	10/12 Times Roman
Display:	Helvetica
Printer:	Princeton University Press/Printing
Binder:	Princeton University Press/Printing